Mint Errors to Die For

A Sampling and Explanation of More Than 250 Error Coins That Escaped the U.S. Mint

Mat,

Good luck on your search for those error coins!

Joseph P. Cronin

Mint Errors to Die For

A Sampling and Explanation of More Than 250 Error Coins That Escaped the U.S. Mint

Published and Copyrighted © 2021 by Joseph P. Cronin

Inquiries for usage of photos or illustrations created by the author can be addressed to him directly at josephcronin@protonmail.com

Important Notice: All of the research and information in this book, including opinions and analysis from both the author and other numismatic Mint error experts who were quoted and referenced, was crafted with the utmost care to ensure accuracy. Nevertheless, the possibility of an error or difference of opinion always exists. The author does not assume responsibility and cannot be held legally liable for economic losses or other damages resulting from the purchase, trade, sale, or other transaction of items based on the information contained within this book. The estimation of values for many of the coins presented was based on recent sale prices from sources including online resources, private sales made by the author, and national coin show auctions in the United States. Even so, a multitude of factors can and often do influence demand which can lead to significant variations in pricing even when the exact same coin is sold again within a very short time period. It is up to the individual collector to do his/her own due diligence and research before purchasing any coin. Factors including an error coin's specific type or types, condition, grading, damage, eye appeal, rarity, authenticity, recent sale prices, and other factors must be considered before buying, selling and trading error coins.

Printed by Herrmann Unlimited
Printed in Pittsburgh, Pennsylvania, USA
First Edition 2021
ISBN: 978-0-578-81990-7

Front and back cover designs created by Joseph P. Cronin with professional input from Mark C. Kinan.

Photos on the front and back cover and within the book were taken by Joseph P. Cronin unless otherwise specified.

Dedication

To my loving and caring parents,
Donald and Caterina "Cathy" Cronin:

Thank you for your love and patience through
the years. I will always remember how both of
you read to me as a toddler and how much I
enjoyed it. This book is dedicated to both of
you, and I am proud to have you as my parents.

With eternal love,

~ Joseph

Acknowledgements

Writing a book is never a solitary task. Thankfully, the following people helped me complete my first book by offering suggestions, analysis, edits, donated coins, information, supplies, tools, and procedures to help make this a wonderful resource on Mint errors. I cannot express in words how much this truly means to me. Thanks to all of you for making my dream come true and for always being willing to share your valued opinions: Barry and Marie Interisano; Jill Cornell-Slater; Kenneth J. Ramell; Troy Moxley; Steve Lansdale at Heritage Auctions; Rebecca Tran at PCGS; Erin Whitson at Stacks & Bowers; Mr. Rice and the gang at Harold B. Rice Coins & Stamps (Kenmore, NY); Jack Hunt Gold and Silver (Kenmore, NY); Allen Morgan; Robert Risi; Pete Apple; Dwayne Kelly; Tom Miller; Edwin "Paddyman" Padilla; Nick Reisweig; John Amirault; Jim Zimmerman; Ronald Fern; George F. Winters; Saul Teichman; Dustin Nussbaum; Ed Fuhrman and his "Half Cents" Facebook page; Joy Matherne; Counterfeit watchdog and award-winning counterfeit researcher, Jack Young, and his "Dark Side Counterfeits & Fakes" Facebook page; Ken Potter; Error dealer and all-around good guy, Jon Sullivan; "Skip" Fazzari at ICG; and all my friends in the various online groups I belong to. In addition, a special "Thank You" goes to numismatist, coin researcher, error collector, and professional numismatic writer, Mike Diamond, for analyzing some of my coins in-hand. You have one of the best numismatic brains in the world and I'm honored you volunteer your time for me and others on my Facebook page "Joe Cronin's Mint Errors Explained."

I would also like to express my gratitude to the professional reviewers and content editors of my book, including: Long-time collector and well-known Mint error guru, Steven Mills, who was one of the original columnists for *Error Trends Coin Magazine* and currently runs Mint-Errors.com; to Bill O'Rourke who has written articles for both *Coin World* and *The Numismatist*; and the person who inspired my interest in errors in the first place, PCGS Mint error authenticator, author, Mint error dealer, and one of the best and friendliest people in the business, Fred Weinberg, at FredWeinberg.com. You're all very enthusiastic and knowledgeable experts who always make time to talk and are great ambassadors for the hobby.

Of course a huge "Thank You!" goes out to my best friend of 40+ years, Mark C. Kinan, for all the time and patience you've given me at every stage of this process. I know you wish you could have done more, but I am grateful for everything you've done to help me complete this book. Thank you, Mark! You're the best!

But most of all to my loving and beautiful wife, Andrea, thank you for being patient and understanding, and for your encouragement to get me to write and complete my very first book. I love you always and forever, we will laugh every day, we will get through anything, and "Lovies X 3" for ages and ages. I honestly don't know what I would do without you in my life. Thank you, my Love! You mean the world to me and always make me proud!

Table of Contents

PLEASE DO NOT CUT
BAG WHEN OPENING
RETURN TO

U. S. MINT

QUARTER

$1000

D 1 00 GSR 24997

QUARTER

TREASURY DEPARTMENT
UNITED STATES ASSAY OFFICE
NUMISMATIC SERVICE
350 DUBOCE AVENUE
SAN FRANCISCO, CALIF. 94102
———————
OFFICIAL BUSINESS

1943

If you aren't already a member of CONECA, please consider joining today at **ConecaOnline.org**

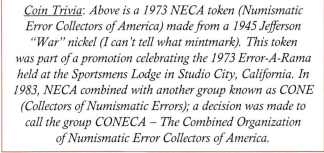

Coin Trivia: Above is a 1973 NECA token (Numismatic Error Collectors of America) made from a 1945 Jefferson "War" nickel (I can't tell what mintmark). This token was part of a promotion celebrating the 1973 Error-A-Rama held at the Sportsmens Lodge in Studio City, California. In 1983, NECA combined with another group known as CONE (Collectors of Numismatic Errors); a decision was made to call the group CONECA – The Combined Organization of Numismatic Error Collectors of America.

CONECA logo used with permission granted 1/14/21

Preface

No one strives to be ordinary in life. Whether applying to colleges, being a finalist for a job, putting in for promotions, attracting a key client, or hoping to get a date with that special someone, it is often crucial to stand out above the rest. Your success in life up to this point is likely due in part to your ability to get noticed from the other 7.6 billion people we share this Earth with. Companies and marketers do not promote "ordinary" products, and as consumers we often love having something different that few others have and will pay good money to achieve that status. Some people go beyond wanting something "different" and actually prefer the unique, the bizarre, and the unexplainable. Whether we like it or not, it breaks up a mundane day when something peculiar comes along. "Ordinary" really means "boring," right? And who wants to be or have something defined as "ordinary?"

It is that exact reasoning why I shifted to collecting Mint error coins. At first it was fun completing sets like silver Roosevelt dimes and Franklin halves when I was younger, but soon it became "ordinary" with nothing more than the same cookie-cutter coin with dozens of the same design; the only variances were different dates and mintmarks. With Mint errors, each one is almost exclusive showcasing attributes like whacky shapes, wrong metals, and/or missing designs unlike the millions – or even billions – of others that were minted that year. It sparked more of an interest in how coins are minted, why metallic compositions changed over the years, how errors happen, and how to detect fake and altered coins. I shifted from having a passing interest to a passion where these can't simply just be looked at but need to be studied individually. Soon a few examples grew into a fairly extensive collection of various error types. Many of my errors are in this book, along with some from a few friends of mine and a bunch from reputable auction sites. These all help make up what you'll see in my very first book, *Mint Errors to Die For.*

However, I did not start out with a desire to be an author. In fact, initially I just wanted to keep a simple list of my growing collection. But as I started documenting a few pieces to inventory them, I thought to myself, "If something were to happen to me, no one in my family is likely going to understand what I have here, nor will many other coin collectors or dealers!" Even worse, someone might know *exactly* what I have and try to take advantage of my family if – God forbid! – they are ever forced to sell them. So due to the esoteric nature of my collection, it was essential for me to tell my family exactly (a) *what* this assortment consists of and (b) *why* these pieces are classified as Mint errors.

It didn't take long to realize a simple catalogue listing wouldn't be good enough for others to understand what's wrong with each of these coins. Some like that nickel on the right might look normal, yet it's a major error worth around $800 (it will be featured later in the book). Therefore I started adding enlarged photos to illustrate where and what the mistake is, as well as including some non-error comparison photos. But even enlarged photos without explanations aren't always helpful, so I needed to annotate them and provide some background on why they look different. In addition, coin collecting vocabulary tends to be a bit arcane, so I provided some definitions, references, and processes in layman's terms to further one's understanding. It was at this point I realized I am writing a reference book!

Then as this project neared completion, it became evident to me that something more was needed in this book for fellow error collectors. Rather than focusing solely on presenting and explaining why certain coins *are* Mint errors, I wanted to provide a great resource on why and how so many coins which appear to be genuine errors *are not* (e.g. fake, altered, and damaged coins). Thus I have dedicated an entire chapter of this book to address the types of phenomenon which can cause a coin to appear – either accidentally or on purpose – as a genuine Mint error.

By undertaking all of this work and explaining things in a way that non-collectors can more easily comprehend, hopefully there will be a better appreciation of these "freaks" and "oddities" for more than just their bizarre appearance and monetary value. I already love showing off these pieces anyway and explaining their abnormal state, and it is entertaining to see and hear reactions from people who cannot believe these creations are both possible and authentic. So why not put everything into a book and make this easier for everyone? Thus I decided to write *Mint Errors to Die For,* which I hope you enjoy and maybe you'll even learn something new. However, I must warn you there are some bad coin puns (as in the title) and other *coiny* jokes in some of the pages ahead. Lastly, unless otherwise noted, all coins featured in this book are mine and were photographed by me. Those not photographed nor owned by me (e.g. some comparison photos from auction sites) are credited when they initially appear.

About the Author

Joseph P. Cronin was born in Niagara Falls, New York, and has been collecting coins for almost thirty years. His father, Donald, got him started as a teenager by not only showing Joe his collection of silver and gold coins but also sharing his historical knowledge about them (e.g. who is on them, why, what certain symbols on them mean, etc.). Though his dad's collection was not extravagant and it contained no particularly rare or exceptional pieces, it became something fun for them to work on together as father and son. Stopping at local coin shops on their travels was something the pair always looked forward to and Joe still enjoys that to this day.

Within the last few years, Joe branched out to Mint errors as they are much more unique and all seem to have more of a story to tell. It also helped him learn more about the minting process, the differences between genuine, altered, counterfeit, and damaged coins, how and where to research accurate information, and even catch mistakes made by third-party grading companies. His collection is quite extensive with some rare error types consisting of only a handful of known examples, and has even had some of his coins featured in national publications like *Coin World* and CONECA's bi-monthly journal, *Errorscope*.

Reading and learning from nationally recognized experts is a passion for him, but so are opportunities where he can share his knowledge and promote the hobby. Almost every day he has coworkers, current and former students, people on coin blogs/forums, and/or dealers nationwide asking him to check out their possible errors and give his thoughts. Joe is also an administrator and moderator for a couple Mint error blogs, has run seminars for coin clubs, and is frequently asked to provide educational exhibits on Mint errors at coin shows in the Western New York area and out of state.

Mr. Cronin graduated *Summa Cum Laude* from the State University of New York at Fredonia with an undergraduate degree in Social Studies Education and earned his Masters degree at Niagara University. Currently Joe is a full-time History teacher in the Buffalo area and is a former U.S. Treasury Department/Homeland Security officer who worked in Buffalo, New York as a Customs Inspector. Joe is a proud member of the American Numismatic Association, the Buffalo Numismatic Association, the Niagara Frontier Coin Club, and is both a member and NY State representative of **CONECA** – Combined Organization of Numismatic Error Collectors of America. All of these groups revolve around the hobby officially referred to as **numismatics** – the collection and/or study of coins and paper currency.

Contact Joe Cronin:
Email: josephcronin@protonmail.com
Facebook Page: Joe Cronin's Mint Errors Explained
Website: MintErrorsExplained.com (Coming soon!)

Curved Clips

Coin Trivia: The U.S. Mint in
Denver started striking coins in 1906.

Which of these Lincoln cent Mint errors is considered a "die clash" and why?

Not sure exactly? You'll know by the end of this book.

Historically, coins are and have been one of the most popular collectibles in almost every country on the planet. In fact, they have been collected for centuries even before the birth of Jesus Christ (for those few who could afford to save them back then. This is why coin collecting is called the "Hobby of Kings"). Regardless of when someone chose to collect coins, it is probably safe to say a common goal among the coin collecting community throughout the world (which I lightheartedly refer to as the "collectorate") is to acquire coins in the best condition possible that their budgets permit. With that in mind, many collectors don't want nor care to understand errors because their very nature involves having defects in some way. Thus it's people like us who make up the minority within this hobby who enjoy collecting coins with defects, some of which are classified as Mint errors. (I jokingly call those who collect errors and die varieties the "defectorate"). But collecting genuine Mint errors is not as easy as you think, so before you start bidding and buying, it's best to educate yourself on what a Mint error actually is and isn't in addition to knowing how to tell the difference.

The term "Mint error" at first may seem oxymoronic and confusing. For example, *if mint means "perfect" and error means "flaw," how can something be both "flawed" yet "perfect?"* Because in this case, the word **Mint** alludes to a specific place where these coins were struck – one of the United States Mints – although "mint" can also refer to condition. (When capitalized, I am referring to the place; lower case will mean condition.) The word **error** refers to (a) mistakes/flaws occurring during any stage of the minting/striking process and/or (b) some kind of problem with the metal itself. Once coins have exited the striking chamber, any damage, staining (not natural toning), alterations, etc., are now referred to as **post-Mint damage (PMD)** and they lose most or all of their collector/numismatic value.

Now there is some debate as to when the process of minting a coin really ends. For example, does it end when the hammer die comes down but before the ejection process? The point where ejection begins? Or is it when it's completely out of the chamber? What if it is damaged during the Mint's packaging processes after striking? Again, I feel any coin with a flaw occurring after it exited the chamber should be considered "damaged." (Edge-lettering gaffes happen post-ejection on modern dollars, but those are still considered errors.) My book features mostly certified errors that occurred at Mint facilities, which consequently makes them "Mint errors."

However, even among more experienced collectors there is some confusion about what exactly constitutes a "Mint error." *Are all mistakes featured on coins considered "Mint errors" if they occurred before they fully exited the striking chamber?* Actually, no. It makes a big difference what type of flaw it is and when it occurred. Imperfections and gaffes created *during* the striking process are different from those which occurred as the coin dies were being prepared and *before* they started striking planchets. At the risk of being too technical, coins with faults/flaws on them due to being struck with dies bearing those exact same faults/flaws *before even one coin was minted* are actually *not* considered "Mint errors" but are known as "die varieties." (The differences will be explained in more detail later in the book.)

OK, what specific circumstances make something a Mint error? There are dozens of error types, but some of them featured in this book include those that are: struck off-center; struck more than once; struck on the wrong type of metal; struck on the correct metal but the wrong thickness; struck on the wrong-sized disk meant for another denomination; struck by two different dies of different denominations (e.g. both 10 cent and 1 cent dies); or weren't struck at all and are completely blank. They also include coins partially missing metal (including being split in half), those that have greatly expanded in size/diameter, started to split, and/or have missing designs. Some are even a combination of these or other error types. The list of possibilities is virtually endless.

Unfortunately many genuine errors are dismissed by untrained eyes as garbage or junk coins because they can appear altered and/or damaged. Some wind up horribly disfigured, discolored, misshapen, split in half, have backwards designs, or become clipped and look like a crescent moon. Quite a few look so ugly and deformed that those who don't understand the nature of Mint errors might callously discard them on the sidewalk or spend them just to avoid seeing them in their change purse or vehicle cup holder. What a shame that not everyone will appreciate or understand what have historically been referred to as "freaks," "irregularities," "defects" and "oddities" – or "FIDOS" as some collectors call them.

On occasion I have to work hard to convince some people their coins are errors and not considered damaged, but usually the exact opposite occurs. There are significantly more people who think they have a genuine Mint error when what they really have is just a damaged coin. Sometimes coins subjected to heat or chemicals in Chemistry classes, buried underground at baseball fields, squeezed in a vise, or run over by steamrollers can mimic various error types. In many cases, just a few simple tools can help you make a quick and accurate determination.

There is a lot to learn about Mint errors, and with this hobby the learning never stops. I still occasionally come across errors, or combinations of errors on a single coin, that I haven't seen before. Many times I have to decide for myself if it is a true Mint error based on my knowledge, skills, and experience. I'm not perfect and make mistakes sometimes, but it's important that you learn from them. My goal is to explain and show you some popular Mint errors that maybe you haven't seen before or knew were possible, especially so you aren't the next person who unwittingly buys a damaged, altered, or counterfeit error or turns a genuine one away at a great price. Perhaps you will start checking your change a little more closely after reading this book as some very expensive Mint errors have circulated around before they finally got noticed and were properly identified.

Though I do not have all or even most error types, I do have types I like personally. With what I do have you will most certainly see some cool, weird, and head-scratching examples in the coming pages of over 250 genuine Mint errors. I even included a few die varieties as well as some altered, counterfeit and damaged coins to illustrate comparisons to genuine errors. In addition, I provided little bits of "Coin Trivia" on several pages throughout the book to really help you tap into your inner coin nerd.

If you are just starting out as a collector and think you may have found a Mint error, bring it to your local coin shop, ask an experienced collector, or post it on an online coin forum for review. However, be prepared to hear it is not valuable nor even an error at all despite what a loving grandparent told you about it long ago. If you are told it is an error and might be worth some big money, get a second opinion and even a third before you sell it or spend the money to get it certified (if you feel the need to). Though the chances are slim, you just might have one of the next great *Mint Errors to Die For*.

What are some basic tests you can perform to see which of these Mint error quarters might be missing an obverse clad layer?

If you don't know the answer now, you will by the end of this book.

Do Coins, Including Mint Errors, Make Good Financial Investments?

I decided to bring up this question first before the book starts officially because (a) I want it to be one of the first points you read about and (b) it leads me to perhaps the best piece of advice I can give to a new and/or inexperienced collector. My advice to you is this: Coins – including Mint errors – should not be purchased as investments. In fact, quite often they make terrible investments. Now some people will say, "Well, only people who can afford the super rare and expensive errors will ever make a huge return," but even people buying million dollar coins have suffered catastrophic losses. To prove my point, let's take a look at what happened with the sale of one of the most astounding and highly-publicized Mint errors of all time.

Though it looks like a normal copper 1943-D Lincoln cent, this coin below to date holds the record for the highest price anyone ever paid for a Mint error. *Ok, what's so special about it?* Well, in 1943 Lincoln cents were to be minted only on steel planchets, not copper ones. (I explain why and how the error occurred later in the book.) However about twenty have been discovered struck on copper planchets, but only one is known that was struck at the Denver Mint. News of this coin made international headlines including media reports from places like Saudi Arabia, South Africa, Australia, and Japan. It was sold to an anonymous buyer in America for a whopping **$1.7 million** in 2010. Imagine what it will sell for next time!

Photos used with permission by PCGS® at PCGS.com/CoinFacts

Meanwhile, Ten Years Later...

Well the "next time" was in January 2021, but now it was open for bidding at the one of the most respected auction sites in the world: Heritage Auctions. Once again the publicity of its availability was strong, and despite the global economic blow caused by the coronavirus pandemic, numismatic experts noted there was still a strong market for rare and expensive collectible coins. With just the passing of time this coin has to break its own record in terms of a sale price. Surely it was a great investment, right?

WRONG! Not only did this coin not break nor even tie it's record of $1.7 million, the final bid came in at **$840,000.** Now that's not chump change, but it's less than half what it sold for in 2010. In other words, the buyer (assuming the original buyer is the one who sold it) suffered a 50% loss totaling around $860,000. (Plus he/she had to pay about $160,000 in listing fees.)

If we can learn anything from this heart-breaking case study it's that coins do not make a reliable investment. Sure, you can make a profit sometimes, but the market is extremely volatile. I say treat coin collecting for what it should be – a hobby. Do it because you enjoy it, and go into it with the understanding that you might never get back what you paid for your coins. If you are merely in it to chase profits, you may become disillusioned and broke sooner than you think.

What will make a great investment and pay dividends for you is to take the time to learn about this hobby. There are plenty of great books out there on a variety of coin-related topics (like this one!), and wise collectors spend more time reading and studying coins than they do going around looking for coins. Knowledge is power!

"Excuse Me, Sir. Are Any of These Genuine Mint Errors?"

For those of you who collect Mint errors, I am certain you hear the above question regularly. There are very few days out of the year where someone doesn't ask me that as I am frequently presented with coins to examine from friends, colleagues at work, dealers, fellow collectors, coin show attendees, and/or those who post photos on my Facebook page ("Joe Cronin's Mint Errors Explained"). It's gratifying that people have confidence in me and I love studying every single coin to help give them my best answer. But what's even more satisfying is being able to *teach others how to teach themselves* the answers to their questions. Over the years, I am shocked at how even many experienced dealers and collectors don't know how to tell the difference between a Mint error and post-Mint damage, altered

coins, counterfeits, enhanced errors, and other coins merely posing as genuine Mint errors. In fact, this is one of the reasons why I wrote this book; it isn't just to show you part of my collection.

For example, let's test your skills. Below are five coins someone has brought to you to determine which is a genuine Mint error. Do you know which one is: (a) A genuine Mint error; (b) An "enhanced" error; (c) Environmental damage; (d) Counterfeit; (e) Altered to resemble an error? Can you explain why for each one with confidence? What information and tools would you need to give the best answer? Hopefully you'll know the answers and be able to explain why before you finish this book. (Page numbers to find the answers for each coin are in parentheses.)

1. Off-center $1 (268)

2. JFK Half Partial Obverse Clad Layer (227)

3. Cent with Retained Gold Flakes (203)

4. Cent on Dime Double Denomination (253)

5. Nickel on 1 Cent Copper Planchet (282)

Not Every "Strange-looking" Coin is a Mint Error

People do lots of bizarre things to coins and Mother Nature can be just as cruel. Whether accidentally or intentionally, coins subjected to many forms of abuse and misuse can wind up looking quite strange. However one of the most difficult concepts for new error collectors to understand is this: Just because a coin looks strange, it doesn't automatically mean it's a Mint error. In fact most strange-looking coins you'll find are not Mint errors and have simply been damaged in one way or another. Some were likely damaged intentionally in an effort to make them look like genuine errors to scam error collectors.

Regardless, many new collectors (and even many experienced collectors and dealers) will not accept their prized "error" coin isn't an error and can be quite obstinate, rude, and even combative when they're challenged. Discussions with these people can devolve quickly into a comical episode, especially when they become aggressively condescending, arrogant, and insulting. One tactic ignorant people like this use quite frequently is to require anyone questioning their assertions to "prove" how the coin came to look as it does. I have news for people like this: *The burden of proof is on you to prove it is an error, not for someone to prove why it isn't one.* It often isn't possible to say definitively how a coin became damaged. I have never run over a coin with a lawnmower, put one in a blender, shot one with a rifle, used it as a washer for a screw, cut one in half, put one in corrosive materials, burned one with a torch, glued one to a floor, ground one down with a grinder, or Lord knows what else to destroy a coin. However, I do know damage when I see it usually. I don't have to explain how or why the damage occurred and it doesn't matter anyway. It is YOU who needs to prove why it's an error, and for that you need an understanding of the minting process.

My advice in dealing with collectors like this is to try to be understanding and patient with them. We've all been there as new collectors, we've all made mistakes, and it's likely we will be wrong again (but hopefully less frequently as time goes on, especially after reading this book!). When they become insulting and combative after you've tried politely to help them, just ignore them and don't argue with them. Let them learn the hard way when they have to give refunds to the people they sold them to or when they send their coins to grading companies; that can sober people up very quickly. Remember that when you argue with an idiot, it will quickly become difficult for others to tell who the real idiot is. So when you see the next strange-looking coin like these below, it would be wise for you to be open to the possibility it isn't a Mint error.

| Severe Circulation Wear | Squeeze/Vise Job | Cut with Metal Shears |
| Shipwreck Coin (Spanish) | Used as a Washer? | Coin Art |

Basic Tools/Resources Error Collectors Should Have

Mint errors are fun to look at and collect, but before you start collecting/buying them it is imperative to understand not only *what* you are looking at but being able to comprehend and explain the *why* and *how* by yourself. Relying solely on dealers, experts, and labels on certified coins telling you what the error is does not help you acquire those skills. Many dealers aren't experts, the experts can sometimes make mistakes, and I have seen dozens of labels on certified coins that had either missing information on them, the wrong information on them, or both. You also have to be on the lookout for faked, altered, and damaged coins. Without a good working knowledge, you will always be at the mercy of others and thus more vulnerable to making some very costly mistakes. Below are some good tips on how to get started as an informed Mint error collector, but remember it takes time and patience.

1. Read up about the minting process and take tours of the Mints when in town. Knowing the stages, the processes, and how the processes have changed over the years is one of the best ways to help understand how and why coins look the way they do. It also helps you better detect damage, altered coins and counterfeits. (As of this writing, only the Philadelphia and Denver Mints do official tours.)

2. Learn how to grade coins yourself. There are many great print resources including *The Official American Numismatic Association Grading Standards for United States Coins* which provides photos and details of what to look for, and online pictorials like PCGS' Photograde which is great for seeing many series of coins in high definition color photos with different grades. You should also know how factors like Mint luster, strike, and contact marks can affect grades. Test your skills often on both certified coins and pocket change for practice, practice, PRACTICE! And then practice some more!

3. Read books, articles, and online sources written by nationally-recognized experts that cover errors and non-errors. Anything from Mike Diamond, Q. David Bowers, JC Stevens, Jason Cuvelier, BJ Neff, Arnold Margolis, R.S. Yeoman, Bill Fivaz, Alan Herbert, Ken Potter, Jon Sullivan, and Fred Weinberg is a great start. My personal favorite book is *100 Greatest U.S. Mint Errors* by Brown, Camire, and Weinberg, which also explains the minting stages and processes in the Appendix. Also, a copy of *The Official Red Book: A Guide Book of United States Coins* by R.S. Yeoman is a must (I prefer the MEGA large print edition). *Coin World* and *Numismatic News* are always great reads. Error-ref.com (Mike Diamond) and Mint-Errors.com (Steven Mills) are also solid error reference sites with explanations and photos. Lastly, Mike Byer's *Mint Error News*, which you can download free copies of, is a quarterly publication featuring mind-blowing errors and articles on error-related topics.

4. Look at multiple certified and uncertified examples of error coins for sale from nationally-known error dealers. Fred Weinberg's and Jon Sullivan's sites are my personal favorites featuring close-up photos, brief explanations, and prices of some of the wackiest errors you'll ever see and never thought imaginable.

5. Buy yourself a magnet, a 5-10X magnifying loupe, a digital caliper, and an electronic jeweler's scale that goes to 1/100th of a gram. A loupe for seeing details up close, a caliper to measure thickness and diameters of coins, a scale to verify weights, and magnets to check for fakes are all useful tools. These aren't the end-all tools, but they are a good start and great gadgets that a smart and proactive collector owns to help stay one step ahead of all the predatory scammers.

6. Join local and national coin clubs including the **ANA** (American Numismatic Association) and **CONECA** (The Combined Organization of Numismatic Error Collectors of America) both to network with other collectors and for member privileges including access to valuable archived resources (including ANA libraries to borrow copies of books), discounts or free admission to local and national shows, and other goodies.

7. Most importantly, have an open and intellectually curious mind. Read, examine, analyze, compare, and ask questions. Practice your skills often and test your hypotheses. Learn from your mistakes and don't be arrogant. Use the experts and their vast experiences as tools as they all love sharing their knowledge. Over time, you'll be able to teach yourself what is and isn't a Mint error and maybe even become the next expert!

How Do You Find Mint Errors?

Despite what you might read or see on internet video channels, the chances of coming across a genuine, significant Mint error or die variety in circulation is astronomically low. Sure, once in a while someone finds that $50,000 coin, but it's important to temper those expectations and be realistic. *Can you find some genuine Mint errors in circulation?* Yes. *Will most of them still be worth face value?* Yes again. It's not hard to find a few minor laminations, misaligned dies, die cracks, and die chips (these will be explained later), but most of them carry little to no premium.

However, *someone* had to be the first person to discover a significant error. *So how are they found other than buying them from dealers?* One popular yet tedious method is to buy rolls of coins (or people's hoards of coins) and search through them, one by one, using loupes, digital scales, and calipers in what is known as coin mining or **coin roll hunting (CRH)**. This method requires a heck of a lot of work. You have to go to a store or bank, hope they are willing to sell you rolls of coins (which many banks do not like doing if you don't have a business account), carry them out (these get heavy fast!), search through them, roll them back up, and then cart them back to the bank hoping they will buy them back from you. (I have heard from many CRHs that even their own banks where they have personal accounts have refused to sell them rolled coins. In fact, bank tellers I know personally hate dealing with the CRH crowd simply for all the work it creates for them regardless if you are extra nice.) Keep in mind that several error types won't be found in rolls. *Why?* Because some errors become so misshapen and/or enlarged that they can't get processed by coin counting machines nor fit in rolls (see bottom-left photo).

Similar to CRH is when you used to be able to buy small, sealed, canvas **Mint bags** of coins to search through (see center-left photo). Here, coins were not rolled but bagged as loose coins and is where most significant errors were first found. Unfortunately since 2002 coins all leave the Mint in huge ballistic bags (and are rolled by 3rd parties) and new technology to both quickly identify and prevent errors from occurring has greatly reduced most significant errors from leaving the Mint. (Be very cautious of scammers offering old "unopened" Mint bags above face value to search through as it is not hard to resew them after removing high grade coins and/or Mint errors and then switching them out.)

Next is a strategy known as **cherry picking**, which is when you search through dealers' junk boxes or online sales to find an error or die variety that a seller didn't catch. I even search through "normal" boxes of coins at coin shops/shows because many don't know enough about errors. This strategy is enjoyable and less intensive than CRH but requires a much deeper numismatic knowledge. Like CRH, high-valued finds are few and far between but the potential is there.

Lastly, don't forget to also check coins secured in Mint sets, Proof sets, and other special releases. This is by far the toughest avenue to discover a significant, valuable error or die variety. *Why?* Because many expert eyes have already examined those Mint and proof sets very closely looking for non-error gems or popular die varieties like 1955 and 1972 doubled die cents. *Is it still possible to find some errors and die varieties in Mint/proof sets?* Let's find out on the next couple pages!

(Below) This off-center cent is too physically distorted to fit in a roll of cents. Based on its date (2000) it was likely first found in a sealed Mint bag.

Yes, it is possible to find errors and die varieties in Mint and proof sets. In fact, I have one Mint set with the error featured here and a proof set with a major blunder (a die variety) on the next page. Though this 1965 Roosevelt dime error isn't considered to be jaw-dropping, it isn't insignificant either. Many collectors will pay extra on top of the current going rate for errors for those found in Mint and Proof sets simply because (1) they never circulated and (2) finding them in sealed sets is very, very rare…and cool! (Beware: I have seen evidence of people tinkering with sets to place errors inside them knowing those found in sets sell for higher premiums; I call this sneaky move "plastic surgery.") Always inspect all packaging, seals, and corners carefully for signs tampering.

Despite slim odds, for many it's the thrill of the hunt that makes it fun no matter how you choose to search for Mint errors. Again, reading up on the minting process and specific error types should help increase your chances. At a minimum you should know standard weights, metallic compositions, and when design changes occurred. And don't forget: A wise numismatist spends most of his/her time researching and studying coins than looking for coins to buy.

1965 Mint Set Containing a Roosevelt Dime with Clashed Dies

A die clash is when dies strike each other absent a planchet which can then leave slight markings of the opposite die on both dies. Notice you can make out the clear outline of FDR's head on the reverse, and some of the leaves and "PL" of PLURIBUS on the obverse, albeit backwards. (Rare; $85 for the Mint set)

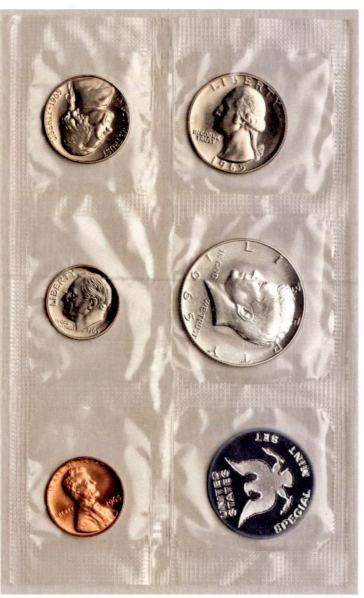

Close-up of the Roosevelt Dime Die Clash Error Sealed Inside the Mint Packaging

Coin Trivia: One of the first periodicals dedicated to covering Mint errors was Error Trends Coin Magazine; *it was published by Arnold Margolis from 1968-2011. Arnie passed away in 2012.*

1983 Proof Set:
Contains a "No S" Mintmark Roosevelt Dime

Finding major errors and major die varieties in proof sets is considerably more difficult than discovering them in Mint sets seeing that proof production and packaging is done with significantly more control and care; there are also far fewer proof coins minted than those produced for circulation. Although someone erred by not putting the "S" mintmark on the Roosevelt dime die that struck this proof coin, technically this blunder and other coins missing their mintmarks are die varieties – not Mint errors. Unfortunately "No S" die varieties still in their original government packaging are slowly becoming extinct as fortune hunters will often break them out of sets hoping to get an elusive PF70 grade from grading companies. Other known "No S" proof dimes include 1968, 1970, 1975. There is also a 1990 cent, a 1971 nickel, and even a 1976 Eisenhower dollar (Type 2) missing the "S" mintmark. (Rare; $700)

| Close-up of the 1983 "No S" Dime | Close-up of a Normal 1983-S Dime |

Coin Trivia: There are only 2 known 1975 "No S" dimes. One of them, graded PR-68 by PCGS, sold for $456,000 in 2019 at a Heritage Auctions sale.

Never, Ever Clean Coins Yourself!

OK, so you've found some interesting coins, possibly even a couple you think may be errors. Depending on how they were stored, what type of metal they are, and how old they are, they could have dirt, gunk, dark toning, stains, carbon or rust spots, or God knows what else on them. *If that's the case, I should just clean them myself, right?*

WRONG! Regardless of what cleaning product you read about or cleaning demonstration you saw online, it is never, ever a good idea to clean a coin yourself because the odds are astronomically high you will cause permanent damage to it. A coin's surface and its surface finish are very sensitive and experienced collectors will examine them carefully. Though you might think it looks good after you've cleaned it, you likely left fine hairline scratches or more serious abrasions, a loss of Mint luster, discoloration, and/or a loss of detail that can totally kill a coin's appeal and value. Serious collectors do not search for improperly cleaned coins to add to their collections and prefer their natural look even if there is a spec of dirt or harmless debris on them. Experienced dealers don't want to buy cleaned coins because they are incredibly tougher to sell; you might be lucky simply getting melt value for them. I have lost count how many times I saw a very rare error but quickly disregarded it because someone cleaned it improperly.

Is there a way to properly clean or restore a coin? Yes, but you need to leave this to the few professionals who know how to do it properly. Both PCGS and NCS (a parent company of NGC) have restoration services that can do a very good job if they are able to bring your coin back to life, however in most cases damage you or someone else caused can not be reversed (e.g. scratches). The cost for both services is very reasonable at around $25 per coin (depending on the coin's value) and though it's about $20 more than the cleaning supplies you might try and use, it is well worth the added expense. If you don't want the heartache that comes with being told you just ruined the very rare and valuable coin you found, please, never, ever clean coins yourself! And, yes, this means you!

1964 Silver Washington Quarter: Struck on a Thin Planchet (4.9 Grams) ~ Improperly Cleaned

Errors on precious-metal coins are always a great find and generally sell for more money than those on modern clad coinage. Regrettably someone ruined this coin by improperly cleaning it (notice all the scratches on the close-up below) possibly to remove the natural toning some silver coins tend to develop. What could have been about a $75 coin has been reduced to its current melt value of roughly $3. If you don't know what you're doing, leave it to the pros.

1947-S Philippines 50 Centavos (Non-error)

Some collectors love toning on coins even if it hinders a coin's designs, while others hate it and find toned coins to be ugly. Below is a heavily-toned Filipino 50 Centavos coin featuring U.S. General Douglas MacArthur.

Know What "Rare" Means (and Doesn't Mean)

"Look! I found a rare Mint error! Wow! I'm rich!"

Not really. This minor curved clip is only worth approximately $10.

By now you should have a good understanding of how to look for Mint errors and that you never clean coins yourself. However there are many misconceptions about collectibles – including coins and Mint errors especially – that are important for you to be aware of. In my opinion, among the biggest fallacies in numismatics is the belief that *someone who has been collecting or selling coins for a long time knows more than someone who hasn't.* Wrong! In any field, the length of time you've been doing something does not necessarily mean you are good at it. What matters is whether or not your information is correct and your knowledge base is strong. I know many coin dealers who have been in business for decades yet they can't tell a good fake from a genuine coin, or a damaged coin from a real Mint error. At the risk of sounding arrogant, I promise you'll know more about Mint errors from reading this book than many experienced dealers and collectors out there.

Other popular misconceptions revolve around usage of the term "rare," and some of them can cost you dearly. I see so many inexperienced collectors buying what they think are "rare" errors with the hopes of flipping them for ungodly profits only to see them lose money. In fact, many errors I see online marketed as "rare" are actually not rare; they're "scarce." *So what exactly does "rare" mean? How is it different from "scarce?" Does "rare" equal "valuable?" Are coins with lower mintages always more valuable than those with higher mintages?* Some of these answers may surprise you, and hopefully they will save you some pain.

For starters, the terms "rare" and "scarce" are not synonyms but instead reflect differences in known quantities. A coin is considered **scarce** if is has considerably fewer in number than those which are **common** (plentiful, affordable, and easily attainable by any collector). If a particular coin is significantly lower in number than a scarce coin, it is considered to be **rare**. However if a coin is so rare that there is only one known to exist, it is referred to as **unique.** If we rank these in order of fewest to most known in existence, it goes as follows: Unique, rare, scarce, and common. (Some go even further with subcategories like "ultra-rare," "very scarce," or "somewhat-common.")

But some coins can be considered scarce or even rare even if there were large production quantities. *Wait. I'm confused. Are you saying a coin with a very high mintage could simultaneously be considered scarce or rare? Yes. How is that possible?* Because *how many were produced* does not matter as much as *how many are still known to exist,* known as **extant.** For example, the Mint has previously either melted or scrapped hoards of coins for various reasons that never even circulated. Some dates and mintmarks were destroyed by the hundreds of thousands, thus they went from being common to scarce. Another reason is that although some coins had large mintages *and* many still exist, there are few known *in certain grades*; this is known as **condition rarity**. Some coins are so rare in higher grades that they skyrocket in value by thousands or tens of thousands of dollars over those just one or two grades lower. (A few numismatists have actually developed "rarity scales" with specific numbers to help differentiate rare, scarce, and common coins. However they all have their issues in terms of how reliable they are.)

Another fallacy is that "rare" always equals "very valuable." What makes anything valuable is *not the number that exist* but *what the level of demand is* for an item. For example, there are some coins (e.g. 3 cent non-silver nickels) where certain years had fewer than 25,000 produced and sell for only hundreds of dollars. In contrast, there are a handful Mercury dimes with mintages at 264,000 or 1,000,000+ that even in the same high grades (and more known examples) sell for tens of thousands of dollars. The reason is that there are considerably more people who collect Mercury dimes than 3 cent non-silver nickels, which of course that higher demand drives up prices. The same concepts apply to Mint errors. In relation to the millions or billions produced for a given coin each year only a micro-fraction become errors. Thus you can make the case that all Mint errors are "rare" or even "unique" since no two errors are *exactly* the same. But very few people collect Mint errors, and several error types like modern curved clips (like the 1985-D cent above), broadstrikes, and minor off-centers on smaller denominations like zinc cents, nickels, and non-silver dimes don't even sell for $15 in MS grades. (Many people actually consider these "scarce" and not "rare" since there are often dozens of them for sale.)

If you didn't before, hopefully now you understand the difference between "rare" and "scarce," that "rare" does not always equal "very valuable," and that some coins with more known examples can sell for much more money than those with fewer in existence (even in the same grade). So don't assume you hit the jackpot if you happen to find a Mint error, and avoid get sucked into some marketing ploy where a seller promotes a coin as being "rare" to induce you to buy it. Knowledge is power which can both save and make you money.

What Should a Good and Complete Error Collection Include?

Whether you collect coins, stamps, action figures, Civil War artifacts, Salvador Dali paintings, or antique Fords, it is natural for most beginners to want to acquire a good, complete collection. However, several conversations can be had about the meaning of the words "good," "complete," and even what the word "collection" means. With collecting Mint errors, these definitions can become even more ambiguous to people.

When I tell people I collect errors, one of the first questions I am asked is usually, "Is it a good collection?" Well, that depends on what "good" means to the people who asked. Do they mean "good" as in "valuable?" Well, I have a few that are incredible errors but aren't very valuable. Are they not considered "good" if they're only worth $25? Maybe they mean "good" as in "eye-pleasing?" Some in my collection are completely blank on both sides yet worth over $1,000. Others are struck on both sides but are just plain ugly-looking to some. Are these "good" error coins? But "good" could also refer to "Mint condition," "rare," or a "complete set." Who gets to decide what is "good" and what isn't?

Now we have another problem. What is meant by a "complete" set? For traditional non-error collectors, "complete" could mean every single year and mintmark for every Lincoln cent made. OK, but are you including "oddities" like all the many doubled dies (e.g. 1955, 1969-S, 1972, 1983, etc.), the 1922 "No D," years that have both small and large dates (e.g. 1960, 1970-S, 1982, etc.), and all the repunched mintmarks? Some do and some don't, so which is actually "complete?" The same applies to Mint errors. If I have every coin series except a Morgan dollar that is 10% off-center or more, is my set "incomplete?"

This leads to yet another discussion. At what point can someone say they have a "collection?" Must it be a complete set of something? Does it have to be in a coin album or in 2x2s, or can I just throw everything in a coffee can? Do I have to be actively looking or can it be just what I happen to find in pocket change? Let's say I only want to collect different metallic combinations from the Jefferson nickel series, of which there are two: (1) 75% copper +25% nickel and (2) the 35% silver war nickels. If I have both, can I say I have a "collection" if it only consists of two coins? Is it "complete?"

As you probably figured out, the words "good, complete" and "collection" mean whatever you – the individual collector – want them to mean. A collection can be a complete set of all Lincoln cents ever released by the Mint, only the "Wheat" cents, or even just a few from your birth year. You decide if it is good or not despite the fact that others will judge it from their own personal standards. Of course, the same is true for Mint errors. Personally, I like off-center and wrong-metal coins and don't find rotated dies interesting. Does that mean my collection is good but your collection of rotated dies is not?

So what should a good and complete error collection include? Are the Lincoln cents on the left considered "good" errors? Can they be part of a "complete" collection? Can it even be called a "collection?" Because we have the power to determine what these words mean based on personal tastes, it consists of whatever you personally say is a good, complete collection.

How Should I Build an Error Collection?

Exactly how you should build an error collection is up to you, but I do recommend you have a theme to it. Buying random Mint errors with no sense of purpose can create a disorganized mess. As for suggestions on organized error themes, the number of choices is limitless and is why error collecting can be much more fun. One common theme people pick includes any and all errors from their birth year, while others only pick silver dollar errors. Below are just a few more choices that are quite common with error collecting.

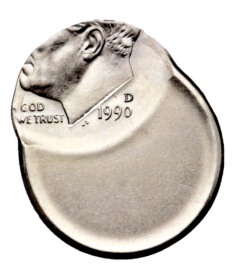

Same Error Type, Different Denominations

Same Denomination and Series, Different Error Types

Same Denomination, Series, and Error Type, but with Sequential Dates

13

Know a Coin's Anatomy

A few beneficial things to grasp in understanding coin collecting includes their anatomy and what certain features mean on them. Hopefully addressing these terms first will help avoid questions as they come up later, including: *Are edges and rims the same thing? How is an obverse different from a reverse? And since when does a coin have "fields?"* Definitions are provided below. (The coin displayed is an error that was struck on a Type 1 blank.)

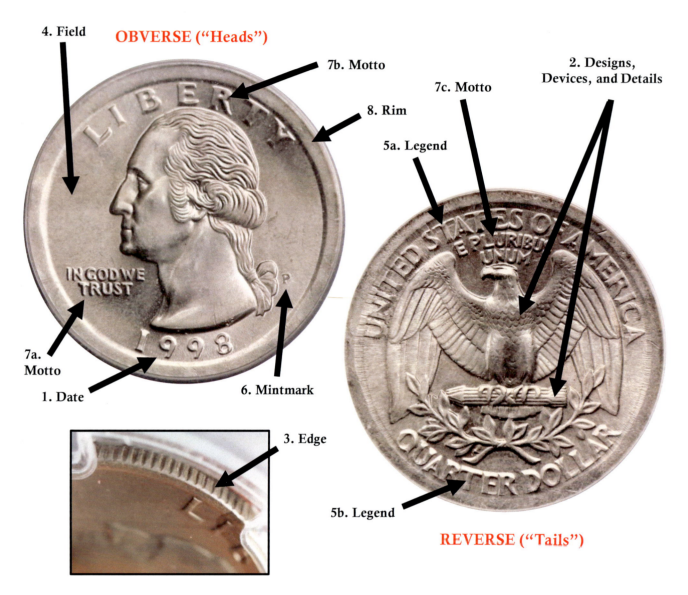

OBVERSE ("Heads")

4. Field
7b. Motto
8. Rim
7a. Motto
1. Date
6. Mintmark

2. Designs, Devices, and Details
7c. Motto
5a. Legend
3. Edge
5b. Legend

REVERSE ("Tails")

1. Date = Indicates the year a coin was issued. Keep in mind that doesn't always mean it's the year it was actually minted. Coins have been produced both the year before and after its date throughout the Mint's history. (Weird, eh?)

2. Designs/Devices/Details = Features struck on a coin, including busts, animals, buildings, etc.

3. Edge = The outer border and "third" side of a coin.

4. Field(s) = Area not used for designs, lettering, etc.

5a & 5b. Legend = Lettering/numbering on a coin stating country, denomination, dates, etc.

6. Mintmark = Letters indicating at which Mint the coin was struck: P = Philadelphia, PA; D = Denver, CO; S = San Francisco, CA; O = New Orleans, LA; C = Charlotte, NC (older gold pieces); CC = Carson City, NV; W = West Point, NY; and at one point D also = Dahlonega, GA (older gold pieces). Locations have varied among different denominations throughout the years. (Note: Coins lacking a mintmark denotes production in Philadelphia, PA.

7a & 7b. Motto = A word/phrase describing a nation's values or principles (e.g. Liberty, In God We Trust, etc.).

8. Rim = Raised borders on coins to help prevent wear.

Why Edges and Rims Are Important For Coins

Edges: For some coins minted today like dimes, quarters and half dollars, you may have noticed the edges have a pattern of ridges or lines; this is known as **reeding.** Over the years other patterns along the edge have been featured, including decorative designs and even lettering and numbering displaying mottos and dates of mintage. *Is reeding just for decoration?* No, and its purpose has been important over the years and remains so to this day.

Back when many circulated coins were composed of 90% gold and silver (with 10% copper), their face value had to equal their weight. In other words, a $5 gold coin had $5 worth of gold in it at the time. Before coins had reeding, scammers figured out they could shave off some gold or silver, sell it as scrap, and continue using those altered coins at face value. It didn't take long for merchants and bankers to learn they were occasionally getting ripped off, and a lack of faith in the value of coinage could have led to serious financial repercussions both here and abroad. Many governments responded to this problem by putting edge patterns on precious-metal coins to both restore public confidence and to better prevent altering and counterfeiting them. Though some attempted to continue shaving them down and carving on fake reeding (for example, the "Rackateer" nickel), the pattern seldom was uniform and tampering was spotted more easily.

OK, but coins meant for circulation today aren't made of precious metals, so why do they still apply reeding? One of the reasons is not just tradition but also to help those who are blind/visually impaired to know which denomination they have. Quarters and nickels aren't that far off in diameter, but the feel of a reeded edge helps you know immediately which it is. Cents and dimes are also similar in size, and again the reeding pattern helps make that distinction. Though nickels and cents are similar in diameter and neither have reeding, nickels are much thicker. Even some modern Sacagawea and Presidential Series dollars have "lettered" edges recessed/incused into the edge which you can feel (though some are missing it! I have some!). So, yes, edge design is important even today.

For coins that have reeding, the process is done at the time of striking inside a reeded **collar** that holds the unstruck planchet in place as the dies strike it (bottom left). As the die pressure is applied, the coin expands slightly while pushing against the reeding pattern inside the collar (bottom right), which leaves the reeded pattern on the edge. If the coin is not seated properly inside the collar, nothing is preventing it from expanding in size and the reeding may be partly or totally missing. You will see examples of these issues later with coins missing reeding which should have it and coins featuring it which aren't supposed to. So don't forget to always inspect edges, too!

Above are photos of a 90% silver dime and quarter which illustrates their edge reeding pattern.

Above is a JFK half dollar missing edge reeding as it was not seated properly inside the reeded collar.

In this bottom row are photos of a Roosevelt dime collar (left) and a close-up of the reeding pattern inside of it (right). The edges of an unstruck planchet push into the reeding pattern when the dies strike it, which then leaves that pattern on the edges of struck coins.

Rims: *Are rims really necessary?* Yes, and the rim should be the highest part of the coin's surface. *Why?* First, it makes coins easier to stack and put in rolls. Second, by making the rim the highest part of a coin, the constant handling of them thousands of times over will help reduce wear and enable the coin to stay in circulation longer; this also reduces replacement costs.

Some coins in particular had poorly engineered designs with virtually useless rims resulting in faster than normal circulation wear, especially for Buffalo nickels. With these, the coin's **relief** (the level which the coin is raised above the surface and appears three dimensional) was too high – mainly the date – and years of circulated use wore the dates and other high points off completely. (See photos below.) Despite later making the date's numbers thicker, the Mint never really solved this problem for this series. Though dateless Buffalo nickels are still worth five cents, they are useless in terms of collector value and appeal.

**1937-D
Buffalo Nickel**

<u>**Condition:**</u>
About Uncirculated

**No Date
Buffalo Nickel**

<u>**Condition:**</u>
God-awful!

NY

Nickel City

Coin Trivia: Many cities have nicknames (e.g. The "Big Apple" for New York City, the "Windy City" for Chicago, etc.), and Buffalo, NY is no different. Known as "The City of Good Neighbors" for its historically friendly residents and the "Queen City" because it was once one of the largest and most prosperous cities in the Great Lakes region during the late 19th to the early 20th centuries, it also earned another nickname in 1913: "Nickel City." Why? The release of the new Buffalo nickel that year featured an image of what many think is a Buffalo on the reverse with an Indian chief on the obverse. However, the animal featured is technically an American bison – not a Buffalo – so the nickname for both the nickel and the city are actually misnomers.

Differences Between Series, Types, Varieties and Die Varieties

Series: Throughout our history as a nation – including the colonial period under England – there have been dozens and dozens of different designs featured on numerous denominations with some only lasting a few years. Both the process of producing them and the design for each coin is an art. They are part of a nation's culture which usually reflects the values of its people (or a dictator's values), and often great consideration, study, debate, and even temper tantrums occur before an official design is chosen to represent a specific denomination.

Most coins are referred to by the real or fictional people or other image on the obverse, including Washington quarters, Liberty nickels, and Eisenhower ("Ike") dollars. A few are referred to by their designer, like Barber dimes, quarters and half dollars (Charles Barber) or Morgan dollars (George Morgan). Yet others are referred to by things like the figure's hairstyle (Flowing Hair or Braided Hair large cent), body position (Seated or Standing Liberty quarters), monetary value (2 cent copper piece, 3 cent nickel, or $3 gold piece), or an animal featured on them (Buffalo nickel, Flying Eagle cent). To be clear, a specific denomination's basic design elements over a period of time is known as a **series**. For example, since 1866 there have been FOUR series of 5 cent nickels, so knowing which series one is referring to is not just helpful but essential. Some people even choose to collect coins by simply acquiring one coin from each series of every denomination, but this can get difficult and pricey when including gold pieces.

Coin Trivia: The U.S. three cent silver piece, also known as the "trime," was the first U.S. coin where the stated value was actually worth more than its metallic value; it was 75% silver rather than 90% for other silver coins. It is also the smallest silver coin in diameter that the U.S. ever minted. (Trime photos courtesy of Heritage Auctions/HA.com.)

"Children of the Coin"
Below are all the 5 cent nickel series produced by the Mint.
(All but Buffalo nickel photos courtesy of Heritage Auctions/HA.com)

Shield (1866-1883)

Liberty (1883-1913)

Indian Head or Buffalo (1913-1938)

Jefferson (1938-Present)

Types: Most people recognize what denomination a coin is simply by looking at it with a quick glance. It is when designs are changed that people many now have to inspect their coins more closely, especially if they didn't know a change in design(s) was coming. Among the most recognizable coins in America for well over a century is the Lincoln cent, but it has gone through a string of design modifications as well as different base metals. These significant, intentional alterations to the basic designs or metallic compositions within a series are known as **types.**

Why change the design and/or metals? One popular motive is to commemorate a historical person's life. For example, 2009 represented 100 years of the Lincoln cent's production and the 200th anniversary of his birth. To honor President Lincoln, a special bicentennial type featuring four different reverse designs was released depicting various stages of his life. Other reasons include commemorating an event like America's bicentennial in 1976, switching metals to reduce cost (e.g. copper prices are rising), or due to production of a special series like the 50 State Quarters or Presidential Series dollars which have different obverse or reverse designs every year.

For Lincoln cents there are six types within this series which are featured below: (1) Copper "Wheat" reverse; (2) Steel "Wheat" reverse; (3) Copper "Memorial" reverse; (4) Copper-plated zinc "Memorial" reverse; (5) The 2009 "Bicentennial" for which there are four different reverse designs. (The proof and "Satin Finish" examples are 95% copper; the others are copper-plated zinc); and (6) Copper-plated zinc "Shield" reverse. In addition, their composition has changed a few times: Copper to steel, back to copper after one year, then it changed to copper-plated zinc roughly 40 years later which continues today. Other examples include Jefferson nickels which had silver *added* to them for a few years during World War Two, and a few series have collector pieces made from 40% or 90% silver and even .9999 fine gold. I guess change is a tradition! *(All except the "Steel Wheat" photo courtesy of Heritage Auctions/HA.com)*

Different Reverse Types of the Lincoln Cent (1909 – Present)

Copper Wheat

Steel Wheat

Copper Memorial

Zinc Memorial

2009 Commemorative Minted in Zinc and 95% Copper (Formative Years; 1 of 4 Reverse Designs)

Zinc Shield

Varieties and Die Varieties: Sometimes there are modest, subtle alterations to a die that happen without changing the overall design. These can be *intentional*, like changing the size of letters or numbers (e.g. 1960 large & small date cents). When minor variations are what Mint designers intended to change, these are known as **varieties.** (Also known as "intentional die varieties.")

Yet other times there are changes to a die as it's being produced that were *unintentional* – flaws – which then strike those imperfections on to planchets; these are known as **die varieties**. Among the most expensive of these are **doubled dies** where the coin hub used to make dies was not aligned properly above the die after the first engraving. What results are doubled letters, numbers, and/or designs with one set being slightly off-center, but the die hubbing process has since changed to better prevent mistakes. One example is the 1934 Washington Quarter Obverse Doubled Die with strong doubling on IN GOD WE TRUST. (Rare; $440; AU-58 by ANACS)

Though die varieties are considered mistakes, they aren't technically "Mint errors." *Why?* Because a die variety involves a flaw on the die(s) *before a planchet is even struck,* whereas a Mint error results from the planchet *not being struck properly* or *flaws with the metal*. For example, before the 1990s on circulated coinage, mintmarks used to be hand-punched right on the working dies using a mallet and punch. If a second hit on the punch was needed, the engraver had to be sure it was at the exact same spot as the first. If the punch moved even slightly, there would be two mintmarks (or possibly more) with one (or more) off-center. Every planchet struck from that die with a **repunched mintmark (RPM)** would also feature that flaw until a new die replaced it. It's the die that is flawed, not because the metal was imperfect or that the striking process was compromised; thus, RPMs are die varieties, not Mint errors. The 1943 D over D Lincoln Cent (FS-501/FS-019) is among the most prized of all RPM Lincoln cents. (Rare; $700; MS-65 by PCGS).

1934 Washington Quarter Doubled Die Obverse

1943 "D/D" Lincoln Cent
Repunched Mintmark (RPM) FS-501

Differences Between Alloy, Clad, and Plated Coins

Aside from early American copper cents and half cents which were all one metal (100% copper up until 1858), each coin today minted for circulation is composed of more than one metal. The reasons different metals are/were combined includes everything from making the metal harder to reduce wear, to adjusting for the rising values of certain metals, to reducing costs, and for conserving metals for wartime use. How they come together to form one solid piece of metal is what differentiates alloy, clad, and plated coinage. Let's learn the differences below.

<u>Alloys</u>: When you make a cake, some of the ingredients you'll need includes vegetable oil, eggs, milk, and sugar that are mixed with flour. Once the cake is mixed and baked, it is not possible to distinguish or identify exactly where particles of each ingredient are; they all blended together and fused into one "cake." This same concept is true for **alloy** coins, where two or more metals are melted, mixed, and form one solid mass of metal. A few alloy coins include Lincoln cents from 1909 to mid-1982 (95% copper + 5% from other metals, except 1943 which are zinc-plated steel and aren't alloys), nickels (75% copper + 25% nickel), and pre-1965 dimes, quarters, and half dollars (90% silver + 10% copper). Like the cake, in the right column you cannot look at the nickel or silver quarter and see any copper, nor can you detect particles of zinc on the 1982 copper cent. However, there are some rare cases where parts of the metal did not melt or mix properly and can be identified in spots; if so, they are considered Mint errors.

> *Coin Trivia: Created in 1792, The United States Mint Police protects employees and its assets with roughly 300 officers throughout its various facilities across the country. (Badge photo credit: USMint.gov)*

75% Copper, 25% Nickel Alloy Jefferson Nickel

90% Silver, 10% Copper Alloy Washington Quarter

95% Copper, 5% Zinc Alloy Lincoln Cent

There were both copper alloy and copper-plated zinc cents minted in 1982. In most cases weighing them can identify which is which. (3.1 grams for copper alloy cents and 2.5 grams for copper-plated zinc cents.)

Clad: In 1965, the U.S. Mint ceased producing 90% silver alloy dimes, quarters, and half dollars for circulation and instead began making clad coins. **Clad** metal consists of separate metallic layers that are pressed into each other with rollers which bond together to form one solid metallic mass.

Since 1965, dimes and quarters consist of a pure copper center sandwiched by two layers of a copper-nickel alloy – one on each side (see quarter photos below). Half dollars from 1965-1970 (and some from 1976) are 40% silver clad and made from three separate silver-copper alloy layers, but half dollars transitioned to the same style as dimes and quarters by 1971. Other clad coins include dollars like Eisenhowers, Susan B. Anthonys, Sacagaweas, and Presidential Series dollars.

With the exception of 40% silver coins and some of the older Sacagawea and Presidential dollars, you can see the individual clad layers on a coin's edge (center). One issue with clad coins is that improper bonding can lead to layers separating or even detaching completely or in sections from the center before or after striking which drastically changes their color from gray to red.

Reverse Clad Layer   **Copper Center**   **Obverse Clad Layer**

90% Silver Alloy Quarter

Clad Quarter

Coin Trivia: Dies used to be dipped in melted wax or plastic to prevent them from getting scratched and to block dust and other debris from settling on them. This quarter set is for a 1985-S proof. (Scarce; $60 for the pair)

Plating: Starting in mid-1982, the U.S. Mint transitioned the metallic composition of cents from 95% copper to a zinc core **plated** with a thin copper layer using an electroplating bath. Basically, an electric current from a circuit is applied causing negatively charged zinc planchets to attract copper ions while submerged in an electrolyte solution; the copper then covers or "plates" the zinc planchets. Since this change, instead of Lincoln cents being 95% copper they are now 2.5% copper and 97.5% zinc. *Why the change?* Because soon there would have been more than 1 cent worth of copper in a 1 cent coin, and is the same reason the Mint discontinued silver coinage in the 1960s. Technically, despite both copper-plated zinc and 1943 zinc-coated steel cents having different layers of metal, these are not considered "clad" because they aren't solid metallic layers pressed together.

Unfortunately, the surfaces for both zinc and steel cents are prone to deterioration when their ultra-thin plating is compromised. For current copper-plated zinc cents, the copper layer is so thin that sometimes trauma causing expansion (e.g. broadstrikes) can lead to cracking of the copper plating which will expose the raw zinc below it (top row); this is known as **split-plate doubling** and is confined only to copper-plated cents. With the zinc exposed to the elements, environmental factors/conditions can lead to its deterioration and corrosion more quickly causing "zinc rot" (center row); it is one reason why many collectors hate the change to a zinc core and sarcastically refer to these as "zincolns." For 1943 steel cents, many lost some of their zinc outer layer from years of handling and/or damage and left the unprotected, low-grade steel areas susceptible to rusting (bottom row). Oh, the humanity!

1999 Broadstruck Copper-plated Zinc Cent

Split Plating of Copper Layer Exposing Zinc Core Due to Being Broadstruck

1993 Copper-plated Zinc Cent with Severe "Zinc Rot"

1943-S Zinc-plated Steel Cent

1943 Zinc-plated Steel Cent with Rust

The Metallic Makeup of Modern U.S. Coin Denominations

Lincoln Cents

From the first Lincoln cent in 1909 through 1942 (as well as Indian Head cents from 1864-1909), cents were an alloy of 95% copper and a 5% mix of zinc/tin (with tin being removed for several years). Since 1942 several compositional changes occurred, which include:

* 1943 → zinc-plated steel
* 1944-1946 → 95% copper + 5% zinc (tin removed)
* 1947-1961 → 95% copper + 5% zinc/tin
* 1962-1982 → 95% copper + 5% zinc (tin removed)
* 1982-Present → 2.5% copper and 97.5% zinc.
* 2009 Special Collector's Editions of Lincoln Bicentennial Cents (Proofs & Satin Finishes only) → 95% copper + 5% zinc/tin

Jefferson Nickels

Despite naming this denomination a "nickel," it is actually only 25% nickel combined with 75% copper which are melted together to form an alloy; they are not plated or layered. The exception to this composition was the production of "**war nickels**" during part of World War Two (1942 –1945, with 1942 having both a Type 1 copper-nickel and a Type 2 silver) where they were made of 35% silver, 56% copper, and 9% manganese. War nickels are easy to spot by the large mintmark above Monticello's dome on the reverse (P = Philadelphia, D = Denver, and S = San Francisco).

Roosevelt Dimes and Washington Quarters

Starting in 1965, dimes and quarters were created using a three-layered coinage strip resulting in layered blanks and planchets called clad coinage. This makeup now consists of a layer of pure copper sandwiched between two outer layers of alloyed metal composed of 75% copper and 25% nickel.

Kennedy Half Dollars

Unlike dimes and quarters, 50 cent pieces from 1965–1970, as well as collector versions of the dual-dated 1776-1976 halves are silver clad with an overall composition of 40% silver. The outer layers are composed of an 80% silver and 20% copper alloy bonded to an inner layer made up of 78.5% copper and 21.5% silver. Since 1971, circulated Kennedy halves feature the same copper-nickel clad composition as both dimes and quarters since 1965.

Eisenhower "Ike" Dollars

Minted from 1971–1978, circulated Eisenhower dollars are the same makeup as other clad coins.

Silver Versions of Roosevelts, Washingtons, Kennedys, and Eisenhowers

Collector versions of 1776-1976 dated Washington quarters, Kennedy halves, and Eisenhower dollars, as well as collector versions of Eisenhower dollars from 1971-1974, were also produced the same way as the 40% silver clad Kennedy halves. Beginning in 1992, the Mint also produced collector versions of Roosevelt dimes, Washington quarters, and Kennedy halves using a 90% silver and 10% copper alloy.

Susan B. Anthony Dollars

Only minted from 1979–1981 and again in 1999, the clad makeup for Susan B. Anthony dollars is the same as Ikes and current dimes, quarters, and half-dollars minted for circulation (non-silver).

Sacagawea / Presidential / Native American Dollars

These gold-colored coins have a pure copper center bonded to a clad alloy layer on each side made up of 77% copper, 12% zinc, 7% manganese, and 4% nickel.

Learn How Coin Values and Grades Are Determined

One of the toughest tasks about error collecting is determining the value of a Mint error. *Why?* Because there really is no "official" weekly or monthly price guide as rare non-error coins have (e.g. *The Grey Sheet*). In addition, even though some publications have generic prices for some error types, some error coins contain more than one error. Sale prices are also much less consistent for errors. So the best way to determine the value of any coin at a particular moment is through recent sales of similar items, which you can research at reputable auction sites including **Heritage Auctions, Stacks & Bowers, Great Collections**, and to some degree even EBay. Generally, the more significant, pronounced, rare, and eye-catching the error, the higher the value. However, as you will see, some plain and boring unstruck pieces can be much more valuable than dramatic and eye-catching specimens.

Along with being difficult to pinpoint an exact value, it can be equally challenging and subjective when it comes to assigning an error coin's **condition** (the state it is in) and **numerical grade** (number out of 70). Unlike non-errors in high grades, error coins often have features and details that are misshapen, cutoff, or missing entirely despite being in mint condition. One side might not be affected much, yet the other side may be fantastically distorted. Because strike quality and degree of details are so unique to each error piece and many have multiple errors, assigning grades uniformly is tougher and can seem somewhat idiosyncratic.

Since the 1970s, the universal system used to grade all U.S. coins based on their quality/condition is an American Numismatic Association (ANA)-modified version of the **Sheldon Scale**, which runs from 1 (poorest condition) to 70 (flawless under 5x magnification). Coins graded 60–70 are considered **Mint State (MS)**, meaning they are judged as uncirculated with no wear. **About Uncirculated (AU)** is the tier below MS with grades ranging from 50 to 58 with light wear, followed by the rest of the descending grades. (See the chart on the top right.)

A "PR" designation with a number (e.g. PR-62) signifies a proof coin that was graded. The word **proof** is not actually a "condition" or a "grade" but a method of production featuring its own special planchet, strike, die, and polish which leaves a mirrored or matte finish. Proofs are struck for collectors in low mintages and released in special Mint packaging (like proof sets), and though legal to remove and spend, they are not intended for circulation. The bulk of coins minted are meant to be used and spent by the public, known as **business** or **circulation strikes**, and are produced in far greater numbers. *So why aren't most modern proof coins worth a lot more if their mintages are lower than very rare, low–mintage business strike coins?* Because as explained earlier, with coin collecting low mintage by itself does not necessarily mean a coin is more valuable than one with a higher mintage. What really makes values escalate is *a high level of demand in relation to the available supply.*

Prefix	Condition	Grade(s)
PR	-	60-70
MS	Mint State / Uncirculated	60-70
AU	About Uncirculated	50, 53, 55, 58
XF	Extremely Fine	40, 45
VF	Very Fine	20, 25, 30, 35
F	Fine	12, 15
VG	Very Good	8, 10
G	Good	4-6
AG	About Good	3
FR	Fair	2
PO	Poor	1

Some of the grading companies came up with a **"plus" grade** for coins (e.g. MS66+), meaning it is on the higher end of its particular grade in addition to having above-average eye appeal. (An icon of a star or an eye is also used for eye appeal.) Although there are collectors who like this new designation to differentiate coins with the same numerical grade, many collectors see this move as nothing more than a clever marketing gimmick.

(Label photo courtesy of Heritage Auctions/HA.com)

Know What Third Party Graders (TPGs) Are and What They Do

TPGS: Because both buyers and sellers each have selfish reasons for having differences of opinion on a particular coin's condition and grade, an idea was developed to have some independent experts examine coins impartially and make those determinations to try and settle those issues. Beginning in 1972 with ANACS, companies started forming to meet this market demand which became known as **third party graders (TPGs).** Four popular grading companies that certify coins today are **Professional Coin Grading Service (PCGS), Numismatic Guaranty Corporation (NGC), American Numismatic Association Certification Service (ANACS)** and **Independent Coin Graders (ICG).**

If a coin meets the graders' standards to certify and encapsulate it, and to maintain the integrity of the coin and its label, it is placed in a protective, tamper-proof plastic holder informally called a **slab**. Labels on slabs identify at minimum the **denomination** (1c, 5c, etc.), year (if a date is present), mintmark (if any), condition/grade, and a reference number indicating things like what coin series it is, the number in that series, and company info which can normally be typed in on each company's homepage for verification. Other pertinent information can also be included like the weight, series, type, error, die variety, or variety it is.

Encapsulation is not cheap. *How much does it cost to submit them?* Depending on which TPG you use, this service costs an average of around $30-$60 per coin (not including the shipping costs) depending on the series/year/grading company. With error and die variety coins, for an additional fee of around $15 they will also list/abbreviate the type of Mint error or die variety it is (e.g. **O/C** for off-center, **DDO** for Doubled

Die Obverse, etc.). However, some which have multiple errors might not all be listed on the label because (a) they won't all fit on the label or (b) the submitter didn't pay extra to have the error/die variety examined and attributed. This is why it is a good idea to inspect all coins carefully in TPG slabs, but especially error coins.

NGC Mint Error Slab

PCGS Slab

Check labels carefully! The label for this coin is wrong before *and after* the obverse later separated. (More on this later.)

Breakdown of a PCGS Mint Error Label

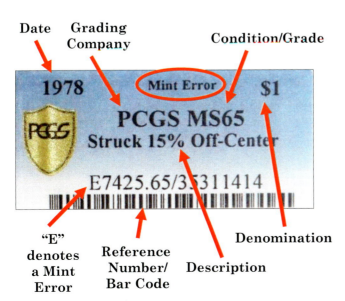

Date | Grading Company | Condition/Grade

"E" denotes a Mint Error | Reference Number/ Bar Code | Description | Denomination

An NGC body bag with the label listing the reason for rejection.

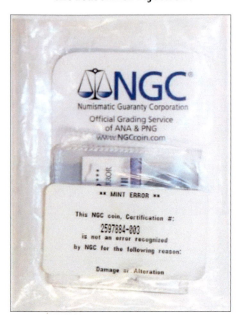

NGC "Damaged to Resemble Error" Label

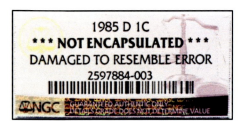

NGC "Questionable Authenticity" Label

Thanks to Jim Zimmerman for the label

An NGC "Details" Label

Some Things TPGs Try to Determine Include:

1. Is the coin a genuine Mint product? As technology improves, so does the technology for forgers to make fakes and alter genuine coins. With some incredibly rare coins being worth millions, the incentive to cash in is high. Popular coins like Morgan dollars and Lincoln cents with rare dates and mintmarks, plus valuable errors (e.g. 1943 copper cents) and die varieties (e.g. 1955 doubled die cents), are frequent targets.

If it is determined your coin is 100% fake, it will be returned with a rejection label (e.g. "Not Encapsulated") indicating the reason why (e.g. "Not Genuine"); you are not refunded the grading fees if it is fake. Some of the TPGs return them inserted in a flip and placed inside a plastic bag known unceremoniously as a **body bag**. If the TPGs cannot prove definitively a coin is genuine, it will likely receive a "No Decision" or "Questionable Authenticity" label (3rd photo from top); some of the grading companies will refund the grading fee minus a small service charge if this is the case. Then again maybe the planchet/coin is genuine but someone modified it somehow (e.g. adding/removing a mintmark or plating a coin). In other words, the coin came from the Mint but someone altered it for whatever reason. These are also placed in body bags with a label indicating the reason for rejection (top two photos) and you are not refunded your grading or shipping fees.

2. Is the coin damaged? Sometimes the issue is not a question of a coin's authenticity but whether or not the level of damage makes it unfit for grading. Coins so badly damaged that they can't be evaluated for grading will likely be rejected and sent back in body bags. Then there are coins which have some noticeable but very minor forms of post-Mint damage (e.g. hairline scratches, small gouges, etc.) which might get slabbed with a dreaded **Details grade** if you tell them it's acceptable. *What does that mean?* It means though a coin was determined to be genuine, it has an observable flaw(s) which occurred after minting and won't receive a numerical grade. You'll likely see a label stating "AU Details" rather than a grade of "AU-55" (depending on the sharpness of details) along with the flaw's description of on the label (bottom photo).

What every collector hopes for when they submit their coins is that they get **straight-graded,** meaning they are determined to be problem-free (a.k.a. "clean") and receive a numerical grade on the slab label. However, many collectors find there is often inconsistency (even within the same grading service) when it comes to evaluating what constitutes "problem-free" and "damaged," and when a coin should or shouldn't be straight-graded or given a Details grade. As expected, coins in Details holders are much less desirable and sell for exceptionally less money. Some within the hobby feel coins with Details grades shouldn't be slabbed at all.

Lastly, some counterfeit and altered coins can have educational value. One grading service – ICG – will actually slab counterfeit and altered coins for educational use. ICG inserts a cautionary yellow label with the word "FAKE" in different languages in the background of the description. Of course there is debate within the numismatic community as to whether or not any counterfeit coin should be slabbed as some feel it only promotes the nagging problem of counterfeit production.

"Not Genuine" Doesn't Always Mean "Counterfeit": The Difference Between Altered and Counterfeit Coins

If by chance a TPG determines that your coin is "Not Genuine," keep in mind that doesn't automatically mean the coin is "counterfeit." I know for simplicity's sake many collectors tend to think the word "counterfeit" applies to *any coin that isn't genuine*, but that word should be used only if certain criteria are met. In my opinion, a "counterfeit" shouldn't be confused with an "altered" planchet/coin even though both are "Not Genuine." *What's the difference?*

An **altered** planchet/coin differs from a counterfeit in that *it was at one time a completely genuine Mint-made product – from the creation of the planchet to the coin's designs/die strikes – before someone or something modified it.* For example, below is a genuine copper cent planchet. However, it was placed between two Roosevelt dimes and squeezed together leaving artificial brockages on both sides. Since the copper cent planchet is genuine despite the post-Mint modification, this coin should be considered "altered" and not "counterfeit."

In contrast, a **counterfeit** is a planchet/coin where absolutely nothing about it is (nor ever was) genuine. Someone not only created their own planchet *but also* forged all the designs/die strikes on that coin. For example, someone poured lead into those fake 1939 Mercury dime molds to make the counterfeit coin on the bottom right. The entire coin from the planchet to the raised designs is fake and therefore 100% counterfeit. (Some experts feel a genuine unstruck planchet that was struck entirely with fake dies should also be considered a counterfeit coin.)

What difference does it make if a coin has been altered or is counterfeit since both are "Not Genuine?" Because by learning how an altered/fake coin was forged, we can then check to see if other suspect coins share similar characteristics and markings (e.g. many fakes have their own die markers). We can also better determine if the quality of a forged coin is getting better over time, and if so, how and why. Perhaps we can even narrow it down to a country/region of origin or even a specific person. A wise collector doesn't just care *if* a coin isn't genuine; he/she should also want to know *why*.

Counterfeit 1939 Mercury Dime Dies (Brass Molds)

Altered Genuine Copper Cent Planchet: Vise Job with Roosevelt Dimes (Artificial Brockages)

Counterfeit 1939 Mercury Dime

Should I Submit My Coin to a TPG?

Aside from being asked if someone's error coin is genuine, the next most popular question I get is *"Should I submit my coin to a TPG?"* Well, that really depends on why you want your error coin certified, graded, and **attributed** – having the error or die variety identified. For example, what exactly do you plan on doing with the coin when you get it back? I'm amazed how many new collectors think it's automatically "just something you do" when you find a Mint error, yet some can't articulate why that is. Below are some factors that should help you decide if sending your error to a TPG is worth it or not.

Reasons You May Want To Submit Them

1. Rare/high-grade coins are often easier to sell and tend to sell for more when they're slabbed than if raw.

2. It can help prevent disputes about a coin's grade.

3. It provides more confidence a coin is genuine.

4. It provides more confidence a coin isn't damaged.

5. Slabbed coins are better protected than those left in paper or plastic flip holders.

6. You feel the TPG's conservation service can properly restore the coin and prevent further damage.

7. You want the coin to have a more professional look when using it for presentations, displays, and seminars.

8. You want to make it easier for your heirs to know what your rare and valuable error coins are and that they are genuine. By having them certified, there is less of a burden on your family to find out what you have and should make it easier for your local coin dealer to help you out.

Reasons You Might Want to Leave Them "Raw"

Not all collectors want their coins slabbed and there are some very good reasons why they don't. I seldom send in coins for grading. *Why?* I feel I have a good grasp if a coin is genuine and what error type is present, so I don't need to spend money to have someone else tell me what I already know. Below are a few reasons why you might consider not submitting them to grading services and leaving them **raw** (i.e. loose/unslabbed).

1. Depending on the TPG, the cost is around $30-$60 each to grade it, and then there are more fees for error attributions, plus your shipping costs. Is the coin even worth that much?

2. Refunds are not given if your coin is found to be "Not Genuine" or if you're not happy with the grade.

3. Slabbed coins take up much more room to store and limits how they can be displayed.

4. Some genuine errors have several different error types on a single coin. However, space on a slab label is limited so TPGs might not be able to fit all the error types on it. This can cause disputes when going to buy/sell/trade a coin.

5. Some error collectors I know don't trust some of the TPGs enough to properly attribute their error coins.

6. Plastic slabs tend to scratch easily which can ruin eye appeal. You can get them re-holdered, but there's a fee (plus shipping). Some TPGs do offer scratch-resistant holders, but there are also downsides to those as well.

7. Sometimes conserving coins to remove toning/surface debris can reveal other flaws which might become much more prominent (e.g. corrosion/pitting, scratches, etc.).

8. I have heard some people say they don't trust TPGs because a few counterfeits have been slabbed, but this happens very, very rarely. Overall they do an excellent job determining if a coin is genuine.

So should I submit my coin or not? That's up to you, but hopefully you have a better understanding of the pros and cons. It truly depends what you're looking to get out of it and what you plan to do with them.

I send fake/altered coins like this one to ICG
to get slabbed for use in educational seminars.

1944 Lincoln Cent: Struck on a Transitional Steel Planchet (2.7 Grams)

Dealer Asking Price: $3,000

When examining a coin, always remember to check the edge or "**third side**" for damage and to help verify its authenticity.

O.K., let's assume this 1944 steel Lincoln cent off-metal error is for sale at your local coin show. The dealer is asking $3,000 and you have the cash in your pocket to buy it. Other attendees there are starting to express interest in it, but their offers are a little too low for the dealer. You remember a similar one sold for over $45,000 a while back. So you ask yourself, *"Is it possible this dealer doesn't fully appreciate just what it is he has here? Will it finally be my turn to find the score of a lifetime?"* However, one nagging issue concerns you: This coin isn't certified. Are you able to determine if it's genuine without the help of a TPG? Keep in mind that as an error collector you might be one of only a few people at any local show who collects errors. It's also possible you might be the most knowledgeable person in the entire building with no one beyond your understanding of errors to get a second opinion. Situations like this are where you as a buyer assume the greatest risk of winding up with a fake; the higher the coin's price, the greater the risk when buying them raw/uncertified. As you're mulling over if it's authentic or not, the dealer senses your curiosity and says, "It might be years before you come across another one. Do you have any questions?" Yes, there are some very good questions you need to ask, but chances are a dealer who doesn't specialize in errors either won't be able to answer them or will give you wrong (or partially-wrong) information. Here are some good questions the average error collector might ask: (1) What does it weigh?; (2) Can you scan its metal content?; (3) Is this steel cent magnetic as it should be?; (4) What's the thickness and diameter?; and (5) What do the edges and rims look like?

Though these are great questions, what's troubling is that some counterfeits are so good they'll pass all of these diagnostic tests. For example, many 1944 steel cent fakes have the same weight (2.7 grams) as genuine errors, are made of steel and are magnetic, have the same thickness/diameter, and have smooth, rounded edges with raised rims. Many rare copper, silver, and gold coin fakes will scan at the correct metal content because forgers melted down badly worn and/or common dates of genuine coins and then made their own planchets and dies. Missing/fuzzy details and a lack of any Mint luster are usually the best clues a coin is fake, but many genuine errors will appear to have significantly weaker details including some off-metal errors. Also, some high-quality fakes were (likely) made at professional and/or government minting facilities whereby the counterfeits produced have both strong details and original Mint luster; a few were even certified and slabbed by TPGs.

So how can I ever tell if it's genuine if all these diagnostics can be faked? Well, if you aren't 100% certain, DON'T BUY IT! Also, you should study how a series you like has been minted over the years, how it's changed, and research common counterfeiting methods. There's plenty of good information out there to help you stay informed, and many wise collectors will tell you to **"Buy the book before you buy the coin!"** *So is this coin genuine or a counterfeit? What clues do you see here?* Let's find out on the next page!

Counterfeit 1944 Steel Cent

Answer: 100% COUNTERFEIT

**Fake Planchet
and
Fake Die Strikes**

Genuine 1944-S Steel Cent *(Used by permission
PCGS ® www.PCGS.com/CoinFacts)*

<u>Above</u>: Rough edges with a "cut and
tear" texture are normal for blanks, not
coins with raised rims. This alone makes
the coin immediately suspect as a fake.

<u>**Reasons Why It's Counterfeit**</u> :
1. The details are way too soft, particularly those on Lincoln's head and face (especially his hair).
2. The shape of some of the lettering, especially the "O" in GOD and the "B" in LIBERTY, don't match up.
3. The "4s" in the date on the suspect coin not only don't match those on the genuine coin, they are different from each other; they're also slanted clockwise. In addition, the shape and tail of the "9" doesn't match the genuine coin.
4. The designer's initials "VDB" (green arrow) are missing on the suspect coin (red arrow).
5. The edges on the suspect coin have that "cut and tear" look despite having a rim. Since the process to add the rim smooths out those edges, there is no way this planchet is genuine.

1960-D Lincoln Cent: Multi-struck (3.11 Grams)

Dealer Asking Price: $300

Another problem besides the existence of completely counterfeit errors (i.e. both the planchet and die strikes are fake) are genuine Mint-produced coins which have been modified to resemble errors; this can happen both intentionally and unintentionally. For example, the clad layers on a dime can be removed by force (e.g. prying them off when a clamshell separation exists, use of an acid, etc.) or via environmental damage (e.g. being buried in acidy soil for a prolonged period of time). Regardless of the cause, these altered coins show up often on dealers' tables and online sites which are marketed as genuine errors; many wind up being sold.

Between counterfeit and altered error coins, it is much more difficult to authenticate a genuine coin that was altered. *Why is that?* For starters, genuine coins will have the correct lettering, numbering, serifs, reeding, designs, and other very fine details on their strikes that most forgers of counterfeits find nearly impossible to replicate. Also, the planchets used by the Mint will obviously meet the specifications for being genuine, whereas many fakes are struck on metals the U.S. Mint doesn't even use for circulated coinage (e.g. lead, aluminum, white metal, silver/gold-plated planchets, etc.). Among the scariest situations in U.S. Mint history was when one infamous forger used genuine planchets (and real error coins) which were struck by some masterfully-created fake dies to create mind-blowing errors. Unfortunately a small handful of these even fooled experts at the TPGs, but eventually they caught on (more on that later).

Now let's get to the coin in question which appears to be a multi-struck 1960-D Lincoln cent. Notice while some strikes are off-center, others seem to be the result of rotated-in-collar strikes. Like the 1944 steel cent on the previous page, the same dealer also has this one for sale but for only $300; it's also uncertified. Here are some of the questions you need to be considering to make an educated decision: (1) Is the planchet genuine? If so, how do you know for sure?; (2) Are any of the strikes genuine? If so, which ones?; (3) Does the asymmetric shape provide any clues? If so, what are they?; and (4) The rims appear damaged and flattened in spots. Should that concern you? Now keep in mind that many coins struck off-center will lose their symmetry, and coins struck more than once can have flattening/damage to the rims if struck off-center. Additional strikes can also come out either stronger or weaker than the original strike. Also, don't forget to check out those edges.

Well, you want the coin and think it's a decent price. So, what do you think? Can you tell if the actual coin is a genuine Mint product? If you think it is, what about the additional die strikes? Were those struck at the Mint or on someone's workbench? Go ahead and turn the page to find out!

Reasons Why It's an Altered Coin:

1. The original strike has strong details/lettering, the edges are smoothed, and the rims are rounded. The planchet and the first strike are good.
2. The formation of the numbers on the date on the additional strikes are off. The "1" leans to the right while the shape and loop of the "9" don't match (bottom right). Additional strikes are also very weak.
3. Only part of the coin has damage from additional strikes. For example, notice how LIBERTY on the obverse is totally unaffected as well as UNITED STATES on the reverse; this means die pressure was not applied evenly despite there being no signs of an obstruction.
4. Warping on the rims from additional strikes (from fake dies) is wavy and inconsistent; this did not come from a Mint die strike.

Answer: Altered Coin

Genuine Planchet/First Strike
with
Additional Fake Die Strikes

Above: The edges are smooth and the rims are rounded. This is how a genuine planchet should look if a rim is present.

Below: Observe how on the original strike the number "1" is vertically straight while on the additional strikes it leans to the right; the "9" is also an entirely different shape.

Answer: Altered Coin

What Exactly Does "Damaged" Mean?

One of the most horrifying and gut-wrenching words coin collectors can hear about a coin they want or already own – other than it's "fake" or "altered" – is that the coin is "damaged." However its meaning really depends on the context "damaged" is being used. I have dozens of "damaged" coins and paid good money for them, that's if by "damaged" you mean "coins that are imperfect from the norm." In that respect, I guess all Mint errors are "damaged." But within numismatics, what differentiates an authentic Mint error from a coin that suffered post-strike or post-Mint damage depends on a couple of factors.

First, *when*, *where*, and *how* the damage takes place is critical in determining if a flawed coin is a "clean" Mint error or a "problem" PMD coin. Imperfections including laminations, clips, and strike-throughs are Mint errors if these flaws occurred *before* the completion of the minting process. Trauma happening *after* the minting process was finished – corrosion, dents, gouges, PVC residue, etc. – are considered post-Mint damage. (However, laminations can occur years later.) In fact, one of the ways TPGs have helped differentiate "good" damage and post-Mint damage is by identifying on a slab label that a coin was struck on a "pre-damaged" or "defective" planchet. (Keep in mind, some forms of damage can be difficult to tell exactly when they happened. For example, sometimes coins can become scratched as they're ejected from the chamber. Thus even though some of these imperfections were the result of striking malfunctions

or flaws from how the planchet metal was prepared, they can sometimes mimic PMD like staple scratches and wind up with "Details" grades.)

Second, not everyone agrees on what post-Mint damage is or should include. *Why? Shouldn't it be obvious what damage is and isn't?* Not always. For example, do you consider fingerprints as damage? I do, but for others fingerprints don't bother them; some people even love them if they've toned over into blazing rainbow colors. Speaking of toning, is that damage? How dark does it have to get, what color does it have to be, and what patterns must exist for a toned coin to then become damaged? I know people who only collect toned coins and they don't think they're ruined. I also know people who hate them on modern coins. And then there's **bag marks** (abrasions on coins caused from contact with each other, including during the bagging and shipping process), **reeding marks** (abrasions left on coins from contact with reeded edges), silver coin **milk spots** (remnants of a rinsing solution left on a coin which was used to remove contaminants and make them brighter), and brown **rinse spots** on zinc cents as well as **plating blisters**. Are these forms of "damage" even if they are naturally occurring and happened during the minting process? Does it matter how severe they are or where they're located for a coin to be judged as damaged? Not everyone agrees. On the next page are forms of damage that most collectors can agree upon.

Laminations
Caused by bad mixtures, impurities, and/or trapped gasses; can occur long after production; are considered Mint errors and not "damaged." However, non-error collectors don't want laminations on their coins and do consider them as damaged coins.

Reeding Marks
Some don't consider these as forms of damage; I do and I avoid coins with them. (These are not the same as "struck-through detached reeding" errors which occur in the striking chamber.)

Dreaded Examples of Damaged Coins

How does damage occur? Well, there are more ways than I can list. Some PMD arises naturally (e.g. exposed zinc on a cent starts corroding), others are done intentionally (e.g. modifying a coin to be placed in a jewelry setting), and then there is accidental damage (e.g. improper storage and mishandling leading to staining or corrosion).

Though some coins with damage can be restored by trained numismatic conservationists (some even going from a Details grade to being strait-graded), most forms of PMD are usually permanent. Of all the dreaded types of damage on this page, only the nickel has a chance to be restored to a straight-grade depending how bad the corrosion is underneath. Wheel marks aren't always labeled as Details coins on slab labels, but they should be (many aren't on older slabs).

PVC Residue ("Green Death") can form on coins via prolonged contact in plastic flips containing PVC. Sometimes removing the green film will wind up exposing possible pitting and corrosion and still be considered a damaged coin.

Rim dings – This proof SBA $1 planchet is worth hundreds less regardless of its cause.

Wheel marks happen if a coin makes contact with the spinning wheel of a coin counting machine. These vary in severity and size with some more noticeable than others. *(Photo courtesy of Heritage Auctions/HA.com)*

<u>Left</u>: The **"Ring of Death"** is caused by a spinning crimper sealing the paper rolls shut.

<u>Right</u>: **Staple scratches** are caused when a coin makes direct contact with a staple, likely when removing coins from a stapled paper flip.

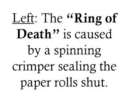

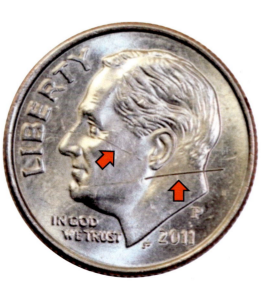

Pre-Strike Damage = "Good" Damage

2000 Lincoln Cent: Struck 5%
Off-center on a Pre-damaged Planchet

Should every damaged coin be given a dreaded "Details" grade? Absolutely not! Believe it or not, some coins are more desirable by error collectors if they actually are damaged. Now I don't mean "damaged" in the sense that a coin has wheel marks, staple scratches, or PVC residue. All of those forms of damage happened *after* the coin exited the striking chamber and left the Mint; they're "bad" and undesirable types of damage (PMD). *OK, so what differentiates "bad" from "good" damage on coins?*

The key difference is discerning *when* the damage occurred. For it to be considered a "good" coin that would get straight-graded rather than be rejected or given a "Details" grade, damage must have occurred at some stage of the minting process *before* the coin was fully out of the striking chamber. *Is there a way to tell if it was before or after ejection?* For some cases, yes. Sometimes you can even pinpoint at what stage it occurred. For example, improperly annealed coins occur when they are overheated in the annealing ovens, edge strikes happen during the striking process, and laminations are caused by improper mixtures and/or impurities in the metals when the planchet metal was prepared.

Now let's take a look at the off-center 2000 Lincoln cent on the left. There's no question both sides are damaged, but is it pre-strike or post-strike? Despite not knowing with 100% certainty at what point this damage occurred (I suspect it occurred as it was entering the striking chamber), there is a way to tell definitively this is not post-strike damage. *How can you tell for sure?*

What at first looks like a coin that was dragged over a rough surface like a sidewalk, on the lower reverse you can see the thin copper plating detached and folded over. However, the raised lettering is *on top* of that flap. This could only have happened if the flap was there *before* it was struck, not after. Though this isn't a very valuable error, modern coins with pre-strike damage aren't easy to find. (Scarce; $40)

Uncirculated Coins with "Bad/Post-strike" Damage

Oddly enough, a coin can have post-strike/Mint damage even if it was never released into circulation – including before it leaves the Mint and in original Mint packaging! Notice the "tread" marks on the reverse of this 1965 nickel which is sealed in a 1965 Mint Set. The cause is likely from the sealer which "ran over" the coin leaving those markings on it. As a result, this coin is not a "Mint" error since the damage occurred after ejection; technically it is a "packaging" error.

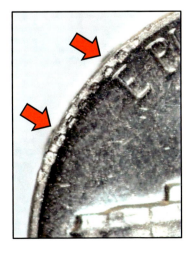

Reasons Why You Need to "Buy the Coin, Not the Holder!"

To help minimize mistakes, TPGs have multiple experts involved in each step of the process as your coin is being examined. For example, usually 2-3 people are going to authenticate/grade your coin while a completely different person (or people) will be attributing the nature of the error. If your coin was encapsulated, it is checked yet again before being shipped back to you.

But despite this exhaustive process, mistakes are going to happen once in a while. Some may feel their coin was considerably undergraded or that it shouldn't have been designated as a problem coin (e.g. a Details grade), while others might claim the label or error attribution is wrong or missing information which now cripples the coin's true value. (There are people who actively search for certified coins with these issues. It is not uncommon for them to remove or **"crack out"** coins and resubmit them with the hope of receiving a more favorable grade in an attempt to make a quick buck.) I've also seen the wrong denomination, date, type, and mintmark as well as spelling errors on labels. One coin dealer friend of mine got his two coins back from PCGS, but each coin had the other coin's label inside. (TPGs will fix these issues for you). If you can believe it, I know several collectors personally who collect certified coins in mislabeled slabs.

My intention is not to gratuitously beat up on the grading companies; nobody is perfect all the time. However, if all you're doing is reading labels and not inspecting the actual coin itself carefully, you could be in for some incredibly painful learning experiences. These next few pages will illustrate why it is critical that you **"Buy the Coin, Not the Holder."** As you will see, TPG carelessness is not the only reason to be vigilant; there are criminals looking to cash in on your carelessness as well.

1. Labelling Errors

Eisenhower 90% Silver Dollar Unstruck Blank

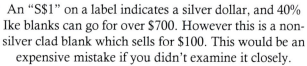

An "S$1" on a label indicates a silver dollar, and 40% Ike blanks can go for over $700. However this is a non-silver clad blank which sells for $100. This would be an expensive mistake if you didn't examine it closely.

2. Wrong Error Attributions

(1943) Zinc Coated 1 Cent Steel Planchet

1943 steel cent planchets can sell for $150, but this is really an unplated zinc cent planchet which go for around $15. There are several of these misattributed planchets inside "Manhattan Collection" labels.

3. Straight-graded Damaged Coins

1976 Washington Quarter (Clad): Flip-over & Double-struck in Collar; Straight-graded at MS60 by PCGS

Healthy debates exist as to what should be considered "damaged," mainly because it can be difficult to pinpoint an exact cause and time a flaw happened like a gouge or scratch. Some unsightly defects are also only visible when a coin is held at certain angles, including the rather large obverse wheel mark on this quarter below. If you only went by the label, you might miss this is a "problem" coin that should've been given a "Details" grade by PCGS. Jon Sullivan is an honest dealer and was clear in noting it had the wheel mark when it was listed for sale, but not every collector is bothered by them.

Photos courtesy of Sullivan Numismatics

4. "Details" Grades Which Should Have Been Straight-graded

1965 Roosevelt Dime Struck on a 90% Silver Dime Planchet: Transitional Error; Graded "AU Details" for Rim Damage by NCS/NGC

Clearly there is rim damage on the reverse side of this remarkable "transitional" error (1965 dimes should be clad, not silver), but the damage on this coin was pre-strike. This transitional error should have been straight-graded and described as a "pre-damaged planchet," which makes a world of difference price-wise for an error of this magnitude.

Photos courtesy of Heritage Auctions/HA.com

5. Genuine Coins Inside Fake Slabs

Not only do you need to be mindful of mislabeled slabs or misattributed coins from grading companies, you also need to be on the lookout for altered and counterfeit slabs (in addition to altered, damaged, and counterfeit coins). For example, surmise the two slabs below. Both Morgan dollars are in fact genuine, but one of the slabs and its label are fake. *Can you spot the fake? What are some problems with it? And why would someone put a genuine coin inside a fake slab?*

Answers: The fake slab/label is on the left. First, the serifs on the numbers and letters are incorrect for that generation of NGC slabs that started in 2016; so is the size of the label itself. Also, the hole where the coin is placed is too small, and the prongs don't taper down. The most obvious blunder is the spelling of the word "GUARANTY" (but on the fake it's spelled "GUARANT*EE*"). As for why someone might put a genuine coin in a fake holder, the most likely reasons are (1) perhaps a coin is damaged and would never get straight-graded, or (2) to inflate a coin's grade, which is likely the case with this fake slab. The coin inside the fake slab is actually closer to an MS63 just as the coin in the genuine slab is. However, while a clean MS63 sells for around $45, an MS66+ grade goes for about $400. Of course, if you went by the rule of "buy the coin, not the holder," and learned how to grade Morgans yourself instead of relying on labels, you should've passed on it anyway. I bought it for $50 but I knew the holder was fake. Several dealers I showed it to had no idea. It's scary, but it's a good educational item.

6. Altered Coins Which Were Straight-graded Dubiously

1983-D Lincoln Cent: Unplated; Straight-graded at AU50 by ICG

Determining the authenticity of a genuine zinc cent missing its copper plating can be challenging even for some experienced error collectors and coin dealers, but there are some rather obvious signs you should be looking for which I will get into later. This particular coin should have been an easy call that it was chemically altered, especially for authenticators at a grading service. I purchased this coin for $100 just to get a closer look at it as I was confident it wasn't a genuine error. The seller insists the error is genuine but still refunded my money and he wasn't upset at my request. Unfortunately he will likely sell it to someone else who won't know this coin has been altered.

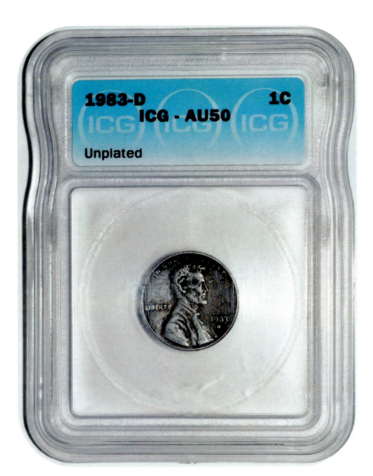

Both of these close-up photos below illustrate strong evidence this zinc cent not only once had its copper plating applied, but that it was removed intentionally using an acid. Based on the photos, what do you see that should have you questioning the authenticity of this "error?"

7. Counterfeit Coins Certified as Authentic by Grading Services

Let me start off by saying that this situation is very rare and I almost didn't even want to bring it up in this book. By no means do I want to shame, discredit, sensationalize, or create unnecessary paranoia within the hobby that TPGs can not and should not be trusted to authenticate your coins as genuine U.S. Mint products. When I submit a coin to any of the major grading services, the last thing I am concerned about is them certifying a fake.

However, I would be remiss if I didn't mention it's happened before, including a small number of inauthentic errors and Early American Coppers (EACs) like this 1806 "C-1" half cent below. This coin is on loan to me from Jack Young, a respected expert on fake U.S. coins. I highly recommend that you join his Facebook group "The Dark Side: Counterfeits and Fakes" to help stay informed.

1806 Draped Bust Half Cent
C-1 Small 6, No Stems
Straight-graded at XF-45 by NGC

Mr. Jack Young, an award-winning counterfeit researcher and expert, is well known and respected in detecting fakes. He loaned me this fake half cent for use in educational seminars
(Close-up photos courtesy of Jack Young)

Know The Difference Between Blanks & Planchets

Throughout the book, two terms used frequently are "blank" and "planchet." *What are they?* These are the unstruck, round metal disks that will eventually become coins once they are struck by the dies. (Technically, they are not "coins" until after undergoing the striking process.) *OK, but what's the difference between a blank and a planchet?* Simply put, a **blank** is an unstruck disk that lacks a rim and the surface area is completely flat (left). In contrast, a **planchet** was a blank but had a raised rim added (right). *But why are these pieces considered Mint errors?* Because the intention was to strike them with coin dies to add their features, but somehow they escaped the Mint's many layers of quality control and wound up in circulation (or the Mint gave them away as promotional items). It is incredibly rare to come across either of these somewhere other than a coin shop or flea market, especially for larger denominations like half dollars and dollars. Also, blanks are considerably more rare than planchets in all denominations as they had to not only bypass the process to add the rim but also went unstruck by the dies. On occasion blanks are actually struck and sneak out of the Mint, but only a well-trained eye can spot these very rare specimens. Though many struck blanks sell for less than $50 for modern denominations in MS grades, others can reach several hundred dollars (a few are actually in this collection) or even thousands depending on the condition, grade and denomination.

But before they become blanks or planchets, they were once part of a long, rolled sheet of metal 13 inches wide by 1,500 feet long with a thickness specified to each particular coin. These sheets known as **planchet strips** are fed through a machine which punches out round disks; these are immediately now called "blanks" or "Type 1 blanks." What's left of the metal after the blanks are punched out is called a "webbing" strip (a few from different denominations will be featured in the next chapter). A blank will soon have a raised rim added that literally squeezes the coin through a channel slightly smaller in diameter than the blank. The pressure resulting on each blank forces metal along the perimeter to shift up on both sides forming a raised rim. Once this occurs, it's no longer called a blank but is now a "planchet" or a "Type 2." Again, blanks don't have rims while planchets do, and the rim should be the highest point on coins.

Manganese Dollar Blank (No Rim)

Manganese Dollar Planchet (Rim Added)

Blanks have a rough "cut and tear" look to their edges while planchets have smooth, rounded edges. Can you tell which is which from these two unstruck clad Kennedy half dollars on the left?

Welcome! Within the pages of this first chapter you will see several different blanks and planchets of various denominations and even small sections of the strips of metal they came from, as well as what the coins should look like if they were struck by the obverse and reverse dies. You might also notice how banged up these unstruck examples are. Believe it or not, these are actually in excellent shape and most would be considered uncirculated. If you think about it, these specimens were tossed around throughout various stages of the minting process, including being smashed on top of one another while plunging into several different bins to be **annealed** (heated), **burnished** (polished), washed, and dried; it's a wonder some of them look as good as they do! Once they are struck by dies featuring some former presidents or other iconic Americans, mythical individuals, birds, and government buildings, most of these scratches and marks will disappear from a remarkable die press facelift. But blanks have to be made before any of this happens, so let's take a look at where they come from first with what will be the official start of *Mint Errors to Die For.*

1 A. Webbing Strips

Featured first are five examples of **webbing strips** which is what remains of the planchet metal sheets after the blanks are punched out by blanking dies. Nowadays these are supposed to be shredded into much smaller individual pieces, sometimes referred to as "bow ties" due to their shape, which are later recycled to make new metal sheets. These strips are actually considered Mint errors because they are not supposed to be circulated. Some denominations are easier to find than others, with half dollar and dollar strips being among the toughest. Silver and gold webbing strips are astronomically rare if they even exist outside the Mint. Lastly, though each webbing strip is consistent with the U.S. coin featured on each page, keep in mind the U.S. Mint also minted coins for many foreign countries. Anyway, enjoy the strip show!

95% Copper Indian or Lincoln Cent Webbing Strip

The following is an enormous copper webbing strip used to punch out flat, rimless Type 1 blanks for either Indian Head cents (1864-1909; top left) or Lincoln cents (1909-1982, except 1943; bottom left), depending on how old this strip actually is. The Mint made both copper and copper-plated zinc cents in 1982, but this strip is copper. In fact, since copper-plated zinc cents are not plated until after they are punched out and given a rim, this strip could not be copper-plated zinc. Despite making multiple billions of copper cents, large copper webbing strips very rare. ($400)

Indian Head Cent

Photo courtesy of Heritage Auctions/HA.com

Lincoln Cent

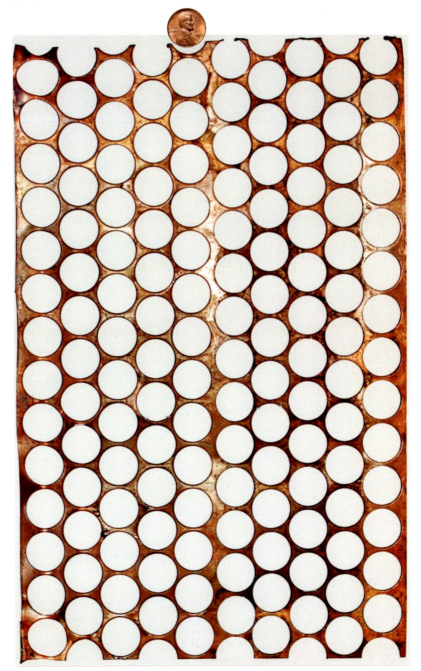

Zinc-plated Steel Cent Webbing Strip

This is a rather large section of webbing strip which had blanks punched out to produce 1943 Lincoln steel cents (informally referred to by some as "**steelies**"). One way to know if this strip is authentic is to see if it sticks to a magnet, as do all authentic steel cents. Zinc-coated steel planchets replaced copper ones for cents in 1943 as copper was needed for military-related items during World War II. Some experimental planchets tested to replace copper included: Copper-plated steel; brass; manganese; aluminum; lead; various plastics with different colors; rubber; a "red fibrous material"; and even tempered glass. (Rare; $150)

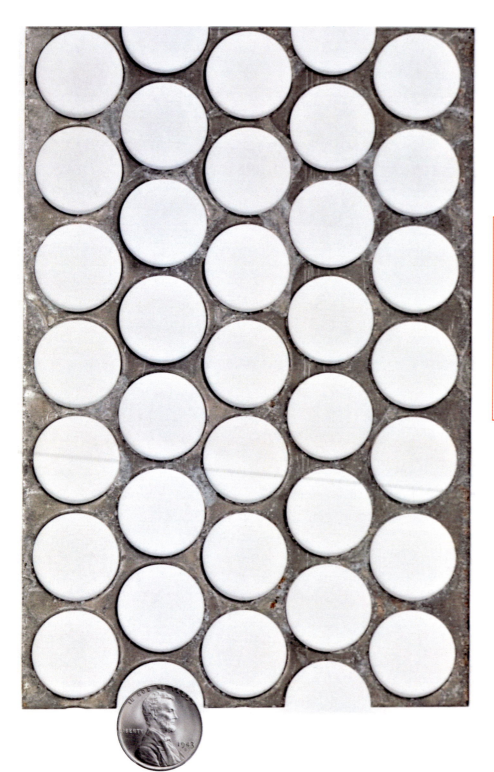

1943-D Steel Lincoln Cent

Coin Trivia: *In anticipation of Germany's occupation of Belgium ending towards the end of World War II, the U.S. Mint in Philadelphia produced 25,000,000 of these 1944 two franc coins (below). If their composition looks familiar, it's because they were minted on leftover zinc-plated steel planchets that were used to make 1943 Lincoln cents.*

1944 Steel Belgian 2 Francs

5 Cent Nickel Webbing Strip

The composition of this webbing strip – 75% copper and 25% nickel – is consistent with that of 5 cent U.S. nickels, likely the Jefferson series due to its nice condition and slight toning. Nickel webbing strips are among the rarest of all non-precious metal strips in lower denominations. It should also be noted that struck coins are slightly wider in diameter than the blanks punched out, which explains why struck coins normally don't fit inside the webbing strips they came from. (Rare; $425)

Above: Edge view of a nickel strip illustrating how blanks are actually punched and torn out of the planchet strips.

Jefferson Nickel

1964 photos courtesy of Heritage Auctions / HA.com

Coin Trivia: In 1988, Hollywood Brands created a marketing gimmick where they packaged a 1988 nickel in approximately 12.3 million PAYDAY candy bars for sale. The one featured on the right is a 1988-D. (Scarce; $10)

Clad Roosevelt Dime Webbing Strip

Featured here is an uncommonly large section of a clad dime webbing strip. Since Roosevelt dimes are the only clad dimes made for U.S. coinage, a specific series can be attributed. Dimes changed from 90% silver to clad in 1965, and you can see the copper core (top right) on the edges. Though clad dime webbing strips are rare, even more rare (and which I have never seen in person) are 90% silver web strips for any denomination – if they even exist! (Rare; $225)

Edge View of a Clad Dime Webbing Strip

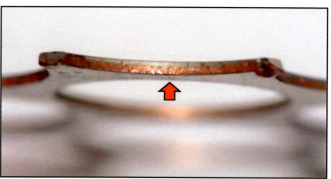

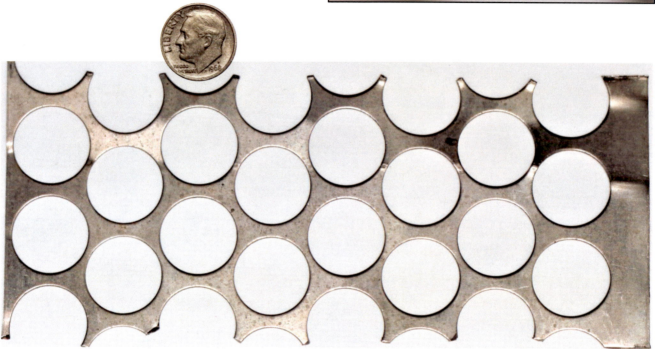

Clad Roosevelt Dime "Bow Tie" Webbing Scrap

Normally webbing strips are shredded into small pieces like this – known as a **bow tie** – which are recycled to make new planchet strips. These can be found for most modern U.S. denominations except proof and precious metal coins/bullion. ($5)

Undated Lincoln Cent Struck on a Clad Dime Bow Tie Scrap

This clad dime bow tie scrap made its way into a chamber striking Lincoln cents. Graded MS-65 by PCGS, this incredibly rare error type sold for $3,450 at Heritage Auctions in 2009.

Photos courtesy of Heritage Auctions/HA.com

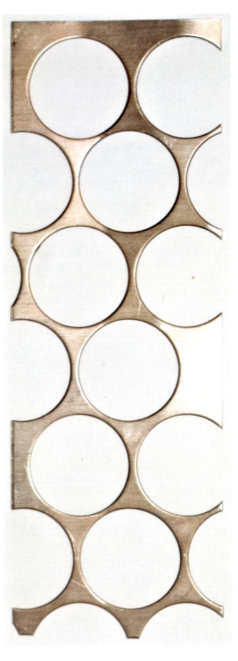

Clad Washington Quarter: Unpunched Planchet Strip and Punched Webbing Strip

Both of these strips on the left are for clad quarters. While the far left strip was never struck with the blanking dies, to its right is a webbing strip that was. Neither is particularly shiny like the struck 1974 quarter below because blanks from strips aren't polished until after they're punched out. In order, they are punched, heated, washed/polished, dried, affixed with a rim, and then struck with dies to add their designs. (Unpunched strip; Rare; $150; Punched webbing strip; Rare; $200)

Washington Quarter (Clad)

1968-S Proof Washington Quarter Cancelled Dies

Coin Trivia: The U.S. Mint destroys old coin dies to prevent unauthorized minting. To the right are the obverse and reverse "cancelled" dies for a 1968-S proof Washington quarter that was torched. (Scarce with this much detail remaining; $100 for the 25 cent die pairing.)

1 B. Unstruck Blanks and Planchets

1849-1857 Copper Half Cent
"Braided Hair" Unstruck Planchet

The half cent is the lowest denomination ever minted by the U.S. and features four different types. However, this planchet could only be a survivor from the last one, known as the "Braided Hair" half cent, produced between 1849-1857. *How can that be certain if most of the four types weighed the same at around 5.44 grams?* Because this last type is the only one that had a diameter of 23.0 mm, as does this piece. And though there were proof specimens made from 1840 through 1857, this unstruck example is not a proof planchet which has a different surface. Since we know how many years this type was produced, we can give a specific time period.

It is also 100% copper as are "large" cent pieces. Major changes came by the end of 1857 as both the production of half and large cents ceased, and in 1856 the new and smaller cent pieces were now alloy coins (nickel was added). *Why the transformation?* Copper values were rising so steadily that the metallic value of copper was worth more than the coin's face value. Consequently, some people began melting their copper coins to sell them as scrap. Some feared the entire nation was going to experience a coinage shortage. Seeing that most transactions were done in cash at this time, there was concern that commercial activity might come to a halt which could lead to an economic disaster. By producing cents smaller in diameter and adding nickel to them, both the metallic value and the incentive to melt them decreased.

Why were copper values rising at this time? One reason was the booming Industrial Revolution in America which created a greater need for all industrial base metals (iron ore, copper, etc.). Another was the discovery of gold on the West coast. *What does that have to do with copper prices?* Because copper bonds well with gold – which is a very soft metal – and the addition of copper makes it harder. Designs on coins/jewelry won't wear so fast, and the more gold you find the more copper you will need. Only a handful of these unstruck examples exist and is the rarest and most valuable piece in the Cronin Collection. (Extremely rare; $1,900; ungraded as NGC doesn't give blanks or planchets grades; *struck images courtesy of Heritage Auctions/HA.com*)

Braided Hair (Obverse)

Braided Hair (Reverse)

Unstruck Half Cent Planchet

1795-1857 Copper Large Cent Planchet

This unstruck planchet could be as old as 1795 when George Washington was in office or its last year of mintage in 1857 when James Buchanan was sworn in. On the right are the five types this planchet could have become. Can you spot changes in design on both sides over the years? However, oftentimes designs are copied for different denominations. Note the "Braided Hair" large cent on the bottom right has the same obverse and reverse design same as the "Braided Hair" half cent on the previous page, except of course for its size/weight and its value (Rare; $175; AU-50 by PCGS; *struck images courtesy of Heritage Auctions/HA.com*).

Unstruck Large Cent Planchet

Flowing Hair

Draped Bust

Classic Head

Matron Head

Braided Hair

1856-1864 Copper-nickel Small Cent Planchet

Small one cent production started in 1856 and by the end of 1857 no more half cent or large one cent denominations were made. The first design sported a "Flying Eagle" on the obverse which was only produced for three years (though in 1856 the Flying Eagle cent was struck as a pattern coin and not for circulation); it was subsequently replaced by the Indian Head cent in 1859. In 1864, the Mint again transitioned the metallic content by removing nickel and making them bronze – a 95% copper and 5% tin/zinc mixture. This planchet is extraordinarily scarce with only a handful of certified examples and has retained its beautiful original golden color. (Very rare; $500; ungraded by NGC; *struck images courtesy of Heritage Auctions/HA.com*)

Coin Trivia: According to Greek mythology, a coin needed to be placed in the mouth of the dead as a bribe to Hades' ferrymen, Charon, who would then transport bodies across the River Styx to the World of the Dead. Some believe those without payment were left to wander the Greek shores for one hundred years as punishment until they could eventually cross the river.

Copper-nickel Flying Eagle

Copper-nickel Indian Head

Unstruck Copper-nickel Planchet

95% Copper Cent Blank and Planchet

Either of these copper specimens could be as old as 1864–1909 when Indian Head cents were minted, or from 1909–1982 (except 1943) when copper Lincoln cents were produced. All struck examples below are on planchets. (Semi-scarce; $5 each; *Indian Head cent photos courtesy of Heritage Auctions/HA.com*)

Left:
**95% Copper
1C Blank**

Right:
**95% Copper
1C Planchet**

**Copper
Indian Head
Cent**

**Copper
Lincoln
Cent**

(1943) Zinc–plated Steel Cent Blank and Planchet

These were produced in 1943 during the middle of America's involvement in World War II in an effort to conserve copper. Both America and our allies needed ammunition (among other war necessities) including bullets, which are encased in brass jackets. Copper is the base metal of brass, so you can see why so much copper would be needed during wartime. Both are very scarce, but blanks are more scarce in all denominations. ($175 for the blank; the planchet is $150 certified by NGC.)

In the right column is a struck example of a steel planchet graded MS-67 by PCGS. The small, oval-shaped green CAC sticker on the outside of the slab label indicates approval from the **Certified Acceptance Corporation**, a company that examines coins already slabbed by TPGs. A green CAC sticker (i.e. the "green bean") implies that coin is on the higher end of a particular grade, and often commands 10% to 90% more than those without one. A gold CAC sticker implies the coin should actually be one grade higher than it was assigned (e.g. an MS-60 instead of AU-58), which can command more than double their value. Like the "+" grades, some view CAC designation as simply another marketing gimmick, but many collectors do respect and value their conclusions as being on the higher end of the grading scale. As of this writing, CAC does not evaluate error coins. (Scarce in this grade; $185)

Steel Cent Blank

Steel Cent Planchet

1943-D Steel Cent

LINCOLN 1C
ZINC-COATED STEEL
PLANCHET (2.6g)
MINT ERROR
4218151-011
NUMISMATIC GUARANTY CORPORATION NGC®

1943-D   1C
PCGS MS67
CAC
2714.67/83244707

Copper-plated Zinc Cent Planchet

During 1982, the U.S. Mint changed from a copper alloy to a zinc core plated with a thin copper layer, so 1982 cents could be either copper (3.11 grams) or copper-plated zinc (2.5 grams) depending on their weight. The reason for this change is that Mint officials feared the copper in a cent would soon be worth more than its monetary value. At the top is a copper-plated zinc planchet, and below are struck examples of the new reverse design that started in 2010 known as the "Lincoln Shield."

The Mint no longer produces planchets for cents and is contracted out to Jardens Zinc Products in Greenville, Tennessee, thus the Mint only receives pre-made planchets. Because it is believed that the zinc core is plated after the rims are added (the process there is kept secret), this could likely explain why copper-plated zinc blanks are almost nonexistent and why I don't have one in this collection. (Very common; $1)

2010 Shield cent photos
courtesy of Heritage Auctions/HA.com

Coin Trivia: At times the Mint has actually given away unstruck planchets and struck cents as promotional items as seen here in this Mint cello above (2015–D).

Unplated Zinc 1C Blank   **Unplated Zinc 1C Planchet**

Unplated Zinc Cent Blank and Planchet

This is what copper-plated zinc cents look like without their copper plating and before striking. Sometimes these even sneak through and get struck by the dies (see below) and they resemble both zinc-coated steel cents minted in 1943 and cents struck on silver or clad dime planchets. (Semi-scarce; $10 each)

1983 Lincoln Cent: Struck on an Unplated Zinc Planchet

On occasion, unplated planchets wind up getting struck at the Mint without ever being plated with copper. With a bright bluish tint, it's perfectly understandable if someone assumed incorrectly this was a 1943 steel cent. It's BLUE-tiful! (Very scarce; $175; MS-65 by ANACS)

Coin Trivia: Many people confuse these unplated planchets with slugs made by punching out pieces of metal. One way to tell the difference is to use a magnet as neither plated nor unplated examples are magnetic.

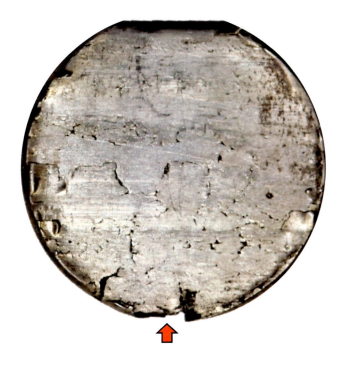

1942-1945 Jefferson "War Nickel"
35% Silver Planchet: 5% Straight Clip
with Laminations and a Ragged Fissure

Unstruck Jefferson "War Nickel" planchets – composed of 35% silver, 56% copper, and 9% manganese – are incredibly tough to come by as their production only lasted four years (1942-1945). Also, though it is relatively easy to identify whether or not other denominations are either silver or clad, ascertaining whether or not a nickel planchet is silver can be difficult and frustrating for inexperienced collectors. *Why is that?* Because both silver war nickels and the non-silver nickels weigh exactly the same: 5 grams. *Then how can you tell if an unstruck nickel planchet is silver or not?* Though some people claim they can tell by the sound they make (which I do not ever recommend doing), the color, or by the nature of their toning (if any is even present), one way to make a solid determination is by putting them on a metallic scanner like a Fischerscope XAN 250 machine. For example,

this planchet above scanned at 33.4% silver which proves it was for a U.S. war nickel. Unfortunately not many people have access to a scanner like I do; they're also expensive. Some jewelry stores and coin shops have scanners, but they may charge a fee to scan them.

What makes this planchet more interesting is that there is a 5% straight clip (likely from being at the very end of the planchet strip when it was punched out) and has multiple laminations and lamination cracks on both sides. Whether due to impurities or bad mixtures, silver war nickels tend to be more prone to laminations than other 20th century coins. I believe it also has a small ragged fissure (red arrows) which may have been caused by a blanking die that punched through an area of planchet metal that was cracked. This is a great example of how a damaged planchet is not really considered "damaged" in the eyes of error collectors since these errors occurred during the planchet's preparation phase and was defective before striking. (Very Rare; $250)

Left: In terms of design, the obverse of a silver war nickel is the same as regular copper-nickel issues (known as Type 1).

Right: The reverse side of a struck 35% silver war nickel planchet. Look for the enlarged mintmark above Monticello's dome (known as Type 2).

Shield/Liberty/Buffalo Nickel Planchet

Identifying what planchet is for what series, especially if it is the same weight, color, diameter, or composition can be very tricky. However, rim formation is actually one factor that can provide a good clue.

Below are two U.S. nickel planchets, but the left one has much more of a pronounced rim. Thus, we can lean heavily in favor of either a Shield, Liberty, or Buffalo nickel planchet. (Very scarce; $40. *Shield and Liberty nickel photos courtesy of Heritage Auctions/HA.com.*)

Left:
Very Pronounced Rim Formation (Shield, Liberty, or Buffalo Nickel Planchet)

Right:
Slightly-raised Rim Formation (Likely a Jefferson Nickel Planchet)

Shield Nickel	Liberty Nickel	Buffalo Nickel

Jefferson Nickel Blank & Planchet

These unstruck escapees were supposed to be minted as nickels, which despite its name is only 25% nickel and 75% copper. Before 1866, 5 cent pieces were called "half-dimes" because like dimes, they were made of silver and had to be "half" a dime's weight. They were not called "nickels" until 1866 when nickel replaced silver in them (there was also a "3 cent" nickel). The diameter, weight (5 grams), and their composition is the same for all four series of 5 cent nickels. However, the condition of the blank and rim formation of the planchet is indicative of the Jefferson nickel series. (Semi-scarce; $5 each)

5C Blank	5C Planchet	Jefferson Nickel

1973 Jefferson Nickel: Struck on a Type 1 Blank

As mentioned previously, raised rims are added to coin blanks not only to help them stack easier but also to slow the progression of wear from people handling them thousands of times over. But not all blanks make it to the upsetting mill where rims are added. In any mass production facility, mistakes and imperfect products can still manage to find their way inside boxes and cans, and even inside Mint bags, rolls, and Mint/proof sets.

This 1973 Jefferson nickel may appear normal but is one of the few that slipped by the upsetting mill where raised rims are added; it then made its way to the striking chamber. Though it appears it has raised rims, it is merely an illusion. One of the easiest ways to tell is to check the edge. *Why is that?* Because the edges on a blank should be somewhat rough as blanks are actually torn out of planchet strips after being punched by blanking dies; the edges are not smoothed out until they are squeezed as they pass through the upsetting mill. Also, since this is a blank, design details – particularly nearest to the rims – tend to be much weaker. Because dies are calibrated to strike a normal, slightly thicker planchet with raised rims on both sides, coins struck on blanks tend to have slightly weaker design elements. Someone had a very keen eye to spot this error type. Even most error collectors likely may have missed this one. Coins struck on blanks aren't very dramatic looking, but they are incredibly rare and actually very affordable in lower denominations. Can you tell the difference below? (Rare; $60; MS-65 by NGC)

No Raised Rims on a Type I Blank

Raised Rims on a Type 2 Planchet

Notice anything funny about this 1950-D nickel? You'll see it again on page 230.

90% Silver Dime Planchet

The last four series of silver dimes have the same diameter (17.9 mm), metal content (90% silver and 10% copper) and the same weight (2.5 grams) except for some dates from the Seated Liberty series. But like the nickel planchets on the previous page, the rim formations can at times provide clues as to which series an unstuck planchet was to become. Based on the rounded but less-defined rims on this planchet, it was likely intended for Roosevelt dimes or possibly some of the later dates for Mercury dimes. (Scarce; $40; 1916 *Mercury dime images are courtesy of Heritage Auctions/HA.com*)

Silver Dime Planchet

Winged Liberty or "Mercury" Dime

Roosevelt Dime

1965 - S. S.

Clad Unstruck Roosevelt
Dime Blank and Planchet

Up until 1965, dimes were made of 90% silver. Dimes then transitioned to a clad composition featuring a copper core sandwiched between two layers of a copper–nickel alloy – a metal made up of two or more metals. Only the Roosevelt series has been struck on clad dimes, so a specific series can be attributed. (Common; $5 each)

Below is an unstruck clad dime planchet sitting on top of a struck dime. The top one has no reeding because it isn't added until the coin is struck by the dies inside a reeded collar; if they aren't struck, they won't have reeding.

Clad 10C Blank

Clad vs. 90% Silver Dimes: Circulated silver coins generally look whiter and duller than clad coins, and they also have a higher pitch when dropped. But of course, please don't go around dropping them!

Clad	**90% Silver**

Clad 10C Planchet

(Above) Also note the differences with their edges as clad coins have a copper streak.

90% Silver Quarter Planchet

This unstruck 90% silver quarter weighs approximately 6.3 grams. Four series of quarters had this weight and diameter, including Washington, Standing Liberty, Barber, and some Seated Liberty quarters (some dates of this last series were 6.74 grams). The rim is pretty pronounced on this quarter, so it is difficult to pinpoint exactly what series it was prepared for, but it's excellent condition indicates it was likely for a Washington quarter. Sadly, quarters minted with 90% silver for circulated use ceased by 1965. (Rare; $150; MS-61 by PCGS, though I don't know how specific numerical grades can be assigned to an unstruck coin. *Struck images courtesy of Heritage Auctions/HA.com*).

Washington

**25 Cent
90% Silver
Planchet**

Standing Liberty

Clad Quarter Blank and Planchet

Clad replaced 90% silver for quarters starting in 1965. These can only be from the Washington quarter series since it is the only one made from clad coinage. Starting in 1999, new design changes occurred beginning with the release of the "50 State Quarters" series. For example, a slightly different bust of George came about, along with shifting the legends UNITED STATES OF AMERICA and QUARTER DOLLAR from the reverse to the obverse, and moving the date from the obverse to the reverse. In addition, each state has its own unique reverse design featuring something significant from each state. In 2009, the series included "Washington D.C. and U.S. Territories," and from 2010-2021 the "America the Beautiful" series will showcase national parks/sites. (Common; $6 each)

	Traditional Design	**50 State Quarters Series (NH)**

Clad 25C Blank

Clad 25C Planchet

Clad Proof Quarter Planchet

Proofs aren't meant for circulation as they are prepared and minted differently than coins struck as business strikes. These traditionally have a mirrored or matte appearance with some having frosted designs/lettering that contrast with mirrored fields and are known as **cameos.** Most proof coins have an "S" mintmark denoting production at the San Francisco Mint. Proof coins are normally a bit more controlled, so exactly how it got out of the Mint is a mystery. Only a handful of these exist. (Scarce; $300; NGC)

Clad 25C Proof Planchet   **Clad 1968-S 25C Proof Planchet**

WASHINGTON 25C
PROOF PLANCHET 5.6 GRAMS
MINT ERROR
1886090-023
NGC

90% Silver Half Dollar Planchet

Up through 1964, half dollars were 90% silver. Beginning in 1965, 50 cent pieces transitioned to 40% silver clad through 1970, then converted to copper-nickel clad in 1971. The Mint would not make any 90% silver half dollars again until 1992 when they began a special collectors set which also included silver dimes and quarters.

As to which series this planchet was supposed to become, there are a few possibilities displayed below. The most recent is the Kennedy series, but only the 1964 half was 90% silver. During the late 1800s up to the mid-20th century, the Mint also produced dozens of different commemoratives honoring a multitude of famous Americans, anniversaries of states admitted to the union, and other significant historical events. Without knowing exactly when this piece was produced (like being found in a Mint-sealed bag with other struck pieces of a particular date), it is difficult to pinpoint what it was meant to be. However, it is most likely for either a Franklin, 1964 Kennedy, or possibly one of the later commemorative halves including those honoring Booker T. Washington from 1946-1951. (He was instrumental in helping to educate freed slaves to learn practical skills as they adjusted to the post-Civil War era; bottom right). Booker T. Washington is also featured on the commemorative half alongside George Washington Carver from 1951-1954. (Scarce; $80; *All struck images courtesy of Heritage Auctions/HA.com*)

Coin Trivia: The only 90% silver JFK half dollar produced for circulation was the 1964 first-year issue.

| **John Kennedy (1964 only)** | **Benjamin Franklin** | **Commemorative (Booker T. Washington)** |

40% Silver Clad Half Dollar Planchet

Starting in 1965, half dollars became silver clad and are composed of a mix of 40% silver and 60% copper; both the individual outer layers and the core are silver-copper alloys. Featured here is the non-proof "business" or "circulation" strike, which is a coin meant to be used as money, whereas proof specimens are minted as collector items.

Only a few dates in the history of silver half dollar production are 40% silver, and thus one is much less likely to come across an unstruck 40% planchet than a 90% one. The years of production for 40% silver half business strikes are as follows: 1965, 1966, 1967, 1968-D, 1969-D, 1970-D, and a special commemorative in 1976. Both the non-proof 40% silver clad 1970-D and 1976 bicentennial were only released in Mint sets, while silver proof examples from 1968-1970 and 1976 were issued in proof sets minted in San Francisco. (Very Scarce; $200; MS-62 by PCGS; *1970-D Half Dollar images courtesy of Heritage Auctions/HA.com*)

40% Silver Clad Kennedy Half Dollar (1970-D)

40% Silver Clad Proof Half Dollar Planchet?

40% silver clad proof half dollars were only minted for the 1968-S, 1969-S, 1970-S, and 1976-S bicentennial issues. Though this planchet has the exact same weight (11.5 grams), scanned at the exact same metal content for a 40% silver planchet, and has more pronounced rims and shiny, pebbled surfaces that proofs have, I can't say for certain this is definitely a 40% silver proof JFK planchet. I am waiting to hear back from NGC as it could also be a planchet for a token or even a foreign planchet. (Very rare; $1,300 if it's the real deal. I've got my fingers crossed!)

40% Silver Half Dollar Proof Planchet

Notice the distinct differences between both the surface finishes and the rim formations. Proofs have a "pebbled" appearance and tend to have rims that are more defined.

40% Silver Half Dollar Non-proof Planchet

Clad Half Dollar Blank

JFK Clad 50C (Bicentennial)

Clad Kennedy Half Dollar Blank and Planchet

By 1971, John F. Kennedy half dollars intended for circulation contained no silver and changed to a copper-nickel clad, though there are special issues made of silver (e.g. the 40% silver bicentennial and 90% silver halves since 1992). Only JFK halves so far have been minted out of clad, so a specific series can be attributed. The struck image on the reverse is on the bicentennial half dollar featuring Independence Hall in Philadelphia, PA. It is there that both the *Declaration of Independence* and the *U.S. Constitution* were debated and eventually signed. (Scarce; $65 each; *Bicentennial images courtesy of Heritage Auctions/HA.com*)

Clad Half Dollar Planchet

Coin Trivia: Starting in 2002, the Mint switched to shipping coins out in enormous ballistic bags. For example, now $1 coins are sold in batches of 140,000 per bag and weigh over 2,500 lbs. You can buy $1 ballistic bags directly from the Mint to search through them, but you need to come up with $140,000, plus pay $11,900 in fees, and make arrangements to go there and pick them up. Gone are the days where you could buy them in small canvas bags like these. (And of course, I managed to find an old half dollar bag printed off-center!)

90% Silver Seated Liberty, Morgan or Peace Dollar Blank

As with all Type 1 blanks (no rims) they are scarcer than planchets (with rims). Three possible $1 series exist for this unstruck blank with a diameter of 38.1 mm and a weight close to 26.73 grams; these include some Seated Liberty dollars minted after 1839 (1840-1873), Morgan dollars (1878-1921), and Peace dollars (1921-1935). Of course deciphering which series a *planchet* is from depends on how the rims were formed. Since this is a *blank* with no rims, I cannot exclude the possibility it could have been meant for a Seated Liberty dollar. (Rare; $900; NGC. *Seated Liberty dollar images courtesy of Heritage Auctions./HA.com*)

**90% Silver Dollar Blank
(Seated Liberty/Morgan/Peace)**

Seated Liberty

Morgan

Peace

Coin Trivia: Silver dollars were once used as the cash prize winnings in Las Vegas slot machines up until the mid-1960s. Many casinos then switched to casino-specific, non-precious metal tokens. Today most casinos' slot machines simply print out paper receipts for winnings that are redeemed for cash – not as thrilling as the sound of silver dollar jackpot winnings hitting the metal trays below.

**40% Silver Clad
Eisenhower "Ike" Dollar**

40% Silver Clad Eisenhower (Ike) Dollar Planchet

In addition to serving two terms as President of the United States, previously Dwight Eisenhower was the commanding officer of Allied forces during the D-Day invasion of Normandy, France. On June 6th, 1944, the Allies stormed the beaches with the goal of liberating France, Belgium, and other Allied nations that were conquered by Hitler's Germany during World Ward II. Eisenhower or "Ike" dollars were only minted from 1971-1978 (no 1975 date as bicentennials were produced for 1975 and 1976), and 40% silver clad examples were struck both as proof and non-proof coins from 1971-1976 but not meant for circulation. This particular planchet, like the proof nickel planchet, is part of what's known as the San Francisco Hoard. (Rare; $625 by NGC; *1972 Eisenhower images courtesy of Heritage Auctions/HA.com*)

**40% Silver Clad
Dollar Planchet
(Eisenhower)**

Coin Trivia: The Hobby Protection Act of 1973 *(and its later amendments) in part requires manufacturers of copies and replicas of numismatic items (coins, paper currency, etc.) to clearly mark the word "COPY" on the item in capital letters and in English.*

Clad Eisenhower (Ike)
Dollar Type 1 & Type 2 Blanks

These unstruck dollars are great examples illustrating the differences between a Type 1 and Type 2 blank. *But I thought "Type 2" meant it has a rim, and is therefore a planchet?* Well, there is a difference between a Type 2 *planchet* and a Type 2 *blank.* Since there is no rim on either, neither can be planchets.

What makes the left one a Type 1 blank is that is has neither been annealed (heated) nor burnished (polished). Notice the very prominent and different surface finishes; the Type 1 is dull and the Type 2 is

almost mirrored. (Some experts even told me the Type 2 could be an "experimental finish" since many test pieces were done at the San Francisco Mint; others think it could be an experimental proof Type 1 blank.)

Anyway, if a blank has not been annealed nor burnished, it is a Type 1 blank; if it has been, it is a Type 2 blank. This distinction is deep in the technical-nerd jargon of numismatics, and most simply understand Type 2s to be planchets, but the difference is definitely prominent. (Type 1 blank: Scarce; $100; Type 2 blank: Very scarce; $175; NGC)

Type 1 Clad $1 Ike Blank

Type 2 Clad $1 Ike Blank

Clad Eisenhower (Ike) Dollar Type 2 Planchet

There are a few marks on this one, but larger coins tend to have more marks on them than smaller ones. Notice the surface difference between this business strike and the pebbled proof planchet below. (Scarce; $100)

Clad Eisenhower (Ike) Dollar
Proof Planchet with a Labeling Error

Because the Mint makes far fewer proofs than business strikes, it is natural that there will be incredibly fewer proof errors than business strike errors. Exactly how this made it out of the San Francisco Mint is unknown, but it is not far-fetched to suggest a Mint employee could have secretly snuck it out. The handling of proof coins is much more controlled, so the likelihood of it making into circulation or found in a Mint bag by mistake without help is unlikely. This is one of only around ten known. (Extremely rare; $1,700; PR-62 by PCGS)

There is also a labeling error on this slab (bottom right). The date range is listed incorrectly as "1971-*1976*" instead of "1971-*1978*" as those are the years clad Ikes were made. 40% silver Ikes were made from 1971-1976, which this one clearly isn't. Thus, we have an error coin slabbed with a labeling error.

Susan B. Anthony (SBA) Dollar Blank and Planchet

The Susan B. Anthony dollar is probably the least popular series ever minted, with limited production from 1979–1981 and again in 1999. Unstruck blanks and planchets are worth much more than most struck business strike and proof specimens even in high grades. (Scarce; $85 each; *struck Susan B Anthony images courtesy of Heritage Auctions/HA.com*)

SBA $1 Blank   **SBA $1 Planchet**

Susan B. Anthony Dollar

Coin Trivia: Frank Gasparro designed both sides of the Susan B. Anthony dollar and both sides of the Eisenhower dollar, with the exception of the reverse side of the bicentennial (which was designed by Dennis Williams). He also designed the reverse sides of both the Lincoln Memorial cent and the John F. Kennedy half dollar.

Sacagawea (Sac) or Presidential Series (Prez) Manganese Dollar Blank and Planchet

Since both of these series use the exact same metal with the same dimensions and weight, they could have been either a "Sac" or "Prez" dollar. (I have seen some dated "2000," but that specific year can only be attributed if someone submitted it that year, which was the very first year this composition was released; it was when the Sacagawea series started). Like the Susan B. Anthony series, these are also not popular and most people hate getting them back as change. (Scarce; $30 each; *Struck images courtesy of Heritage Auctions/HA.com*)

Manganese $1 Blank (Left)

Manganese $1 Planchet (Right)

Sacagawea

Presidential Series (Millard Fillmore)

Unburnished Sacagawea/Presidential Series Manganese Dollar Blank and Planchet

Somehow, these two examples on the top row missed the burnishing (polishing) stage of the minting process, and so they are both very dull compared to their burnished counterparts on the bottom row. These are great examples which illustrate just because something is extremely rare, it doesn't necessarily equate to a high value. *Why?* Very few people collect or even understand these particular unstruck blanks/planchets. (Very rare; $100 each; NGC for both)

**(Left) Unburnished
$1 Manganese Blank**

**(Right) Unburnished
$1 Manganese Planchet**

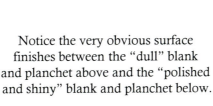

Notice the very obvious surface finishes between the "dull" blank and planchet above and the "polished and shiny" blank and planchet below.

Left:
**Burnished $1
Manganese Blank**

Right:
**Burnished $1
Manganese Planchet**

It is not listed on the label, but the manganese blank inside the slab on the left is unburnished. Ultimately it is your responsibility to educate yourself to stay informed.

$1 Commemorative
90% Silver Proof Planchet (PCGS)

Starting in 1982, Congress authorized the U.S. Mint to once again start minting commemorative coins; 1983 is when modern silver $1 proof commemoratives began production. Some of the many commemorative themes include anniversaries of the U.S. *Constitution* and *Bill of Rights*, our Founding Fathers' birthdays, a celebration of non-political figures like American inventors/innovators including Thomas Edison and the Wright Brothers, and America's first black Major League Baseball player to break through the color barrier, Jackie Robinson, which is featured on the bottom left. (Scarce; $100 as it has few marks and superb luster unlike most others; MS (but should be PR)-62 by PCGS. *Struck images courtesy of Heritage Auctions/HA.com*)

**1997 Jackie Robinson
Commemorative
90% Silver Dollar**

$1 Commemorative
90% Silver Proof Planchet (ANACS)

Despite being the exact same planchet as the PCGS one featured on the upper left, ANACS did not designate this one as a proof planchet on the label as PCGS did. This is another reason to check both the planchet/coin and the label carefully. (Scarce; $100; MS-60 by ANACS)

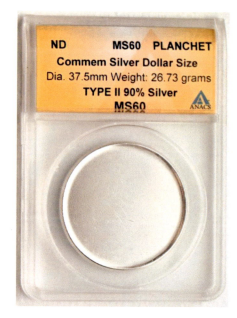

$1 American Silver Eagle
.999 Fine Silver Proof Planchet

Commencing in 1986, the $1 Silver American Eagle continues to be one of the most popular bullion coins produced by the U.S. Mint. The obverse design is borrowed from another very popular coin and arguably one of the best designs in the history of American coinage: The Walking Liberty obverse design featured on Walking Liberty half dollars (1916-1947).

As to why this was graded an "MS" and not a "PR," especially since the pebbled surfaces are indicative of a proof planchet, is not known to me. In fact, how unstruck blanks and planchets can even get a grade at all with no designs to grade is even more puzzling to me. (Scarce; $250; MS-62 by PCGS. *Struck photos courtesy of Heritage Auctions/HA.com*)

Struck Silver American Eagle

Coin Trivia: Although you can buy a single American Silver Eagle from the U.S. Mint if you like, you can also purchase what is known as a "Monster Box" (below). No, there is no actual monster included in your purchase unfortunately, but it will contain 500 American Silver Eagles.

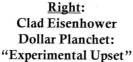

Left:
Jefferson Nickel:
Proof Planchet
with
Experimental
Finish

Right:
Clad Eisenhower
Dollar Planchet:
"Experimental Upset"

Experimental Planchets:
Jefferson Nickel and Clad Eisenhower Dollar

Before a brand new physical change is introduced to a coin like a different metal type or surface finish, and before a brand new series begins production, the Mint runs a series of tests to find out how planchets look after they go through various stages of the minting process. For example, on the left is an "experimental finish" that was tested for proof Jefferson nickels, and on the right is an "experimental upset" (i.e. testing out the rim formation) for what would become the brand new Eisenhower dollar set for release in 1971. In some cases, these test pieces manage to escape the Mint and wind up in a collector's hands…like mine!

You may have noticed that these and a few others in my collection were once part of the "**San Francisco Hoard**." *What is that?* Apparently an employee who worked at the San Francisco Mint during the early 1970s left a batch of mostly unstruck blanks/planchets and some struck proof error coins to his son that were found in a San Francisco bank's safe deposit box. The son later sold them to Mint error expert, Fred Weinberg. NGC figured out and attributed these test pieces in what has become a neat discovery and rare chance to own some historic experimental planchets that may have likely been destroyed. (Experimental Finish nickel planchet; Rare; $200; Experimental Upset Clad dollar planchet; Extremely Rare; $250)

Chapter 2: Annealing Errors

Normal Dime

Annealing is the process where coin blanks are heated in an oven before they are struck by the dies. Depending on the type of coin and its metallic content, oven temperatures range between approximately 1,000 – 1,700 degrees Fahrenheit. *So, coins are baked?* Sort of, but unlike food items placed in ovens to go from raw to cooked and/or to solidify things (e.g. cakes), blanks are heated to soften, strengthen, and enrich the planchet's structure. Without this process they would be more likely to crack or break apart when great force is applied during the die-striking process as they are still very brittle. (Coin hubs and dies are annealed as well for the same reasons.)

Sometimes blanks can be heated too long which can result in some rather drastic color changes. Gray-colored coins like nickels, dimes, and quarters can become partially or completely copper-colored, pink, brown, dark gray, black, or even a combination of colors. (See a normal and improperly annealed comparison to your right.) *I can see getting darker, but why and how would they become copper-colored?* Because without getting too technical, copper is the main ingredient in most modern circulated coinage. It was discovered that if blanks are overheated significantly, copper particles can be drawn outward towards the surface and can sometimes settle there. In some extreme cases, even a raised copper crust can form on the surface producing a shell which can start to flake or separate in sections. Examples which are less extreme might exhibit minor spots of copper here and there or only appear on one side, yet others might have no copper-red color at all. Improperly annealed Sacagawea and Presidential "golden" dollars will usually appear with a dull bronze color, a light gray, or even a very dark gray. Regardless of their color(s), these should be categorized as **improperly annealed** errors. Technically terms describing this condition as being "sintered" (forming a solid mass of metal from particles without ever going to a liquid state) or having a "copper wash" (leftover copper dust in annealing ovens settling on incoming planchets) are not correct concerning how this error occurs, which is from the migration of metal from within. Despite many of these errors featuring some wacky colors, genuine improperly annealed coins should have some degree of original Mint luster on their surfaces regardless of the colors; they should also maintain their standard weight.

Improperly Annealed Dime

Though some improperly annealed coins can look quite dramatic, this error type isn't enthusiastically sought after by most collectors and they don't normally sell at high prices. However, extreme examples in high grades and/or on type coins (e.g. bicentennials) and Eisenhower dollars can sometimes be worth some pretty decent money. Unfortunately many people think their environmentally damaged coins are improperly annealed errors (or missing clad layers) simply because of a variance in color. Environmentally damaged coins generally lack luster, fine details, and can show pitting/corrosion (bottom photo) which can affect weight. Plated coins, especially if copper is used, can also be confused with improperly annealed errors and are typically unnaturally shiny.

Environmentally Damaged Dime

Coin Trivia: The reverse of a Roosevelt dime features a torch representing liberty. On the left side of the torch is an olive branch which represents peace, and to its right is an oak branch signifying America's strength and independence.

Improperly Annealed Jefferson Nickels

1959 "Black Beauty"
Not all improperly annealed coins with copper in them will turn red. Dark gray is another common color, especially for nickels from 1958 and 1959 known as "Black Beauties." Other dates also exist. (Semi-scarce; $25; MS-65 by ANACS)

1997-P
It is impossible to predict what color or to what degree and where any discoloration will be on a coin. As you can see here, it often is not equally distributed on both sides. Inexperienced folks might see this as nothing more than a stained coin. (Scarce; $40; MS-64 by NGC)

1999-P
This one maintains an almost perfectly uniform color throughout and on both sides. Some might mistaken this for being struck on a 1 cent planchet. (Scarce; $60 due to being completely red and lustrous; MS-63FS by NGC)

2004-P "Westward Journey" Series: Keelboat
Mostly red on the obverse but not as deep as the coin above. On the reverse you see a mix of both deep red and dark grey. (Scarce; $60 due to its limited design; MS-66 by NGC)

1960 Jefferson Nickel: Sintered Planchet (Improperly Annealed)

This is a beautiful example of how annealing errors can not only result in different colors, but they can also form a solid, layered crust on the surface. It also displays how one side can develop bright colors (as opposed to simply being a darker gray) while the other side does not. The contrast on the obverse is incredible and pronounced. (It's possible the black spots could be from grease.) Though annealing errors are scarce, those featuring an actual copper shell are rare. Notice how the shell is starting to separate from the planchet on the close-up photo on the right. Thankfully, I didn't *shell* out too much for this at the auction. (Rare with an actual shell; $125; MS-65 by NGC)

Close-up of flaking on the copper shell.

Coin Trivia: President Thomas Jefferson is one of the few people featured on both sides of a bill or coin simultaneously. Below is the reverse of a $2 bill featuring the signing of the Declaration of Independence, *which was written by Jefferson; he is also on the obverse.*

1968 Jefferson Nickel
Struck on a Thin Copper Layer:
Detached After Strike – 0.2 Grams

Possibly Unique

This piece is by far the most unique and bizarre error in my collection, especially because Jefferson nickels do not have a copper color and are not plated in layers as clad coins are. The metals they're composed of – 75% copper and 25% nickel – are melted and mixed together to form an alloy. Unlike the previous example, this one detached from the planchet and is the shell only.

So how did it acquire an outer copper layer? According to Fred Weinberg, a premier expert and authenticator of genuine Mint errors for PCGS, there was "probably [a] buildup of copper pulled from the nickel planchet when it was annealed" leaving an encrusted copper layer/shell sitting on a planchet. Somehow, he said "that thin layer found its way into the striking chamber (probably laying on top of but not being bonded to) a normal nickel planchet." It was then struck by 1968 nickel dies but became detached, "[and] that's why you see an incused obverse on the reverse of this 'shell' " and why no reverse image is present. (Possibly unique; $700; MS-63RD by PCGS)

This copper shell came from a portion of the copper that was drawn out from a nickel planchet which likely had a curved clip; it's not a copper cent fragment.

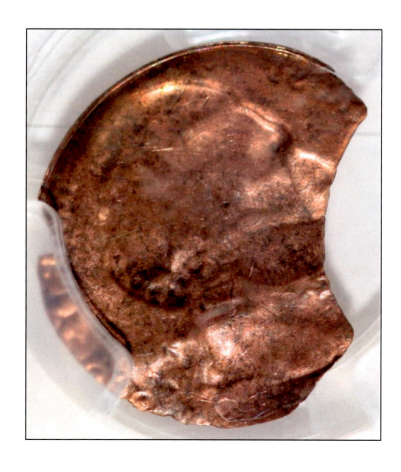

2001–D Roosevelt Dime: Improperly Annealed

Whoa! I guess you can say this improperly annealed dime got *torched*? (Ha ha! Get it?) Anyway, one way to tell if coins with reeded edges (dimes, quarters, halves, etc.) are genuine examples of improperly annealed coins is to check their edges. Upon ejection, the reeding along the coin's edge literally scrapes along the reeded collar. This process partially or completely takes off the discoloration on the edge leaving them looking brighter and lighter than the coin's two sides. If both sides and the reeding are the same color red (or some other off color), it could suggest either plating or maybe environmental damage. For reasons I cannot explain, improperly annealed dimes are much more difficult to find than most other denominations other than Eisenhower dollars. This one is very lustrous, and uniformly copper-red unlike most other improperly annealed coins. (Rare $60; MS-64 by NGC)

2000–D Virginia State Quarter: Improperly Annealed

The State Quarter series is very popular with collectors, and many of my error friends love finding them with errors. Whether it's off-centers, missing clad layers, or even improperly annealed quarters like this Virginia issue, the competition to find them on each state – and the bidding wars which can erupt – can drive up prices pretty quickly. Like the dime above, this quarter has an even copper-red color covering most of the surface on both sides. (Scarce; $90; MS-64 by PCGS)

1973-D Kennedy Half Dollar: Improperly Annealed

Strong and sporadic color differences abound on both sides on this JFK half dollar in addition to raised sections of copper where a shell started forming. Mint luster is present even on the dark gray areas. All in all, what some think is an ugly coin is considered very *a-peeling* to others. (Very scarce on halves; $125)

1974 Eisenhower $1: Sintered Planchet (Improperly Annealed)

You might be forced to make an exception for the ugly dark blotches as there are very few dramatic-looking improperly annealed Ikes. This one got away for only $195 at Heritage Auctions in 2010. Graded MS-65 by NGC. *(Photos courtesy of Heritage Auctions/HA.com.)*

Coin Trivia: Mint Error expert Mike Diamond is credited for providing the scientific evidence proving this error type is caused from the overheating of planchets left in annealing ovens too long. The copper on the surface of these coins is caused by migrating copper atoms within the planchet, not leftover dust from other batches of planchets containing copper that settles on the surface.

2008–P Presidential Dollar Series, James Monroe: Improperly Annealed

Most modern dollar coins don't look so dramatic when improperly annealed as they normally just become shades of gray or at best sport a dull brass color. Our 5th president sadly has forever lost his golden shine, which is probably why President Monroe can't bear to look at us directly here. Observe the very conspicuous contrast between the James Monroe improperly annealed dollar on the left and a non-error coin on the right. (Scarce; $50; MS-65 by PCGS; *Non-error photos courtesy of Heritage Auctions/HA.com.*)

James Monroe $1 (Improperly Annealed)   **James Monroe $1 (Non-error)**

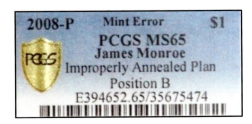

The term "Position B" on the label indicates which way the edge lettering appears if the coin is obverse-side up. If the lettering reads upside down, it is Position A, and right-side up is Position B.

**Quarter Missing an
Obverse Clad Layer**

**40% Silver Clad JFK Half Dollar
Featuring a Reverse Clamshell Separation**

*Coin Trivia: The U.S. Mint estimates a
circulated coin lasts about 30 years in circulation,
as compared to roughly 18 months for paper bills.*

Chapter 3:
Plating and Clad Layer Errors

Starting in 1965, the U.S. Mint started moving away from alloy mixtures (silver dimes, quarters, and half dollars) and replaced them with three-layered clad coinage. The three individual layers are pressed together by rollers which bonds the metals into a solid mass. In mid-1982, cents were next which ceased being a copper alloy and were switched to a copper-plated zinc planchet. (These are plated and not considered "clad.") Today the only alloy coin made for circulation is the nickel.

Despite the immense pressure from rollers to help clad layers bond, the three layers on clad coins don't always remain attached. Issues like impurities or other imperfections on any one of those layers can hinder bonding. Similar problems with zinc cent planchets can also thwart proper copper plating. Clad planchets can start to split apart horizontally (i.e. clamshell separations), bubble, or become completely detached in pieces or entire sides; this can happen before or after die striking. Some of these irregularities can also totally change a coin's color. For example, gray-colored dimes missing a clad layer appear red, while red-colored cents missing their copper-plating appear gray. And although some details may not be as sharp if a layer detached after striking or only the separated clad layer was struck, Mint luster should be present on both sides as well having a reduced weight. Zinc cents missing the copper plating should also have Mint luster but the weight difference is almost undetectable on most small scales.

Lastly, be on the look out for altered clad coins and zinc cents resembling these error types. Many lookalikes were often dropped in some type of acid and/or suffered environmental damage (or they were plated). Watch for mushy details, a lack of luster, extreme thinness, odd weights, corrosion, pitting, and rough or missing reeding.

Zinc Cent without Copper Plating

82

Zinc Cent with Partial Copper Plating

100% Unplated Zinc Cent

Deplated Zinc Cent via Acid (Damaged)

Partially & Fully Unplated Zinc Lincoln Cents

The preparation of 1 cent zinc planchets and the micro-thin copper plating applied to the zinc core are done off-site at Jardens Zinc Products in Tennessee before the striking process, and sometimes a few arrive at the Mint either partially or totally unplated; some of those even manage to get struck by the dies. Unlike coins with clad layers, the copper plating on zinc cents is so remarkably thin that it is nearly impossible to have a detached copper layer – either struck or unstruck – without being intentionally helped/altered.

In general, dull, flat finishes are indicative of deplating (bottom left), while very shiny surfaces suggest post-Mint plating. For either alteration, the original Mint luster is gone and details – particular on Mr. Lincoln – are soft, fuzzy, mushy, and much weaker than normal. Seeing that the weight of the plating is only about .05 grams, weighing these coins is not a very effective measure in determining authenticity, thus one should rely more on surface finish. Beware: These coins are very easy to alter using chemicals and unfortunately many for sale on popular auction sites are not genuine.

Coin Trivia: Sculptor Victor David Brenner crafted the bronze bust of Abraham Lincoln below in 1907, which after consultation with President Theodore Roosevelt it became the inspiration for Brenner's design of the Lincoln cent that debuted in 1909. (Photo below courtesy of Heritage Auctions/HA.com)

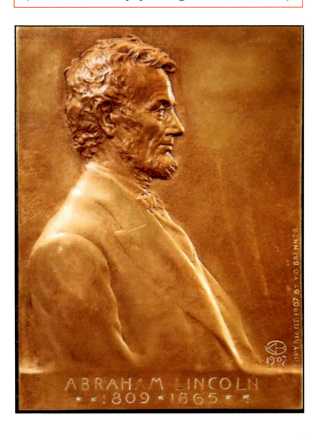

1984, 1985–D, and 1996 Lincoln Cents:
Partial Obverse/Reverse Copper Plating

When plating issues arise for Lincoln cents, the patterns, colors, and percentages of missing copper can vary greatly. For example, observe how the reverse of the 1984 cent has a dark, blotchy unplated area compared to the lustrous missing area on the reverse of the 1996 cent. However, in some cases missing plating can be incredibly similar. Notice how the oval-shaped missing copper is nearly identical on both the obverse of the 1984 cent and the reverse of the 1985-D coin. I assure you all three of these are *Honest Abes*, and fortunately TPGs have ways of detecting alterations via chemicals. Though the culprit for partially plated cents is likely impurities preventing bonding, it's not always easy *Lincoln* an exact cause.

**1984
1 Cent
Partial Plating**
(Scarce; $75)

**1985-D
1 Cent
Partial Plating**
(Scarce; $75;
MS-64 by
ANACS)

**1996
1 Cent
Partial Plating**
(Scarce; $75)

1993 Lincoln Cent: Fully Unplated Zinc Planchet

It might look like a "steelie" from 1943, or a cent mistakenly struck on a silver planchet, but this naked piece slipped by the copper-plating process at Jardens as well as those working at the Philadelphia Mint. Loaded with original luster, it is a spectacular coin illustrating exactly what lies beneath the copper plating on Lincoln cents and in a very high grade. (Rare in this grade; $225; MS-66 by NGC)

2006 Lincoln Cent: Obverse Copper-plated Shell Only (Altered)

Weighing in at .021 grams, this coin is only the obverse copper plating from a zinc Lincoln cent. Though obviously modified, somehow the acid used on it managed to eat away all traces of zinc while leaving behind little discoloration and sharp details on both sides. Even more incredible is that it remains in one piece being that it is micro-thin and has only slight bending in spots. Very intriguing despite being altered.

Obverse: Raised Designs **Other Side: Incused (Sunken-in) Designs**

Missing Clad Layers

Being that clad coins have three layers of metal, it is possible for a clad layer to separate partially or fully, leaving the copper core exposed with its reddish-brown color. (Silver clad coins missing a layer might not even be noticeable as their core is about the same color.) **Missing clad layer** errors are popular and some are quite affordable (e.g. dimes). Prices usually go up as the denomination increases because in general fewer get minted as denominations rise. Thus Kennedy halves are worth considerably more than dimes even in lower MS grades. Ike dollars missing clad layers – especially their obverse layers – can be worth $800+ even in AU grades. Generally collectors prefer obverse missing clad layers, but quarters from the Statehood, D.C. & U.S. Territories, and the America the Beautiful series are the exception as each reverse design is different. Coins featuring both sides missing clad layers are impossibly rare and prices can even reach four figures. (Few exist for any denomination missing both sides.)

Beware! Many inexperienced collectors often confuse missing clad layers with coins that are damaged, usually from environmental factors (e.g. buried underground, under water, stained from rust, etc.). Improperly annealed coins can also have the same reddish color of a clad coin's exposed copper core. One possible way to tell if a coin is missing a clad layer is to weight it, and it should weigh less than its standard weight but even this does not guarantee it is genuine. (Coins are permitted to be a little over/under in their weight, known as a **tolerance level**.) I have seen dozens of examples at shows and auctions that clearly are not genuine and I recommend buying only certified examples if you are a novice (or if you don't finish reading this amazing book!).

Missing Clad Layers: Some Differences Between Layers Missing Before and After Strike

Coins with missing clad layers, either whole or in part, are very scarce compared to the millions or billions produced that still have both sides attached. Of those that have missing layers, most of them were missing before the die strike. *How can you tell if a coin was missing a layer before or after strike?* The answer is easier than you think.

Take a look at the Eisenhower dollar and Roosevelt dime for a few seconds where each has an exposed copper core. What do you notice about the sharpness of the designs and fine details on each coin? You should observe that the Eisenhower dollar is considerably sharper than the dime including the date, lettering, and bust. This is because the dollar had it's obverse layer missing before the strike and the obverse die had a direct strike on its copper core. Conversely, the dime looks fuzzy because it entered the coining press with its obverse clad layer attached and it came off after striking. So wherever the outer clad layer is for this dime, it likely has a sharp strike; seldom will the core be just as sharp as an outer layer and may even appear altered by being dipped in an acid. In either case, Mint luster should still be present.

One other thing you may have noticed is that although the dollar has sharper details than the dime, the strike still appears to be weak. This is common on missing clad layers before strike because the coin is marginally thinner than normal. The clearance between the dies would be set for a slightly thicker planchet, so it's conceivable that the planchet wouldn't get the full impact of a die strike; thus designs might not be as sharp and prominent as those on complete planchets.

As mentioned above, clad coins with an entire side missing a clad layer *after* strike are very rare, yet their rarity doesn't seem to translate into higher sale prices than those missing before strike. I have seen several partially-missing clad layers after strike, but one must examine these very carefully. Many of those I've seen personally seem to have had their layers "helped" off to try and remove more (or all) of the clad layer to increase their value. Look for bending/folding around the edges of the remaining clad layer, tool/gripping marks along the edges, and scratches on the surface of the exposed copper as possible signs the coin was tampered with. Examples of these "enhanced errors" will be covered later. *(Photos of both coins courtesy of Heritage Auctions/HA.com.)*

1971 Eisenhower $1: Missing Obverse Clad Layer (Before Strike)

1967 Roosevelt Dime: Missing Obverse Clad Layer (After Strike)

1978 Roosevelt Dime:
Struck on a Defective Planchet –
Missing Reverse Clad Layer

If you take a look at the exposed copper center on the reverse of this coin, it could provide the reason as to why the reverse clad layer didn't bond to it. Notice it has several "chunks" of copper missing from it (red arrows). Though I can't say definitively that this is why the reverse layer didn't bond, it can't be ruled out as the cause either. (For all I know the missing chunks are attached to the missing reverse layer, wherever it may be.) It's possible that during the preparation of the planchet metal for the copper center that it wasn't mixed properly, that it had impurities in it, or maybe it wasn't rolled properly. Maybe this particular part of the copper strip wasn't pressed with the proper pressure by the rollers because it was at the beginning or end of the feed into the rolling press. (Rollers smooth out the planchet strips and press them to their desired thickness. For clad coins, each of the three layers are first rolled separately, and then they are rolled/pressed together so the layers all bond to each other.) Whatever the exact cause, the reverse layer came off before the strike. Lastly, the ANACS label is incorrect; this dime is struck on a planchet, not a blank. (Scarce; $75; MS-63 by ANACS)

```
1978 10C  MS 63

1978 10C
MISSING REVERSE CLAD LAYER
DEFECTIVE BLANK  2.08 GRAMS
MS 63
                              ANACS
```

Coin Trivia: President Franklin Roosevelt was a founder of the March of Dimes, an organization to help prevent birth defects (and ironically, he is on this defective planchet). A redesign of the dime was done in his honor after his death in 1945, and in 1946 his image appeared on the obverse which remains to this day.

Close-up of the copper Core Defect on the Reverse

2001-D   Mint Error   10C
PCGS MS64
Rev Clad Layer Missing

E5202.64/15046166

2006 P 10C
OBV CLAD LAYER MISSING
MINT ERROR MS 64
2527166-003

NUMISMATIC GUARANTY CORPORATION

2001–D Roosevelt Dime: Missing Reverse Clad Layer

Observe how several letters and numbers nearest the rims appear worn. One likely possibility is that the missing layer caused the planchet to be thinner, thus the full force of the dies may not have fully reached the planchet to complete a full strike that resulted in the weak details. There is also a bizarre pattern in the metal behind FDR's head that resembles a fingerprint. This coin truly has many more mysteries than just the missing reverse clad layer, including a dull white color on the obverse that resembles the appearance of a silver dime. ($60; MS-64 by PCGS)

2006–P Roosevelt Dime: Missing Obverse Clad Layer

Perhaps FDR had nothing to fear but an obverse missing clad layer itself. (Scarce: $60; MS-64 by NGC)

Coin Trivia: The Roosevelt dime was officially released on January 30th, 1946, which would have been FDR's 64th birthday.

88

1972–D Clad Washington Quarter: Obverse Clad Layer Missing

Improperly annealed? No. Though it is very similar in color, the obverse clad layer has simply disappeared exposing the core. Lots of Mint luster here on both sides. (Scarce; $190; MS-65 by NGC)

1974 Clad Washington Quarter: Reverse Clad Layer Missing

At first glance you might think perhaps this was mistakenly struck on a cent planchet due to its similar color until you turn it over, but in reality it is missing the reverse clad layer. (Scarce; $190; MS-65 by PCGS)

Coin Trivia: In 2020 the U.S. Mint released the American Samoa issue of the D.C. & U.S. Territories Quarters. Though many collectors feel this is one of the best designs for the series, unfortunately its timing couldn't have been worse: America and the world shut down their countries and economies to help prevent the spread of the coronavirus by mid-March in 2020. Supposedly the virus originated in China as a result of people there eating infected bats and then passed on the virus to humans.

1967 Kennedy 40% Silver Clad Half Dollar: Missing Obverse Silver Clad Layer

Kennedy halves minted from 1965–1970 (and collector bicentennials) are silver clad. Here, the obverse silver clad layer is missing yet it looks just as lustrous as the reverse side. However you can see faint blotches of copper showing through. Though hardly noticeable looking at it, this piece weighs 2.1 grams less than its standard weight of 11.5 grams. (Scarce; $75; AU-58 by PCGS)

```
1967        Mint Error        50C
      PCGS AU58
Obv Clad Layer Miss. -9.4g
     E6710.58/11467870
```

1969–D Kennedy 40% Silver Clad Half Dollar: Missing Reverse Silver Clad Layer

Unlike the previous half dollar, this one instead is missing the reverse clad layer as well as being graded a little higher. Silver clad halves missing a clad layer are far less scarce than non-silver clads missing layers despite being produced for only seven years: 1965-1970 and the bicentennial in 1976. (Scarce; $90; MS-62 by PCGS)

```
1969 D 50C
MISSING REVERSE CLAD
LAYER (9.3 g)
MINT ERROR MS 63
2681302-009

NUMISMATIC GUARANTY CORPORATION    NGC®
```

1979-D	Mint Error	SBA$
PCGS MS63		
Clad Layer Split Off		
Series: 104		Coin: 2
E9572.63/5670979		

	MS 64	
1979-D $		469683
MISSING CLAD LAYER		

1979–D Susan B. Anthony (SBA):
Dollar: Missing Reverse Clad Layer

The Eagle has landed on the reverse of this first-year issue of the Susan B. Anthony dollar. However, the clad layer did not and the mission to make these dollars popular was aborted after its third year of issue. A relaunch in 1999 fared no better with the public as it still remained an unpopular coin. (Rare; $250; MS-63 by PCGS)

1979–D Susan B. Anthony (SBA)
Dollar: Missing Obverse Clad Layer

Wow! What a bright red and beautiful coin! Known for helping to lead the charge for what would later become the 19th Amendment granting women national voting rights, I am sure Susan would also favor amending the constitution of this coin so she wouldn't be permanently exposed. (Rare; $275; MS-64 by ANACS)

Red-colored Quarter Error Type Exercise: Missing a Clad Layer, Improperly Annealed, Struck on a Cent Planchet, or Environmentally Damaged?

Just because you see a red-colored clad dime, quarter, half dollar, or dollar coin, don't always assume it's missing a clad layer. Most often the issue is that your coin is stained from environmental damage. However, don't always assume that either as you may have found a great Mint error. Clad coins missing a layer should weigh less than a standard coin. For example, a normal quarter weighs 5.67 grams, but those missing a clad layer weigh about 1 gram less. Keep in mind it could also be struck on a cent planchet, a foreign planchet, or might even be improperly annealed. Below is a quick reference as to what you might be looking at if your clad coin appears red in color. (I can't say enough how handy it is to own a good digital scale.)

2000-P Quarter
Weight: About 4.67 grams
Mint Luster? Yes; Designs Cut Off? No
Possible Error Type: Missing Clad Layer

2000-D Quarter
Weight: About 5.67 grams
Mint Luster? Yes; Designs Cut Off? No
Possible Error Type: Improperly Annealed

1972-D Quarter
Weight: About 3.11 grams
Mint Luster? Yes; Designs Cut Off? Yes
Possible Error Type: Struck on a Cent Planchet

1996-P Quarter
Weight: About 5.2 grams
Mint Luster? No; Designs Cut Off? No
Possible Error Type: None (Environmental Damage)

Detached Outer Clad Layers

Being that clad coins are composed of three layers – two outer layers and a copper center – bonding must take place to keep them all together. However, occasionally defects, bad mixtures, and gasses can prevent proper bonding which results in layers partially or fully separating from each other. Sometimes they can start to separate yet still remain anchored to the coin, sort of resembling a partially-opened clam, commonly known as **clamshell separation layers.** (If it is an *alloy* coin like nickels or 90% silver coinage, it is technically referred to as a **clamshell split layer.**)

In other cases they can detach completely from the core fully or in sections, known as **detached clad layers**. These layers can either be struck by both dies,

struck with one die with an incused image on the other side (if it separated from the planchet after striking), or never struck at all and remain completely blank. Clad layers struck by both dies are very desirable but will have very weak features on both sides since the dies are calibrated to strike a normal-width planchet. If an identifiable date along with additional major errors are present, they can sell for hundreds or thousands of dollars depending on a coin's denomination and other possible factors.

Unfortunately some people try to remove a clamshell layer forcefully which often results in damage (e.g. scrape marks, bends or folds on the outer layer, evidence of tool marks, etc.). Yet many cases exist where the outer layers and the core had damage on them before they left the Mint, so these marks do not always equate to tampering.

1969–D Roosevelt Dime: Struck 50% Off–Center on a Detached Obverse Clad Layer

Weighing in at .4 grams, this dime shows just enough of the date to identify it. (Scarce ; $125; MS-64 by NGC)

Roosevelt Dime: Detached Reverse Clad Layer

A nice example of a reverse outer clad layer that split off after striking. (Scarce; $100)

(No Date) Washington Quarter: 45%
Off-center Obverse Clad Layer, Split After Strike

This 25 cent obverse clad layer separated from a planchet after it was struck off-center. Who knows where the rest of it is, but this one – which is now a fraction of the coin's weight – has survived. (Very Scarce; $200; MS-60 by ANACS)

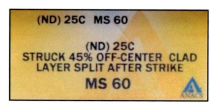

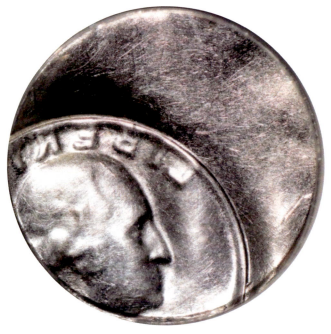

(No Date) Kennedy Half Dollar:
25% Off-Center Obverse Clad Layer

Though struck clad layers aren't the rarest items, they are much scarcer than coins missing their clad layers. Denominations higher than dimes are also very scarce. This layer was struck 25% off-center. Notice the incredibly sharp struck side on the left, and that the opposite, incused side on the right is actually quite detailed itself. This is a gem of a coin for its error type, eye appeal, and its high grade. (Rare; $400; MS-66 by NGC)

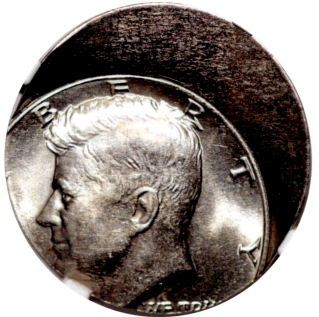

(1968-1969)-D
Kennedy Half Dollar:
40% Silver Clad Layer Struck by Both Dies

Very few struck clad layers exist, but those struck on both sides are rare and become much rarer as the denomination goes up; only a handful of Kennedy halves are known for this specific error type. For this particular coin, it must have separated first and then entered the striking chamber otherwise it would not have designs on both sides. Missing designs can be attributed to not receiving a full and direct strike as it is much too thin. This also prevented many of the small dings and scuffs which occur before striking to be smoothed out when the dies ram them. Many people might consider this coin to be "damaged," but to an error collector it is a thing of beauty.

Though dateless, this half dollar does have a sharp "D" mintmark located under JFK's neck signifying production at the U.S. Mint in Denver, Colorado. Since 40% silver clad half dollars were only produced in Denver in 1968, 1969, and 1970, other dates can be excluded (1965-1967 and 1976). As to why this also couldn't also be a 1970-D, those were only released in special Mint sets. Thus this coin was very likely discovered in a half dollar roll or Mint bag which 1970-D halves were never placed in. (Very rare; $400; Ungraded by NGC)

(1968-69) D 50C
STRUCK OUTER
CLAD LAYER (1.92g)
MINT ERROR
4711184-015
NUMISMATIC GUARANTY CORPORATION

Coin Trivia: President Kennedy is not just featured on the half dollar for American coinage. Below is his likeness on the 2015 Presidential Series $1 coin. (Photo credit: USMint.gov)

1969–D 40% Silver Clad Kennedy Half Dollar:
Was an 80% Clamshell Split layer (Separation)

Is Now Both a Detached Reverse Outer Clad Layer *and* a Missing Reverse Outer Clad Layer

A clamshell separation error exists when a clad layer starts to detach from the planchet and bears a resemblance to a partially-opened clam. However somehow the once partially-detached layer became completely separated from the planchet *after* it was placed in this PCGS slab, and so it is no longer a "clamshell separation" but has since become two different error pieces: (a) a detached reverse clad layer and (b) a missing reverse outer clad layer.

What makes this an exceptionally interesting pair is that not only do we have a detached clad layer which is 40% silver clad but is also a set where both the clad layer and the coin it separated from are both together; this is even rarer and is a lucky find in a nice MS grade. Lastly, the label is incorrect as a "clamshell split layer" denotes horizontal separation for alloy coins, not clad coins. Of course now the point is moot seeing it is no longer a clamshell. (Very rare; $600; MS-62 by PCGS)

Coin Trivia: Starting in 2007, the Mint began issuing a $10 half ounce gold bullion coin honoring the spouses of U.S. Presidents. Below is the obverse side of one of the issues in 2015 featuring Jackie Kennedy – the wife of slain U.S. president, John F. Kennedy. (Photo courtesy of Heritage Auctions / HA.com)

Clamshell Separations

Denom.	Number	Value
Cents	50	.50
Nickels	40	$2.00
Dimes	50	$5.00
Quarters	40	$10
Halves	20	$10
Dollars	25	$25

1965 40% Silver Clad Kennedy Half Dollar: 40% Clamshell Separation on the Reverse Side

It is common to see striation lines on both the separated layer and the planchet when separation of the layers occurs (see red arrows below); this is usually an indication of impurities and/or poorly-prepared mixtures which hindered proper bonding. Unlike how the 1969-D on the previous page appears, this 1965 half dollar is still an actual clamshell separation.

Sadly many of these coins are ruined when people try to pry the separated layers off by force hoping to make them more valuable. Look for evidence of tool marks which can leave scratches and/or indentations from some sort of gripping device. (Scarce; $90; Uncertified)

Coin Talk: Calls for President Kennedy to be featured on a coin came as early as the day of his assassination on November 22nd, 1963. First Lady Jacqueline Kennedy is the one who selected the half dollar as the denomination of choice. It is said that Mrs. Kennedy had an objection to the hairstyle on the 1964 proof coin as she felt the accented hairlines above his ear weren't to her liking; it was later modified by the Mint regardless of who asked for the change. The 1964 "Accented Hair" variety is a popular must-have for JFK collectors.

A **broadstrike** error is a coin that has expanded in diameter because it was resting entirely outside the retaining collar when struck by coin dies. Without a collar (bottom left) to hold the planchet in place to maintain its diameter and symmetry, broadstruck coins generally become wider – or broader – in diameter. Broadstrikes can become so enlarged that they might eclipse coins which normally have greater diameters. For example, some broadstruck nickels can be larger than quarters. Of course the wider they become the thinner they get as well. The compromised and enlarged planchet might even develop splitting along the edges which can leave them resembling a heart or mushroom-shaped appearance.

In addition, to be a broadstruck coin all design elements from the dies must be present. However, at times designs and lettering might appear missing or warped closest to the rims. For example, observe the broadstruck dimes on the top right and top center. Notice how the base of the letter "E" in ONE on the reverse side is missing on both coins and now reads as "ONF." Despite the cut-off letters, they're not missing because the designs ran off the edge like off-centers.

Another feature of broadstruck coins is that those which normally have reeded edges (e.g. dimes) will be missing them. *Why?* Because the die strike causes the planchet to expand slightly with the edges being pushed into the collar's reeded pattern (bottom center). Thus if the planchet is not in the collar, it won't have the reeding added. Planchets resting partially in the collar might have incomplete reeding.

The degree of expansion, the oblong shapes they might assume, and the position of the designs on the planchet can vary from one broadstrike to the next. Those appearing slightly uncentered like the dime on the top right are referred to as **uncentered broadstrikes**, while the dime on the top center is a **centered broadstrike.** Again, it is important to understand that an uncentered broadstrike is not the same as an off-center strike. *What's the difference?* A broadstrike has all the design features on it whereas an off-center coin has details going right off the edge (bottom right).

Normal Strike

Centered Broadstruck Dime

Uncentered Broadstruck Dime

**Collar
(Roosevelt Dime)**

**Reeding Pattern Inside
a Roosevelt Dime Collar**

Off-center Dime

Broadstrikes on Planchets

1996 Lincoln Cent:
Cupped Broadstrike Out of Collar

This bowl-shaped cent literally looks like a small copper frying pan. Because zinc is such a soft metal, broadstruck zinc cents tend to have some of the wildest expansions/shapes. Broadstrikes with this degree of cupping aren't easy to find. (Very Scarce; $200; MS-63RB by PCGS)

Right Column: The outline around this normal 1993 cent below illustrates the exact diameter of the 1996 broadstrike on the left. Just a hair short of being quarter-sized, you can really get a sense of how wide broadstruck coins can become. Unlike the 1996 cent, the 1993 cent was struck inside the retaining collar.

Coin Trivia: There are many phrases in the English language where the word "penny" is used. One of them is the old British saying, "Penny-wise but pound-foolish." In this instance it refers to a situation where someone is careful about spending small amounts of money (i.e. pennies), but not about large amounts of money (i.e. pounds; that is British pounds – their unit of currency).

1999 1C

MINT ERROR MS 66 RD

OBVERSE DIE CAP

4678391-003

NUMISMATIC GUARANTY CORPORATION　NGC

1999 Lincoln Cent: Cupped Broadstrike with a Brockage of the Obverse Design on the Reverse Face; Also Struck with Clash Marks on the Obverse

A genuine two-headed Lincoln cent? Well, sort of, except this coin was not struck with two obverse dies. Instead it was hit by an obverse die on the obverse side, while the reverse side had a previously struck cent smashed into it leaving the incused, mirrored design of Lincoln's bust as a brockage. In fact, error expert Mike Diamond told me and my Facebook group that its mate (i.e. the coin that this cent was struck with simultaneously) would be "a double-struck reverse die cap."

This coin also closely resembles a die cap (and that's how it is labeled), however Mike observed there is "no evidence this coin was struck more than once" and that just because a coin has deep walls, it doesn't mean it's been struck more than once as die caps are. (Very scarce; $325; MS-66RD by NGC)

Below: Not listed on the label are the obvious clash marks on the obverse side of this coin exhibiting the Memorial columns normally found on the reverse side.

Coin Trivia: The width of a cent is 0.06 inches. The width of a zinc cent's copper layer is 0.0008 inches.

100

1945-P Jefferson Silver "War" Nickel: Broadstrike

The production of "war nickels" – those made with 35% silver from the Jefferson series – only lasted four years from 1942-1945, so chances of coming across a significant war nickel error is extremely limited. This particular coin has a decent expansion in size. In addition, it is a superb gem of a coin loaded with shiny original Mint luster and no significant contact marks. The light edge toning only adds to its brilliance and eye appeal. Lastly, as is typical of broadstrikes, notice the warped lettering along the rims on both sides of this coin resulting in misspelled words like "IRUST" on the obverse and "AMFRICA" on the reverse, among others. (Rare; $250; MS-64 by NGC)

1996–P Washington Quarter: Huge Cupped Broadstrike

Broadstruck quarters from the 1990s are a very common and affordable error type, but it is quite rare one comes along looking this large, cupped and nearly half-dollar sized. Incredibly, almost none of the features or letters have been corrupted except on the reverse where the "E" in QUARTER is now an "F" and spells "QUARTFR." A true gem and a very rare find this size with a small die crack near the "1" on the date. (Scarce this large and grade; $150; MS-65 by PCGS)

1944 Walking Liberty Half Dollar: Uncentered Broadstrike

Arguably one of the most beautiful designs ever to grace a U.S. coin is found on the Walking Liberty half dollar. Minted from 1916–1947 and designed by German immigrant Adolph A. Weinman, this coin features a walking Liberty on the obverse with an outstretched and inviting hand and a shining sun in the background, while a perched yet alert bald eagle is spreading its wings on the reverse. As a History teacher, I can't help but notice this series spans some of the most significant events in American and Global history including World War I, the rise of Soviet Communism and Germany's Nazi Party, Prohibition, the Great Depression, and of course World War II.

As for the broadstrike error, one could argue that it's not that significant in terms of its expansion. However major errors of any type are very rare for silver half dollars and their availability is extremely limited. When they are offered for sale, expect to pay a couple thousand dollars at least. This wonderfully-toned beauty sold for $3,120 in 2020 at Heritage Auctions. Graded MS-62 by PCGS.

Coin Trivia: Some numismatic experts believe Weinman's obverse design was inspired by the obverse design on French coins like this one below designed by Oscar Roty – an 1898 French 5 Francs. (Photos courtesy of Heritage Auctions / HA.com)

Photos courtesy of Heritage Auctions / HA.com

Broadstrikes on Blanks

Many broadstrikes also appear on coins lacking rims (i.e. blanks) though it can be hard to tell the difference. Check the edges for that cut-and-tear texture which are found on blanks to help identify them.

Two 1945 Lincoln Cents: A Centered and an Uncentered Broadstrike on Type 1 Blanks

Presented here are two similar yet different broadstruck 1945 Lincoln cents on Type 1 blanks. On the left is a centered broadstrike, and on the right an uncentered broadstrike. As to why these became broadstruck, it's quite possible that since they had no

rim added they were a bit wider in diameter and therefore didn't sit properly in the collar. Though rims seem to be visible, this is merely an illusion. The variance in colors – one with a slight blue tint, the other a burnt orange – is a perfect example of how copper coins can assume a myriad of hues. (Scarce; $65; centered broadstrike is MS-64BN by PCGS)

Centered Broadstrike

Uncentered Broadstrike

1944 Winged Liberty (Mercury)
Dime: Centered Broadstrike on a Type 1 Blank

This cent-sized dime is almost perfectly symmetrical with the same amount of bare planchet around the perimeter. In addition it has no rim because it was struck on a blank. Though the tops of some of the letters are missing on both sides, it is not an off-center strike as the designs do not run off the edge. It also looks like there are full split bands (FB) on the torch which is not on the label. What a beauty! (Very scarce with full bands; $350; MS-65 by NGC)

1990–P Washington Quarter:
Uncentered Broadstrike on a Type 1 Blank

George had a significant expansion in diameter here, though he's not a centered broadstrike like Lady Liberty above. Also, only on the reverse side do you see corrupted lettering closest to the rims while the obverse side's date and lettering are almost completely unaffected. I guess in this case we can forgive George for having that typical *blank* stare since the coin has no raised rims. (Somewhat scarce; $75; MS-65 by PCGS)

1978 Eisenhower Dollar:
Centered Broadstrike on a Type 1 Blank

Broadstrikes on dollar coins are particularly rare, especially if they are nearly perfectly centered and on a blank. Though not very expanded in size, its uniformity is appealing and has few distracting marks unlike most large-sized coins. One small broadstrike for a collector, one giant coin for mankind. (Rare; $275 MS-64 by NGC)

1999–P Susan B. Anthony Dollar:
Broadstrike on a Proof Type 1 Blank

Because fewer proofs are produced than business strikes, it is far less common to come across a proof error. Notice the mintmark has a "P" for Philadelphia and not an "S" for San Francisco where proofs are traditionally made. The reason being is that in 1999 Susan B. Anthony proofs were exclusively minted in Philadelphia. Less than ten known SBAs of this exact error type exist. (Very rare; $600; MS-63 by ANACS)

Coin Trivia: The design on the reverse of the Eisenhower dollar is modelled after the mission patch for the Apollo 11 Moon landing in 1969. (Eisenhower approved the very first space mission in 1955.) For some strange reason the design remained for SBA dollars.

Misaligned Die (MAD) Quarter:
Only one side (obverse) is off-center.

Off-center Cent:
Both sides are equally off-center.

Chapter 5: Misaligned Die (MAD) Strikes and Off-Centers

Among the most noticeable errors even for non-collectors is when a coin is not centered properly. Many people, especially those who are perfectionists, can't stand it when something is off-center, crooked, or not level. I include myself among these types of people as I just can't help myself from straitening an unlevel hanging photograph or painting – even at someone else's house! However when it comes to numismatics, off-center coins are one of my favorite errors.

Now there are many different error types which can result in coins not looking centered. For example in the last chapter you read about uncentered broadstrikes, yet they are not technically considered "off-center" because their designs and details do not run off the edge. Another category includes **misaligned die strikes (MADs)**, however there are three main differences that separate MADs from true off-center coins: (1) Though MADs do have designs that run off the edge, typically they are off-center only *on one side* (though there are some dual misaligned dies strikes out there); (2) MADs are struck *inside the collar* while true off-centers are struck outside the collar; and (3) MADs typically have areas of weakness – or no designs at all – on the exact opposite side of the unstruck area (red arrows). *How do misaligned die strikes occur?* Many experts believe one of the dies – and usually it's the hammer die – was loose/vibrating and struck the planchet while it was tilted slightly. Like many other errors, some MADs can be much more extreme than others.

As alluded to earlier, true **off-center** coins – as well as broadstrikes – are struck outside the collar, but the designs on both sides run off the edge equally on both the obverse and reverse sides. As with most other error coins, those on higher denominations (e.g. half dollars and dollars), discontinued series (e.g. half cents and silver coins), and type coins (e.g. steel cents and war nickels) tend to have significantly higher sale prices. For example, this Mint state 1997-D cent struck about 60% off center with a full date and mintmark could probably fetch around $15-$25, while an off-center Morgan dollar with the same characteristics would likely cost you over $15,000. Lastly, though many error collectors find the range between 40% – 60% off-center ideal (and with full dates), if a coin has good eye appeal outside that range it is often good enough for them to acquire.

5A: Misaligned Die (MAD) Strikes

1970-D Lincoln Cent and 1975-D Jefferson Nickel: Misaligned Die (MAD) Strikes

A "MAD" coin is among the few moderately significant Mint errors that coin roll hunters (COH) can find searching through thousands and thousands of coins. Though not really all that dramatic looking, these two MADs are pretty significant as most others are barely noticeable. On both of these, notice the obverse side is about 3-5% off-center with a portion of the bare planchet showing while the reverse is centered with no bare planchet showing. If you compare the reverse of the nickel and cent, notice there is much more weakness in the affected area on the nickel than the cent despite being the same percentage misaligned. This is likely because the lettering is much closer to the edge on the nickel than it is on the cent. These are *MAD, MAD, MAD, MAD* coins! (1970-D cent; $10. 1975-D nickel; $20; both can usually be found CRH.)

Coin Trivia: The award-winning design for the Jefferson nickel which premiered in 1938 was submitted by a German immigrant – Felix Schlag.

1977-D Washington Quarter and 1979-D Susan B. Anthony Dollar: Misaligned Die (MAD) Strikes

Like other error types, the value tends to go up for an error type as denominations increase. So, all things being equal, if a 1 cent and a $1 coin are both MADs at 5% off-center, the dollar will sell for more money. In addition, with severely misaligned die strikes prices tend to rise the more one side is off-center. Thus if there are two $1 coins where one is 5% off-center and the other is 10% off-center, the latter is generally more valuable.

One thing that can increase the value of a MAD is if other errors are present. Those on off-metal planchets can garner quite an uptick in desirability and price than if no other significant errors are on a coin. For example, examine the SBA $1 on the bottom which has additional errors on it. Can you spot them? What are they? How did they get there? The answers to these questions are covered in an another chapter. Good luck! (1977-D quarter; scarce; $25. The Susan B. Anthony approximate value and its grade are covered later in the book).

Coin Trivia: One of the ways the Mint tried to help people distinguish a Susan B. Anthony dollar from the similar color and size of a Washington quarter was to have a hendecagon – or eleven-sided rim – around the coin. Regardless, the public absolutely hated this series.

Washington Quarter Rim

Susan B. Anthony Rim

1809 "Classic Head" Half Cent: Struck 5% Off-center

This Early American Copper (EAC) coin is over two centuries old, with 1809 being Thomas Jefferson's last year and James Madison's first year as President. EAC off-centers on half cents are incredibly rare, and unlike this one, many have considerable damage and/or are terribly worn. Though the label indicates this coin is 5% off-center, it appears it is closer to being about 10% off-center. This coin boasts a beautiful and uniform chocolate-brown color complete with a full date and very fine details, which I wanted to *half* the minute I saw it. (Very Rare; $1,000; VF-25 by PCGS)

1794 Large Cent, Head of 1795: Struck 10% Off-center

1794 is only the second year the U.S. Mint (which at the time was just the Philadelphia Mint) was producing coins for our newly-independent nation. Major errors on Early American Coppers (EACs) tend to always sell well and at an incredible premium. This large cent, despite its lower grade at F-12 by NGC, went for an astounding $19,995 in 2014 at Heritage Auctions. *(Photos courtesy of Heritage Auctions/HA.com.)*

1857 Flying Eagle Cent (Copper-Nickel): Struck 25% Off-center

Because this series was only minted for three years from 1856-1858 (with 1856 being pattern or proof-only issues), very few major Mint errors on them are known and thus sale prices can be exorbitant. For example, the off-center coin below sold for $6,612.50 at Heritage Auctions in 2004. Graded XF-45 by PCGS. *(Photos courtesy of Heritage Auctions/HA.com)*

1865 Indian Head Cent (IHC)
"Fancy 5" Variety: Struck 25% Off-center

Legend has it that the Indian Head cent's designer, James Barton Longacre, used his daughter, Sarah, to serve as the model for Lady Liberty's face for this series. Many numismatic experts dispute this, and at one time even the designer himself stated it was based on the statue *Crouching Venus*. What is certain is that this Indian Head cent is perfectly struck at 3 o'clock, in great condition with a full date, and exhibits a pleasing chocolate-brown color for a copper coin over 150+ years old. In fact, this piece was minted during the final year of America's War Between the States. Indian Head cents in general are particularly scarce more than 10% off-center. I must say of all my IHC errors, this one is *chief* among my collection. (Very scarce; $700; AU-50 by PCGS)

1917 Lincoln Wheat Cent (Copper): 20% Off-center:

Early off-center "Wheat" cents one hundred years old and older are very scarce in mid to high MS grades, and even fewer are this bright red (though it is slightly gold-colored). The placement is very pleasing as the full bust and almost all of both wheat stalks are still visible. What a vibrant gem that was minted five score and four years ago! (Very scarce; $450; MS-65 by NGC)

1969-D Lincoln Memorial Cent (Copper): 60% Off-center:

This 1969-D has a perfect placement, strike, full date, and a bright red color. One popular method of error collecting is to gather off-center cents by year and mintmark, although it can get tough not only with Wheat cents but also with dates after the early 2000s. Trying to add off-center proof cents to your collection could be a nearly impossible task. Good luck finding them, and even more luck affording them. (Somewhat Scarce; $40)

1865 Three Cent Nickel: 10% Off Center

Wait a minute. A 3 cent nickel? You read that correctly. Before nickels were worth 5 cents, they were worth only 3 cents. But not all 3 cent U.S. coins are called "nickels," nor are all 5 cent U.S. coins called "nickels." *Huh???*

From 1851-1873, the Mint began producing 3 cent coins made with 75% (and later 90%) silver; these became known as **trimes**. However, they also started minting this 3 cent coin on the right from 1865-1889, but it's a combination of 75% copper and 25% nickel (no silver). To differentiate between the two 3 cent pieces, those containing nickel were called "nickels." In sum, 3 cent silver coins are *trimes* and 3 cent coins made with nickel were *nickels* (and switched to *3 cent nickels* once 5 cent nickels were produced).

If you aren't already confused, in 1866 the Mint began producing 5 cent nickels, which since then are just called "nickels." Yet the Mint had also been producing silver 5 cent coins from 1792-1873 called "half dimes" (or spelled "disme" for the 1792 coin.) So because those were made with 90% silver and 10% copper, they were not referred to as 5 cent "nickels" because they contained no nickel. In sum, 5 cent silver coins are called *half dimes* (not including silver Jefferson war nickels), while 5 cent coins made with nickel are called *nickels*.

To put things in perspective of how confusing things were back then, in 1865 there were not only two different 3 cent coins produced but two different 5 cent coins minted as well. One of those 3 cent coins is featured here, which of course is a Mint error! Behold an 1865 3 cent nickel struck 10% off center with pleasing surfaces, a nice even color, and a full Civil War-era date. 1865 is also this series' first year of production. (Very scarce; $500; VF-30 by PCGS)

---

*Coin Trivia: Among the many crises which came about during the U.S. Civil War was a coinage crisis as people started hoarding coins due to rising values of precious metals. In an attempt to alleviate the coinage shortage that could've put commerce to a halt, the U.S. government authorized paper currency in fractional denominations (i.e. less than $1) for a short period of time. Presented here is one example of this **fractional currency** – yet another 3 cent piece!*

Photos courtesy of Heritage Auctions / HA.com

1920 Buffalo Nickel: Struck 25% Off-center

In terms of its artwork and design, few U.S. coins command a perfect mix of beauty and strength like the wildly popular "Buffalo" or "Indian Head" nickel. Unfortunately its significantly high relief made it susceptible to rapid wear leaving many well-circulated nickels with few design details, including many with dates no longer visible.

It is believed the Indian chief on the obverse is a composite of different Native Indians rather than a single person, and the model for the American bison on the reverse was most likely a bison housed in either the Central Park or Bronx Zoos in New York City during the early 1900s.

1920 is one of the more common dates for off-center Buffalo nickels, but few are greater than 10% off-center. Staged almost perfectly at 12 o'clock, being 25% off-center, and boasting a very high grade with a full date makes this eye-pleasing coin an outstanding example of this error type. Notice the die clash marks under the Indian chief's chin (Rare this far off-center and highly graded; $1,000; MS-65 by NGC).

1920 Buffalo Nickel: Struck 40% Off-center on a 1 Cent Copper Planchet

Stunning errors with more than one major error never, ever come cheap. This fantastic double error brought a hammer price of $12,337.50 in a 2017 Heritage Auctions bid. Graded MS-64BN by NGC. *(Photos courtesy of Heritage Auctions/HA.com)*

1989–P Kennedy Half-Dollar: 70% Off-center

This JFK half is perfectly off-center at 12:00 o'clock with a full and complete date. Eye appeal with errors is everything, and this coin definitely has it! (Very scarce; $550; MS-66 by NGC)

1922-S Peace Dollar: Struck 15% Off-center

Major off-center 90% silver dollar coins are considered royalty for those who collect off-center errors, and this Peace dollar is no exception. It's perfect 3 o'clock placement, gorgeous toning with hints of blue and green, and a godly grade at MS-65 by PCGS makes it a coin most collectors can only dream of. For Las Vegas collector/dealer Mike Byers, it's a reality and can be yours for $75,000. Good luck finding another!

Photo courtesy of Mike Byers, Inc.   *Photo courtesy of Mike Byers, Inc.*

Coin Trivia: Under the Coinage Act of 1792, *the U.S. government established the Mint, set the dollar as our standard unit of money, and included other requirements. One of those directed that for all gold and silver coins, the reverse ("tails") is to feature an eagle.*

1978 Eisenhower "Ike" $1: 15% Off-center

The Ike dollar is among the easiest modern series to complete, yet major errors are among the most expensive compared to other modern denominations, especially off-centers. This gem is not only 15% off-center but has a very strong date unlike many other off-center Ikes and has no distracting marks as many larger coins tend to have. We Like Ike! (Rare; $700; MS-65 by PCGS)

1999–P Susan B. Anthony $1: 20% Off-center

SBAs are scarce more than 10% off-center. There is a lot of the planchet and the design showing, and the full date makes it all the more stunning. This is incredibly eye-pleasing and an ideal off-center dollar coin, and the marks at 9 o'clock on the obverse simply add to the intrigue. (Scarce; $260; MS-66 by PCGS)

> *Coin Trivia:* The highest auction price for a Susan B. Anthony Mint error on record is a 1999-P SBA struck on a manganese planchet intended for the new Sacagawea dollar (which was making its debut in 2000); it sold for $15,600. As for the highest auction price known for an Ike dollar error, a mated pair comprised of a 1973-S dollar indented by (and including) a cent planchet rammed into the obverse sold for $40,250. Both coins were sold via Heritage Auctions in 2006 and 2008 respectively.

Chapter 6:
Wrong Stock, Off-Metal, & Improper Alloy Errors

Two Cent Piece: Improper Alloy Mix

Two Cent Piece: Correct Alloy Mix
(Photo courtesy of Heritage Auctions/HA.com)

Coin Trivia: The U.S. 2 cent piece was minted from 1864-1872 and a proof-only year in 1873; they were all struck exclusively in Philadelphia.

Though many Mint errors occur because of machine malfunctions (e.g. broadstrikes), or from flaws within coin metals (e.g. impurities causing clamshells), some errors occur because of simple negligence. For example, feeding the wrong metal meant for a different denomination into a blanking press can only be blamed on people's carelessness, not on a machine glitch. In other cases, incorrect percentages of metals may have been mixed together leading to variations in color, weight, and composition. Among two popular error types that can be caused by human carelessness include both wrong stock and improper alloy coins (though improper alloys can also ensue via experimentation or can occur naturally without negligence).

A. **Wrong stock** errors exists when either:

(1) A wrong type of coin metal strip or "stock" was fed into the blanking and coining presses meant to strike a different denomination. If the blanking dies and coin dies are set to strike nickels, but are instead fed clad quarter stock, you wind up with a nickel composed of 25 cent clad stock. Now like quarters, you will see a thin copper strip along the edge instead of a solid gray color. Though the planchet will be the correct size/diameter, it will be struck on the wrong type of metal.

(2) A coin is composed of the *proper metal*, but was struck on *the wrong thickness* meant for another denomination. For example, both dimes and quarters since 1965 have been struck on clad metal – a copper center sandwiched by two copper/nickel alloy layers. Should a dime be struck on quarter stock, it will be the correct size/diameter and the correct metal (clad) but it will be the thickness of a quarter.

For both 1 and 2 above, the key is that the denomination was struck on the proper-sized planchet. A wrong stock error differs from a wrong planchet error, which is where the obverse/reverse dies set to strike a particular denomination were fed the wrong-sized planchet (and likely the wrong metal type) for a different denomination. Regardless, any coin struck on the wrong metal (not simply the wrong thickness on the correct metal type) is called an **off-metal**.

B. An i**mproper alloy** error exists when either:

(1) All the correct metals to make planchet strips are present, but the percentages/proportions for them are off because people didn't follow the recipe. This can result in coins having abnormal weights, colors, and even metal types (e.g. becoming brass instead of copper). Too much of one ingredient and/or not enough of another generally can be attributed to human blundering.

(2) The metals are the right proportions but were poorly mixed, which may not necessarily be the result of human error. When this occurs on copper coins, sometimes blotches or streaks of different colors appear; these are known as "**woodies**" as they can resemble a wood grain pattern. However, not every coin with streaks is a woodie; they can also be caused by environmental damage or even just lines created by dirty rollers that squeezes coin metal to its proper thickness. Coins can even possess different colored fragments of unmelted metal(s) known as **intrinsic metallic inclusions**.

1987–P Jefferson Nickel: Struck on Clad Quarter Stock (Wrong Stock/Off-Metal)

Nickels should have solid, gray-colored edges, but this one has a copper-red center. *Why?* Because it was struck on 25 cent clad stock. Without checking the edges most folks would never even notice the composition of this Jefferson nickel is wrong.

How'd this error happen? Someone must have fed the wrong sheet of metal – quarter stock instead of nickel stock – into the blanking press when it was set for doing nickels. This particular error is one of less than twenty known. Being worth 18,000 times more than face value, I bet Mr. Jefferson is feeling pretty *clad* about that. (Very rare; $900; AU-53 by PCGS)

Nickel on Clad Quarter Stock

Normal Nickel

The edge on this error has the reddish-brown color of a clad coin, like dimes, quarters, and half dollars. In this case it is 25 cent stock. Notice there is no reeded edge as quarters have. *Why?* Because nickel collars have no reeding pattern.

Presented here is the edge of a normal nickel which should have a very uniform gray color to it. Even "War" nickels containing 35% silver should have that solid gray look. Remember, even if you do see copper-red spots on nickels it could simply be the result of environmental damage or possibly from being overly annealed.

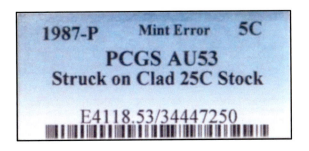

1987-P   Mint Error   5C

PCGS AU53
Struck on Clad 25C Stock

E4118.53/34447250

Coin Trivia: The phrase "IN GOD WE TRUST" is the official motto of the United States. The motto stopped being used on the five cent nickel in 1883, and did not make a comeback until 1938, the first year of issue for the Jefferson nickel.

1968-D & 1969–D Roosevelt Dimes:
Struck on Clad Quarter Stock (Wrong Stock, Correct Metal)

Oops! Though Franklin Roosevelt doesn't quite show it, he has been struck erroneously upon the wrong strip of coin metal. Though the metal is clad as it should be, where a Mint employee(s) erred was by feeding the wrong thickness of clad metal strip into the blanking press set to produce quarters. As a result, President Roosevelt is gracing 25 cent thickness.

Though not technically an "off-metal" error since dimes and quarters are both clad with the same percentages in each of the three metallic clad layers, it is definitely a wrong stock error due to its incorrect thickness. And not only is this dime much thicker than normal (even though few among the public would even notice) but as you might expect these error types also weigh more; it is 3.0 grams instead of its normal weight of 2.27 grams. In fact, the thickness and weight difference could even cause these to be rejected by vending machines and even Coinstar machines. Lastly, though the reason is unclear, dimes on quarter stock are much more scarce then quarters struck on dime stock. (Scarce; $160; AU-58 by PCGS)

Below: Normal dime (top) and the 1968-D dime struck on 25 cent stock thickness (bottom).

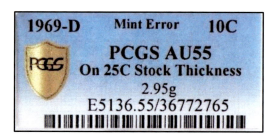

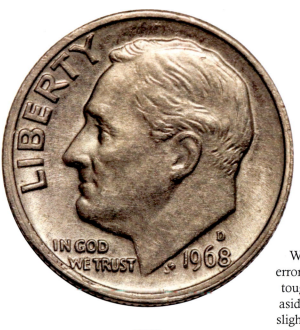

Wrong stock errors can be very tough to spot as aside from being slightly thicker or thinner, there's nothing else visually dramatic about them.

1970–D Washington Quarter:
Struck on Dime Stock: Wrong Stock, Correct Metal

This quarter looks normal, right? The blank was punched out from a press for quarters, struck by quarter dies, is the same diameter, and is even the same type of metal for quarters (clad). *Then what's the problem with it?*

The coin press was mistakenly fed stock meant for dimes. But the quarter dies were calibrated to strike a thicker planchet, which did not quite completely reach it for a forceful strike and left it appearing worn from circulation. Not so! 1970-D Washington quarters struck on dime stock are the most common wrong stock/thickness errors available as thousands are believed to have been made. Because they're so plentiful, these are very affordable even in MS grades. These seldom have a complete and/or sharp date. (Scarce; $175; MS-64 by PCGS)

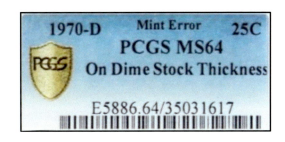

The wrong thickness also affects the ability of the reeded collar to properly complete reeded edges. Notice below part of the coin's edge above has light reeding on the left side but is missing on the right side. How awful that one of our Founding Fathers became a laughing *stock*.

Several dates exist for clad quarters struck on 10 cent thickness, including 1965, 1967, and 1969 to name a few. As you can see below, these can also be found on silver coinage.

Photo courtesy of Heritage Auctions/HA.com

1864 Two Cent Piece: Improper Alloy

This first year issue of the 2 cent piece is a perfect example of a "woodie" and its wood grain look, likely caused by a poorly mixed batch. Mint errors of any kind on 2 cent pieces are very rare. (Rare; $200)

1941 Lincoln Cent on a
Brass Planchet: Improper Alloy

This 1941 cent has 9% less copper than it should, so it is now technically a "brass" cent. Though some speculate it was possibly an experimental metal combination, it likely was just an accidental improper mixture. (Rare; $400; AU-58 by NGC)

1941 1C
ON 86%CU-11%ZN-3%SN
PLANCHET (3.3g)
MINT ERROR AU 58 BN
2819757-001

NUMISMATIC GUARANTY CORPORATION NGC

Chapter 7: Wrong Planchet Errors

A **wrong planchet** error occurs when a planchet intended for one denomination is struck by a set of dies for a different denomination (e.g. a cent planchet is struck with quarter dies; see below for an illustration). Some can be noticeable rather quickly as the coin could be the wrong color, such as when a quarter (gray-colored) is struck on a cent (reddish-brown color). Others may blend in nicely if the coin and its wrong planchet are similar colors or when the proper metallic composition remains (e.g. quarters struck on dime planchets). Many of the most expensive errors are wrong planchet coins.

On occasion there is a drastic difference between the size of a planchet and a die's denomination. When the dies are bigger than the planchet (e.g. half dollar dies striking a dime planchet) the struck coin will almost always be missing details, along with the possibility of stretched out features and even what may appear as scratches or gouging from coin dies. Other details may be weak or missing because the die pressure was calibrated for its matching planchet, metal, and thickness – not the wrong planchet it struck.

Other whacky issues can occur as well. For example, certain denominations have reeding on their edges (dimes, quarters, halves) and some do not (e.g. cents and nickels). Cents and nickels struck in quarter collars where the reeding pattern exists could now possibly have full or partial reeding, whereas a dime struck by nickel dies would not have it. Also, some people are surprised that if a quarter is struck on a cent planchet it remains the weight of a cent despite looking like the diameter of a quarter; it just becomes thinner as the diameter expands.

As with all errors, those featuring full, four-digit dates are much more desirable. And the more extreme the example (e.g. an Eisenhower dollar struck on a dime), normally the higher the price. Wrong planchet errors can also include the wrong country's planchet. The U.S. minted coins for several nations including Argentina, The Philippines, Tanzania, El Salvador, and even Cuba, with several foreign planchet error combinations close in size/color/shape and vastly different in size/color/shape.

How do wrong planchet error coins occur? For example, how can a cent possibly be struck with quarter dies? There are many different and plausible explanations which can be both intentional or unintentional. Here are a few theories explaining their existence:

1. Perhaps a cent planchet was stuck in the bottom of a bin, but when quarter planchets were poured into it the cent planchet came loose and was fed into a press where it was struck by quarter dies.

2. Maybe a cent planchet was hiding in a crevice for years inside Mint machinery, was suddenly jarred loose, and rode along with quarter planchets into a quarter die press. Voila!

3. A Mint employee found a cent planchet and mistakenly threw it into a quarter planchet bin (this procedure has since been changed).

4. A bored Mint employee intentionally threw a cent planchet into a quarter planchet bin.

A quarter die...   **...is supposed to strike a quarter planchet...**   **...but instead struck a 1 cent planchet...**   **...so we wound up with this quarter on a 1 cent planchet.**

The photo of this quarter die was modified to resemble an actual die.

Coin Trivia: In 1874, the U.S. Congress approved the Mint to produce coins for foreign governments. One of the first countries America minted coins for was Venezuela which started in 1875. In all, the U.S. Mint produced coins for over forty countries until they stopped this practice in the 1980s.

1959 Lincoln Cent:
Struck on a Silver Dime Planchet

Wrong planchet/off-metal errors are wildly popular, and those struck on precious metal planchets can get expensive regardless of their grade. For example an AU-58 with moderate eye appeal like this 1959 cent on a silver dime planchet is worth about $700, whereas in Mint State grades it could go for well over $1,000. This coin can fill many holes in one's collection depending on what types of errors are desired. For example, in addition to a silver coin error this coin is also a wrong planchet and an off-metal error as it was meant to be a silver Roosevelt dime. It's also a good example of a **"first year of issue"** error seeing it's the first date featuring the Lincoln Memorial reverse. But that's what makes the hobby fun! Wheat Lincoln cents on silver dimes tend to be much more expensive. (Very scarce; $700; AU-58 by PCGS).

1943 Lincoln Cent: Struck on a Silver Dime Planchet

1943 Lincoln cent off-metal/wrong planchet errors are one of the few FIDOs that can cause the heavy hitters in error collecting – many of whom are associates/friends – to compete aggressively against one another like hungry sharks stalking that last fish from a school. (In fact, World War Two and Civil War era dates in general tend to yield higher prices and can have more competitive auctions.) This is one of those cases where the date really matters, so expect to pay more for a 1943-dated Lincoln cent on a silver dime planchet. For example, the one below with the same grade as the 1959 cent above fetched $3,760 at Heritage Auctions in 2015. AU-58 by PCGS.

1943 photos courtesy of Heritage Auctions/HA.com

Cents Struck on Clad Dime Planchets

1966 Lincoln Cent: Double-struck In-collar on a Clad 10 Cent Planchet

Cent on clad dime planchets can be found if you're looking for them with several different dates available. However, those which are also double-struck are ultra rare including this beauty which is a rotated in-collar double-strike with two dates. Someone got a bargain at $2,115 in 2014 at a Stacks & Bowers auction. Graded MS-64 by PCGS.

Photos courtesy of Stacks & Bowers® at StacksBowers.com

1964 Lincoln Cent: Struck on a Clad 10 Cent Planchet (Transitional Error)

Without checking the edges of this particular coin, one might never know how truly special this Lincoln cent error is. True, it is on a dime planchet, but read the label again and check that date. The date is 1964 which is a year when dimes were still supposed to be 90% silver. However despite the 1964 date, this is a clad dime planchet which contains no silver. It isn't until 1965 that dimes and quarters went from being struck on 90% silver planchets to being minted on clad planchets. (JFK halves transitioned to 40% silver-clad planchets in 1965, and then non-silver clad in 1971.) Errors that occur when a coin is struck on a planchet composition intended for a different year, or struck with dies meant for a different year, are known as **transitional errors.** Among all error types, transitional errors are just about the most expensive major errors you will hear about and usually make national news when discovered (e.g. 1943 cents struck on copper planchets instead of steel planchets). This 1964 transitional error sold in 2008 at Heritage Auctions for $7,245. *(Photo courtesy of Heritage Auctions/HA.com)*

Nickels on 1 Cent Planchets

**1978
Jefferson
Nickel**
(MS-65RB
by NGC;
Scarce in
grades of
MS-65 and
higher)

I sold this
in 2020
for $275.

**1904
Liberty Nickel**
(MS-62BN
by PCGS;
Very Rare)

Sold for
$3,5250
in April
of 2013
at Heritage
Auctions.

**1882
Shield Nickel**
(AU-55 by
PCGS;
Ultra Rare)

Sold for
$8,518.75
in 2014
at Heritage
Auctions.

*1904 and 1882 photos courtesy
of Heritage Auctions / HA.com*

Other Denominations on 1 Cent Planchets

1972–D Washington Quarter:
Struck on a 1 Cent Planchet

By George! Although at first it looks to be missing both clad layers, this 25 cent piece was instead struck on a copper 1 cent planchet. Notice some areas are very sharp (e.g. Washington's face, the arrows on the reverse), while other details fade away like LIBERTY on the obverse and QUARTER DOLLAR on the reverse. This phenomenon isn't uncommon on wrong planchet errors when the dies are bigger than the planchet. Quarters on cents are rare in this grade and higher with a full date. (Rare: $900; MS-65RB by NGC)

1959-D Franklin Half Dollar:
Struck on a 1 Cent Planchet

The larger the denomination and/or the larger the physical size of the coin, the more you should expect to pay for a wrong planchet/off-metal error struck on a 1 cent planchet. This stunning example has a particularly crisp and sharp date on the obverse with the mintmark visible on the reverse. Franklin half dollars struck on the wrong planchets make for quite a remarkable – and expensive – short set of Mint errors. This coin sold for $7,590 at a 2004 Heritage Auction. Graded AU-58 by ANACS. (*Photos courtesy of Heritage Auctions/HA.com*)

1958 Jefferson Nickel:
Struck on a Silver 10 Cent Planchet

What an incredible piece this is! A sharp full date, beautiful color, and problem free surfaces on both sides make this a wonderfully attractive error. Wow! (Rare; $800; AU-55 by PCGS)

1969–S Jefferson Nickel:
Struck on a Clad 10 Cent Planchet

Since this coin has such a sharp strike, some think this coin was struck with proof dies. We the People love this coin! (Rare with "S" mintmarks; $425; MS-64 by PCGS)

Nickels on Dime Planchets

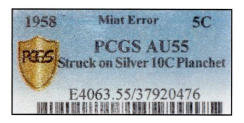

1958	Mint Error	5C
PCGS AU55		
Struck on Silver 10C Planchet		
E4063.55/37920476		

1969-S	Mint Error	5C
PCGS MS64		
Struck on 10C Planchet		
Series: 20		Coin: 78
E4083.64/5543409		

Quarters on
Nickel Planchets

1978 Washington Quarter:
Struck on a 5 Cent Planchet

An untrained eye would miss this error as it is the right color a 25 cent piece should be, but it was struck on the wrong metal and a wrong-sized planchet. As a result, George also weighs in at 5.0 grams instead of 5.67 grams because he was mistakenly struck on a nickel planchet. Notice on the bottom comparison photos that only part of it has a reeded edge that quarters have. *Why?* Because the smaller nickel planchet can't fill up the entire reeded collar of a quarter, and thus won't have edge reeding on the entire coin. (Scarce; $275; MS-65 by PCGS)

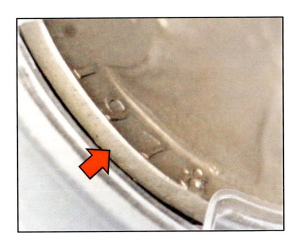

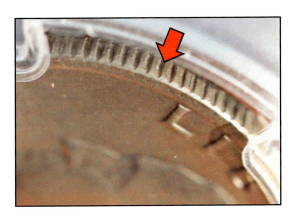

Coin Trivia: Washington refused when he was offered to have his likeness on America's first $1 coin. He felt it was a practice akin to tyrants and dictators and that it would be inappropriate since America is a country of free people.

1978   Mint Error   25C
PCGS MS65
Struck on 5c Planchet
E5904.65/81610377

1979-S Susan B. Anthony $1: Struck on a 1 Cent Planchet
Graded MS-64RD by PCGS, Susan and our Eagle here are now memorialized permanently on a copper cent planchet. In a 2014 auction at Heritage Auctions, the winner forked over $3,818.50 to secure the bid.

(No Date) Eisenhower $1:
Struck on a Clad Dime Planchet

We can't pinpoint a specific date or mintmark on this Eisenhower dime...I mean, dollar...but at least we know what date and mintmark it *can't* be. This series was struck from 1971-1978, however the bicentennial has a Liberty Bell reverse design which this coin clearly doesn't have. We also know it couldn't have been intended to have an "S" mintmark because this dime planchet isn't a proof; San Francisco only made proof dimes between 1971-1978. One thing we do know is that in 2006 this coin sold for $13,800 at Heritage Auctions. Graded MS-63 by PCGS.

Photos for both coins
courtesy of Heritage Auctions/HA.com

1972-S Proof Eisenhower $1: Struck on a Two-coin Set (Dime and Cent Planchet); Mated Pair Chain Strike and Wrong Planchet Errors

Y-*Ikes!!!* (Ha-ha! Get it?) I believe in all my years of looking at and studying major U.S. Mint errors, never have I seen a coin (or should I say "coins") quite like this before. This Ike dollar is not just dramatic but is also mesmerizing. Regardless of what you collect in terms of error types or the budgets you have to work with, there's little doubt that this would be the flagship coin in any collection. Lets take a look at why it's so darn special:

1. It is a proof error(s), which by themselves are extraordinarily rare. The care and control in producing proofs is much more precise than for circulated coins. How did Mint workers possibly mess this up?

2. These coins make up a mated pair chain strike which is a rare error type even for business strikes.

3. Neither coin is the correct planchet as neither is meant for a dollar. How both a cent proof and a dime proof planchet were inside a coning press simultaneously that was set for striking Eisenhower dollars is quite peculiar.

4. Both coins were squarely inside the retaining collar – not off-center, nor fully nor partially on top of each other. They just so happened to be perfectly side-by-side.

5. There is a complete and sharp date and mintmark along with a pleasing placement of both President Eisenhower's face on the obverse and the Eagle on the reverse. Could it be any more perfect?

Well, that's also what makes this coin very suspect; everything seems just *too* perfect. It's hard to imagine this coin is anything but a Mint-assisted error. I am certain someone at the San Francisco Mint – possibly without authorization – produced this coin intentionally to create an absolutely fantastic error. Mind you the coins are not counterfeit; the planchets and die strikes are 100% genuine. It's just that no actual "error" occurred as it was planned and struck to look like this.

I first saw this proof error set listed by error dealer Jon Sullivan for $45,000. Of course it's only natural that I wondered just where this set actually came from, and it has a very neat backstory. Apparently this set and some other coins were discovered in an unclaimed safe deposit box in San Francisco (presumably owned by someone who once worked at the U.S. Mint there). The bank turned the lot over to the State of California, who then sent them to the U.S. Secret Service to determine if these were legal to sell at auction to the public. The Secret Service gave the O.K., California then auctioned them off, and eventually Sullivan was offered some by the auction winner. Sullivan told me that he "figured out they were a set" and "then paid accordingly." This amazing mated pair is now the property of Las Vegas rare coin dealer, Mike Byers.

Dollar on a Cent AND Dime Planchet

Photo courtesy of Mike Byers, Inc.

NGC certified the set with a grade of PF-67 for both coins; the cent is PF-67RD.

Photo courtesy of Mike Byers, Inc.

Coins Struck on Gold Planchets

1913 Buffalo nickel photos courtesy of Heritage Auctions / HA.com

1913 (Type 2) Buffalo Nickel: Struck on a $5 Gold Half Eagle Planchet

Though there are six known Indian Head cents struck on gold Half Eagle planchets, this is the only known Buffalo nickel struck on a gold planchet of any type; in this case, it is likely a $5 gold Half Eagle planchet. Sadly someone cut into the rim on the reverse at 8 o'clock (see photo below) likely to prove it was just another plated novelty coin worthy of only a collector's junk box. Though 99.9% of the time that is the case, please DO NOT EVER DO THAT to a coin to determine its authenticity! Regardless of how rare or even unique a coin can be, damage like this undoubtedly cost the seller thousands of dollars (possibly tens of thousands of dollars in this case). The hammer price at Heritage Auctions in its January 2021 auction was $78,000 – a heck of a lot less than what many experts expected despite the damage.

Above is a 1913 Indian Head $5 gold Half Eagle, which is likely what the planchet for the featured 1913 Buffalo nickel was supposed to become. Seeing that U.S. Mint control of gold and silver planchets was so tight even back then, it is unknown if this is a true error or the result of Mint employee shenanigans.
(Photos courtesy of PCGS ® Used by permission at PCGS.com / CoinFacts)

1959 Lincoln Cent:
Struck on a Philippines 10 Centavos Planchet

For a number of different reasons, the United States in its history has minted coins for dozens of foreign countries; one of those was the Philippines in Southeast Asia. This 1959 Lincoln cent below was inadvertently struck on a Filipino 10 centavos planchet. The coin is slightly gold-colored as its composition is copper-nickel – similar to Flying Eagle and early Indian Head cents, however no 1959 date was minted for a Philippines 10 centavos coin. We can therefore deduce the planchet was likely left over in a bin from striking 1958 10 centavos coins and somehow was fed into a chamber set for 1959 Lincoln cents. Since the Filipino planchet is narrower in diameter, it explains why designs are cut off nearest the rim. As to why the coin looks to have indiscriminate circulation wear, it's the result of the planchet being thinner than a U.S. cent. As a result, the high points didn't make full contact with the deepest parts of the recessed dies during the strike. In my opinion, this should be an MS-grade coin – not and AU – as many details are still quite sharp.

U.S. coins on foreign planchets are very popular among hardcore error collectors, especially if the differences in color and size are quite drastic. For some reason, coins struck on Cuban planchets seem to be expensive regardless of their grades. As to why U.S. coins struck on Cuban planchets are more popular than on other countries' planchets, I guess that answer is just *foreign* to me. (Rare; $500; AU-58 by PCGS).

1958 Philippines 10 Centavos
(Copper-nickel)
2 grams

Double-strikes

1959-D Franklin Half Dollar:
Double Struck (2nd Strike 55% Off-center)

Despite sixteen years of mintage from 1948-1963, major Franklin half dollar errors are incredibly rare. This double-struck Franklin is absolutely stunning with it's pleasing 6 o'clock off-center placement, an even color on both sides with just a hint of toning in spots, and superb eye appeal. Despite the second strike being outside the retaining collar, at first glance it appears to maintain perfect symmetry despite being slightly oblong. I must say it has *Ben* a long time since I have seen a major half dollar error this nice. It's no surprise it sold for $15,600 at a 2019 Stacks & Bowers auction. Graded AU-58 by PCGS.

1959 photos courtesy of Stacks & Bowers® at StacksBowers.com

1921-S Morgan Dollar:
Double-struck (2nd Strike 90% Off-center)

Morgan Dollars are perhaps the most collected silver dollar on the planet despite what many categorize as a blah-looking design on both sides. Though many issued from San Francisco and Carson City can be pricey even in lower grades, major errors on Morgans can quickly be unaffordable for average error collectors. Even those with subtle-looking errors like this minor double-strike are super rare and highly desirable. For example, this 90% off-center second strike sold for $12,000; it's graded MS-62 by PCGS. (My friend had it conserved and regraded as it was once an AU-58. Photographed by yours truly.)

1942 Lincoln Cent:
Double-struck Flipover In-collar

Simply incredible. Both sides have features of their opposite side in what is an impressive war-time error coin. On the top left (obverse), both wheat stalks are clearly visible at 6 and 10 o'clock, as is the "C" in CENT on Lincoln's temple, and UNUM at 3 o'clock are well-defined elements of the reverse. On the bottom left (reverse), Abe's face is shadowed, the word LIBERTY is at 9 o'clock, IN GOD at 11 o'clock, and the "42" from the date at 4 o'clock are all prominent features of the obverse. This is a truly outstanding error with a beautiful color. (Rare; $500; XF-45 by NGC)

1942 1C DOUBLE STRUCK
FLIPOVER IN COLLAR
MINT ERROR XF 45 BN
3034766-002

NUMISMATIC GUARANTY CORPORATION

<u>Above</u>: This overlay should give you a better idea of exactly what you are looking at on this flipover double-struck cent. *(Thank you, Mark Kinan!)*

Coin Trivia: In addition to coins, the U.S. Mint in Philadelphia also produces a wide array of national medals that celebrate the lives and achievements of people who made profound and positive impacts in U.S. and world history. One example is a Congressional Gold Medal honoring Colonel James Doolittle and his Tokyo Raiders for their actions during World War II in what became known as "Doolittle's Raid" over Japan.

Two 1913 (Type 1) Buffalo Nickels: Nearly Identical Double-struck Rotated In-collar Errors

At first appearance both of these coins could easily be disregarded by a Mint error novice as damaged coins destined for a junk box. Au contraire, mon frère! In what can only be explained as an incredible and almost unbelievable coincidence, these two Buffalo nickels not only have the exact same error type but have nearly identical clockwise rotations between strikes. (For example, notice how on each coin the Chief has two eyes with both in the same area.) In addition, despite that neither coin has a visible date they're both 1913 Type 1 coins. *How can you tell?* There's a raised mound under the Buffalo's legs which is only seen on the 1913 Type 1.

Now seeing that these two coins have the exact same error type with the same degree of rotation between strikes, naturally your suspicions should be heightened. However, the coincidence itself should not automatically discount these as fakes or altered coins. In my opinion for both coins the rims look good, the visible lettering for both strikes look good (e.g. spacing, size, serifs, etc.), and designs and details for both strikes look good. I agree with PCGS authenticators that both of these are genuine errors, however the grades seem a lot farther apart than they should. (Top row: MS-63; sold for $5,040 in 2017. Bottom row: XF-45; sold for $3,290 in 2014. Both sold via Heritage Auctions.)

Coin 1: MS-63 (PCGS)

Coin 2: XF-45 (PCGS*)***

Photos for both coins courtesy of Heritage Auctions/HA.com

1964–D Jefferson Nickel: Double-struck Rotated In-collar

Almost at a complete 180 degree rotation after the first strike, this one also has some nice design details from both sides. By remaining in the collar that holds the planchet in place, the nickel did not expand in diameter and kept its round, uniform shape.

To illustrate the double strikc, please see the matching colored arrows: The red arrows show how the coin has two dates and the green arrows point out the "TED" in the word UNITED. You also see the phantom design of Monticello and the words FIVE CENTS near the top of the dome for both strikes on the reverse. This is a beautiful and high-grade example of a popular error type (and note it's diameter and symmetry haven't been compromised), but unfortunately for Thomas, he will likely never declare independence from this holder. (Rare; $400; MS-62 by NGC)

Close-up of the Second 1964 Date

Close-up of the Second FIVE CENTS

```
1964 D 5C
DOUBLE STRUCK
ROTATED IN COLLAR
MINT ERROR MS 62
4679488-004
NUMISMATIC GUARANTY CORPORATION    NGC®
```

Coin Trivia: The Anti-Counterfeiting Educational Foundation is an organization dedicated to helping law enforcement "protect the integrity of U.S. and world coinage by educating officials on the economic impact and growing threat of counterfeit circulating, collectible, and bullion coins." (Source: ACEF Mission statement https://acefonline.org/about-us/)

1964 Jefferson Nickel:
Double-struck, Second Strike
10% Off-center (and Broadstruck),
And Obverse Indent with a Mushroom Split

Many error collectors have noticed there are a disproportionately large number of error coins, and various types of errors, that were created during the early to mid-1960s. *Why is that?* America started experiencing a coining shortage around 1959, and so the Mint had to increase production to meet consumer demand. So, it is expected that as production of something increases, the chances that mistakes occur during production also increases. *But what led to the coining shortage?* Among some of the factors includes America's strong economy at the time (more people buying means more currency/coins needed), an increased use and popularity of coin-operated vending machines, and new industrial uses for silver. With the Mint publicly acknowledging fears of a possible silver shortage and rising prices, many people speculated it wouldn't be long before the silver in a silver coin was worth more in bullion than its monetary value; this in turn led to hoarding and further depleted the coinage supply. Despite ramped up mintage levels to increase supplies, consumer stockpiling of coins continued and worsened with word that silver coinage would be replaced with copper-nickel clad coins beginning in 1965. 1964 is one of those years which saw incredibly inflated production levels, and with it came an increase in the numbers and types of Mint errors including the 1964 Jefferson nickel featured on the right.

Looking like an actual mushroom, this nickel had a normal strike but did not eject properly the first time. It was then struck a second time off-center with a second unstruck planchet between the obverse die and the obverse side of this coin leaving an enormous off-center indent. The stress on this coin from the second strike with the additional planchet on top of it caused such a fantastic expansion that it has a nearly identically-shaped (but reversed) split on both sides leaving it with a mushroom appearance. Topping off this dramatic error is the presence of two full and readable dates. (Rare; $600; MS-63 by PCGS)

Coin Trivia: Though this is not a coin, it can be almost as amusing to find mishaps on other U.S. Mint products, especially those printed on or placed inside Mint packaging. For example, Jerry DeSantis found this Mint token inside a 1972-D Mint set with an extra set of printing placed off-center. Do non-coin errors found in Mint sets make the sets themselves more valuable? The answer is really up to you. People can charge whatever they want for something, but it's only going to be worth what someone is willing to pay for it.

1999-P Jefferson Nickel, Multi-error Type: Double-struck 50% Off-center, Broadstruck, and Very Strong Triple Die Clashes (on First Strike Only)

Among all my Mint errors, this one in particular has drawn the most interest, questions, comments, and looks of shock upon first glance. People seem unable to take their eyes off it, mainly because of the placement and alignment of the two heads on the obverse. Some even theorize it was purposely made this way by a rogue Mint employee or is 100% fake. *What the heck happened to it that left such a bizarre appearance?*

For starters, the initial strike shows evidence of incredibly strong die clashing (illustration below). So, the dies at some point struck each other (and by the looks of it, three times) without a planchet in the chamber where each left designs from the other die struck into them. On the obverse, can you see an upside-down design of Monticello with the last letter "O" from MONTICELLO plus the "S" in CENTS just to the left of LIBERTY? And on the reverse, can you make out the three separated, wavy outlines from the back of Jefferson's hair near the end of the words MONTICELLO and CENTS? Yet on the second (off-center) strike there is no evidence of die clashing, meaning the two strikes came from different die pairings, which by itself is absolutely incredible and ridiculously rare.

The initial strike was also struck outside the retaining collar and shows all the normal indicators of a broadstrike, including lettering being cut off nearest to the rim (e.g. STATFS and AMFRICA on the reverse). Then, somehow, it failed to eject properly and wound up being struck a second time 50% off-center by a different die pairing; this flattened part of the rim which is best seen from 7 o'clock to 11:00 o'clock on both sides. Above all, it is the appearance of conjoined Jeffersons attached at the face that really grabs your attention. Nose to nose, this coin is one of my absolute favorites (Rare; $700).

Coin Trivia: To the right is an electrotype pattern struck on copper-plated silver featuring one of the the proposed reverse designs for the Jefferson nickel. The contest to design what would become the Jefferson nickel in 1938 was fierce, including this submission by sculptor Anthony De Francisci; he lost out to Felix Schlag.

Photos courtesy of Heritage Auctions/HA.com

Triple-struck Coins

1981 Lincoln Cent: Triple-struck (2nd Strike 50%
Off-center, 3rd Strike 70% Off-center) with a Uniface Reverse

It took three *strikes* before this Lincoln cent was *out* – of the striking chamber, that is! Though an additional planchet(s) prevented the two other direct strikes on the reverse, in my opinion this triple-struck uniface reverse would be a *home run* in anyone's collection. In fact when Heritage Auctions *pitched* this coin for sale in 2009, the winning bidder didn't *balk* at the hammer price of $1,305. With two full and sharp dates, a nice even color, and superb eye appeal on both sides, I bet the owner has a *ball* showing this off. Graded MS-64RB by PCGS. *(Photos courtesy of Heritage Auctions/HA.com)*

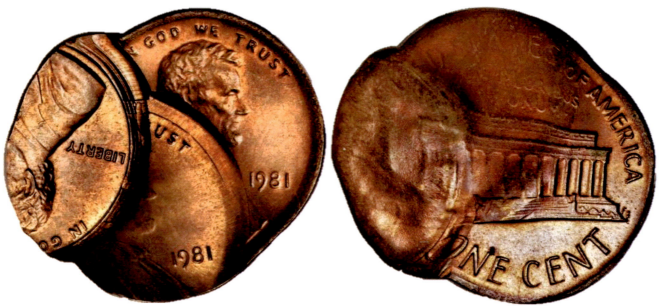

1999–D Jefferson Nickel: Triple Struck
(2 Strikes 80% Off-center, 1 Strike 98% Off-center)

Though it doesn't appear so, it was struck at least three times (the blue arrows point out the third strike about 98% off-center). On the obverse, it is incredible that both Jefferson's face and a full date appear in almost perfect symmetry. Also notice there appears to be a "D" mintmark on the reverse side (see red arrow). Could it be from a previously struck nickel's obverse side that was then struck into the reverse side of this one creating a brockage, or is it a case of pareidolia? (Rare; $125)

> *Coin Trivia:* Thomas Jefferson is credited for proposing that America's coinage should be based on units of ten.

2001-P Washington Quarter: State Quarter Series, New York: Triple Struck (2nd & 3rd Strike 35% Off-center)

Although this looks to be struck only twice, by examining the word UNITED on the obverse you can see clearly it appears three times (see photos below). What great cye appeal it has with its bright luster complimented with hints of blue and gold toning. (Scarce; $450; MS-66 by PCGS)

2001-P   Mint Error   NY 25C
PCGS MS66
3/Stk-2nd/3rd 35% O/C
Series: 39   Coin: 168
E5966.66/2795095

LINCOLN 1C
DOUBLE STRUCK
SADDLE STRUCK
MINT ERROR MS 63 RB
3575031-007

Saddle Strikes

(No Date) Copper
Lincoln Cent: Saddle Strike

On the left is a dateless copper Lincoln cent which has two sets of designs that are off-center on both sides. However just because a coin has two sets of designs, it doesn't necessarily mean it had more than one striking action by the same die pairing. Though there are coins which were struck off-center and then spun around for a second off-center strike, this coin is not one of those. In fact, the featured coin here had only one striking action. *Only one? Well then why are there two sets of designs?*

The reason this coin has two sets of designs – but only had one striking action – is because it was struck simultaneously by two different die pairings which go into action concurrently; this is known as a **saddle strike.** The name is derived from an animal saddle which bears resemblance to this error type. Since some saddle strikes develop a bend or fold in between the die-struck areas while the struck areas resemble a saddle's over-hanging flaps, it is a humorous yet appropriate name for this type of error. Also, if a saddle strike has a fold on it (some do not), it should bend upward toward the side struck by the hammer die. In the case of most (but not all) U.S. coins including this Lincoln cent, the hammer die is usually the obverse die. (A couple exceptions include Buffalo nickels and Mercury dimes where the reverse die was the hammer die and the obverse was the anvil die.)

So what happens with a saddle struck coin is that a planchet entered the striking chamber but wasn't resting squarely in the collar; it was off-center to the dies. But in cases where there are coining presses with more than one set of die pairings (e.g. two or four sets), the planchet could be overlapping two different sets of dies and thus be off-center for each. As the striking action is engaged, each die pairing will strike the coin concurrently leaving two sets of off-center strikes, the force of which can cause the planchet to bend. Again, the coin wasn't struck two different times; it was struck only once with two different sets of dies simultaneously that were side-by-side. Since no other planchet obstructed any of the four dies, both sides have two sets of designs. Most saddle strikes bear no dates, and as a result those few with dates tend to command a higher premium. (Very scarce; $100; MS-63RB by NGC)

Chapter 9: Double Denominations

When a coin has been struck by two different sets of dies from different denominations (e.g. 1 cent and 10 cent dies), this is known as a **double denomination**. Coins like this are incredibly rare even among two of the most common examples: cents on dimes and nickels on cents. Prices go up significantly into the thousands as the example gets less common, like nickels on dimes, half dollars on quarters, and so on. As with all errors, double denominations featuring full dates (especially for both denominations) are worth considerably more, and the more details you see from both and the higher the grade, the higher the premium usually. Sometimes these will appear to have scratches or marks which could actually just be features from the other denomination showing through, so it is best to examine these carefully.

How can this possibly happen? How does a coin already struck wind up being struck again by a different set of dies meant for another denomination? One explanation is that a struck coin was left in a bin that was later reused to transport different planchets for a totally different denomination (this procedure has since been changed). So if a struck dime became stuck in a bin that suddenly had thousands of cent planchets poured on top of it, when it loosens it could be on its way to a cent striking chamber and thus struck twice by two different sets of dies. (Notice that the cent's designs are on top of the dime's designs). Another possibility is that a Mint employee – for whatever reason – tossed a previously-struck coin into a bin of planchets meant for a different denomination. (For the few known proof double denominations, it is hard to believe their creation is anything other than a Mint-assisted error created for personal amusement and/or profit).

1999 Lincoln Cent Struck on a Clad 1999-P Roosevelt Dime: Double Denomination

This is a brilliant example showing incredibly strong details for both the cent and dime in what many collectors informally refer to as an "**11 cent piece**." It is not too often Roosevelt's head shows up this defined, and you can even make out some of his hair lines and his ear on the Lincoln Memorial. What makes this coin even more amazing is that both sides are heads and tails simultaneously. There is also a very clear and identifiable date for each denomination, along with some beautiful toning to add to its eye appeal. (Rare; $800; MS-65 by ANACS)

Left: Sometimes it's not just the coins that can wind up as a double denomination, including this Buffalo nickel / Roosevelt dime Whitman coin folder. (Well, at least the front cover is.) This is one of the most humorous printing errors I have ever seen.

Photo courtesy of Fred Weinberg

1978-D Eisenhower $1
Overstruck on a 1977-D Roosevelt Dime

What a pleasing merge of both the largest and smallest U.S. coins intended for circulation – in terms of their diameter – in modern U.S. numismatic history. You would almost think this combination wouldn't even be possible. And not only that, each denomination has a different date. I mean, how did a previously-struck 1977-D U.S. dime get struck again with 1978-D Eisenhower dollar dies? Can the explanation really be so simple as to theorize this struck dime was left in a bin of unstruck clad dollar planchets? I guess the answer could be that simple, but it's also not unreasonable that such an incredible double denomination with two different dates could have been Mint-assisted. Either way, it's without question the most amazing 110 cent piece I've ever seen. In a 2017 auction at Heritage Auctions, it sold for just shy of $10,000 at $9,987.50. Graded MS-66 by NGC.

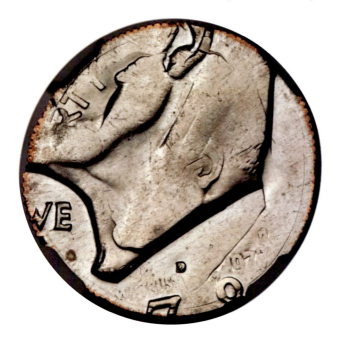

1943 Lincoln Cent
Overstruck on a 1943 Cuban 1 Centavo

For those who love 1943 Lincoln cent errors, this one struck on a 1943 brass 1 centavo planchet from Cuba is muy bueno! And it has two clear dates on the obverse. Querido Dios! Perhaps too perfect to be an accident with its serendipitous placement, regardless it sold for $10,925.00 in a 2012 Heritage Auctions bid; it was sold privately for $25,000 later that year. Graded MS-62 by PCGS.

Photos for both coins
courtesy of Heritage Auctions / HA.com

Chapter 10: Other Error Types & Oddities

Throughout the 200+ years coins have been minted in the U.S. there have been dozens and dozens of different error types and countless numbers of error combinations. So far I've showed you some of the more popular error types collectors love, but there are several others to get to in the coming pages. Perhaps what's coming next might be your favorite, and hopefully there will be some you haven't seen before. So if you're ready, let's *press* onward!

Double Trouble: Machine Doubling (MD) Vs. Doubled Dies (DD)

One of the easiest and least-respected Mint errors to find in circulation are coins exhibiting **machine doubling (MD)**, a.k.a. mechanical, shift, shelf, or strike doubling. Though this form of doubling may appear similar to true doubled dies (DD), there are several significant differences in how they're produced, how they look, and how valuable they are. Sadly many newcomers to the hobby get excited prematurely because they believe they found the next **discovery coin** (i.e. the very first of its kind to be reported) when in reality all they have is MD. *OK, so what's the difference between MD and DD?* Unlike doubled dies where the flaw exists *on the die before a single coin is struck* (and is thus a die variety, not a Mint error), machine doubling *results from a malfunction within the die-striking chamber,* which makes it a Mint error in my opinion.

However, there is debate as to whether coins with MD should be recognized as Mint errors or if they should be considered "damaged" coins. Those who claim MD is not a Mint error believe the minting process ends when the hammer die reaches the lowest point of impact, and anything after that – including a loose die causing machine doubling – is therefore considered "damaged." Though I do respect both sides of this debate and both have some valid points, in my opinion the claim that the minting process ends upon the lowest point of hammer-die impact seems arbitrary and incomplete. I believe the process ends when the planchet finally leaves the striking chamber (or after edge-lettering has been completed for those which have it added after ejection, including some Native American and Presidential Series dollars), mainly because at that point the production processes of making a coin have all been completed. How can the striking/minting process truly be "complete" if the coin is still in the striking chamber? As to which nationally-known numismatic error experts you agree with, it is really up to you to decide who is more persuasive and why. For me, I consider machine-doubled coins as Mint errors. Regardless of your opinion, few consider MD coins to be worth more than face value as they are so plentiful and easy to find, but extreme examples in excellent condition can sell for a slight premium; they're also good to have as educational pieces for comparison.

Anyway, *what kind of striking malfunction causes MD?* It could be anything from a slightly loose/vibrating die to an unstable die press that wasn't maintained properly. What can result is a die strike that bounces, slides, or skids across the planchet leaving a smeared or doubled appearance. Unlike doubled dies which transfer the same die flaw to every planchet, machine doubling from the same die can be unique to each coin or can produce the same flaw in the same area on multiple coins.

Machine-doubled coins and doubled dies also have a different physical appearance. For example, a machine-doubled date will have one of set raised and

rounded designs (green arrows) while its mate will be flat and shelf-like (red arrows). For example, on the 1968-S cent below you can see quite clearly how the doubled designs for each number and letter aren't congruent; one set is raised, the other is wider and flatter. This form of machine doubling is known as "**push**" doubling and happens "when a die bounces off the surface of a coin, shifts position, and lands in a slightly different spot" *(Error-Ref.com).*

1968-S Lincoln Cent with Machine ("Push") Doubling

Below: This 1991 Lincoln cent exhibits push doubling that is more extreme. Unlike the 1968-S cent, the MD here is limited to the bust and not the date or mintmark.

1991 Lincoln Cent with "Push" Doubling

Coin owned by Vincent Eads; photo by Joe Cronin

Doubled Die Vs. Machine Doubling: Side-by-Side Comparison

In contrast to machine doubling, true doubled dies do not occur because of a striking error but rather are born during gaffes involving the die hubbing process. So when you see obverse doubling on a 1955 DDO Lincoln cent, the actual die strike itself was perfectly normal. It only has doubling because there was more than one set of designs carved into the die, but one of those sets was misaligned. Also, both sets of designs on a doubled die will be equal in height, thickness, and length in addition to having a clear line of separation between them unlike machine-doubled coins. The Lincoln cent series has multiple years which exhibit minor obverse or reverse doubling that are affordable to most collectors. Some notable years with much more dramatic obverse doubling are the 1955, 1969-S, and 1972 cents. However the 1969-S is so rare that a recent PCGS certified coin graded at MS-64RD (w/CAC) sold for $126,000 at a 2018 Stacks & Bowers auction.

1969-S Lincoln Cent Doubled Die Obverse (DDO)

A true doubled die like this 1969-S will have two sets of designs which are both raised and rounded; there will also be a clear separation between doubled designs (blue arrows).

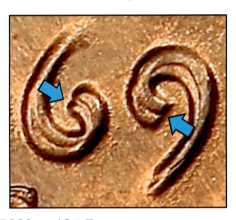

1969-S photos courtesy of PCGS ® Used by permission @ PCGS.com/CoinFacts

1968-S Lincoln Cent with Machine ("Push") Doubling

Each digit and the mintmark on this 1968-S cent lacks a point of separation between the doubled designs (red arrow). They're also not congruent as one set is raised while its mate is flat and shelf-like.

Thanks to Denise Catania for donating the 1968-S for educational use.

<u>Coin Trivia</u>: *A machine-doubled 1969-S sold on EBay.com for $1,100 on March 8th, 2020. I have to believe these unlucky, uninformed people assumed they were bidding on the incredibly rare 1969-S doubled die. Unbelievably, another machine-doubled 1969-S sold for $1,275 on April 17th, 2020. These are going to be some very expensive lessons to be learned when they get their coins back from grading companies. Ugh!*

Die Deterioration Doubling (DDD) and Ridge Rings

1983-P Jefferson Nickel: Die Deterioration Doubling

Of all the error types and die varieties people ask me to examine for them, well over half involve coins they suspect of being double-struck or doubled die coins. Sadly in 99.9% of those cases they have neither. One form of "doubling" they wind up having – which isn't "true" doubling – is a coin with **die deterioration doubling (DDD)**. This flaw develops when a die becomes severely worn (or has "deteriorated") from repeated strikes and its details lose their sharpness over time. Designs tend to flatten out and become distorted, particularly in regions nearest the rim. What can appear as heavy circulation wear and/or doubling on a coin is merely just the result of being struck with a worn-out die which should have been replaced multiple thousands of strikes ago. Though some of these can still look pretty dramatic, most collectors won't even want these in their collection at all let alone pay a premium for them.

Below: The "doubling" present from die deterioration on the letters of AMERICA is very prominent, especially on "ICA."

Special thanks goes out to my friend John Amirault for the loan of this coin.

Below: A **ridge ring,** most commonly found on early zinc Lincoln cents along IN GOD WE TRUST, is likely another form of die deterioration; these also carry no real premium.

Die State Vs. Die Stage

Two terms that some collectors often confuse and misuse are die *state* and die *stage*, which are not synonymous and have entirely different meanings. While coins struck from late die states aren't errors (although some feel not replacing the worn dies in due time is an "operator error" and therefore a Mint error), coins produced from die stages are. *What's the difference between die state and die stage?*

<u>Die State</u>: Because dies are under significant pressure from repeated strikes, over time it is normal for their sharp details to become worn resulting in struck coins mimicking those weak details. For example, the steps of the Jefferson Memorial on the reverse of a Jefferson nickel look sharper and more clearly separated upon a die's initial use than it would at the end of its life. The level at which designs become worn down from striking planchets is known as its **die state.** Sometimes dies can become so worn that coins struck with them appear to have circulated a long time even when fresh off the production line. As can be expected, coins with sharper details are much more desired. In fact, grading companies even have special categories of grades for some denominations and series of coins which exhibit strong details (e.g. "FT" or "Full Torch" for fully separated horizontal bands and fully defined vertical lines on a Roosevelt dime's torch). In contrast, coins struck from late die state dies (i.e. worn dies) are less desired, nor do some consider them Mint errors as they are just the result of a die's normal wear and tear.

<u>Die Stage</u>: In addition to normal wear, dies can also suffer forms of impairment/damage leaving some rather bizarre markings on coins. Planchets struck with damaged dies are referred to as **die stages** and the resulting coins are considered Mint errors. *How do dies become damaged?* Though there is no definitive list, historical forms of damage have included: the dies striking each other (die clashes); die cracks; sections of a die falling out (die chips and cuds); shattered dies; the dies coming into contact with a coin or planchet fragment, foreign object (machine parts, e.g. screws) or a coin/planchet out of position in the chamber that scratches up the dies; scrapes from feeder fingers; and intentional die abrasions from Mint employees attempting to remove imperfections on them.

2019-P Roosevelt Dime: Reverse Die Scrapes

Genuine U.S. Mint 10 cent feeder finger overstruck with dies from Dan Carr's Moonlight Mint. ($80)

On the bottom left is what is known as a **feeder finger**, which is what pushes unstruck planchets into the die striking chamber. From time to time malfunctions in the coining press can cause the feeder finger to make direct contact with the dies and leave scrape marks on them. The damaged die will then subsequently transfer those linear, parallel scrape lines to coins as seen on the reverse of this 2019-P Roosevelt dime above. Coins featuring this type of accidental die abrasion are called **die scrapes.** (Not uncommon; $2)

Die Chips

Though "B-I-E" cents are cool to find in circulation, they really don't carry a significant premium. Even MS examples with much larger chips only go for a few bucks or less despite what some try to charge for them. These and other coins with minor die chips simply don't excite most error collectors because there is no real challenge in finding this particular error type and they lack that dramatic look to them.

1955-S Lincoln Cent: Obverse and Reverse Die Chips

Coin dies are made of hardened steel which are meant to endure a grueling process. For example, one die pairing alone could strike hundreds of thousands of coins at a rate of about twelve per second, and each is struck with dozens of tons of striking pressure. Yet even the strength of hardened steel has its limits and sometimes small pieces of the dies can fall off. *How could part of the steel just fall off?* Well, perhaps a small, sharp piece of steel from a machine part broke off and landed in the striking chamber; that could definitely create a chip on the die face. Or maybe the die wasn't prepared properly and sections of it became compromised after multiple strikes leading to cracks and chips falling out. Also, maybe some parts of the design are so close to other designs (e.g. lettering, dates, hairlines, feathers, etc.) that the small gaps between them become stressed and weaken over time. All of these factors could lead to small divots in the die known as **die chips**; these will then appear as raised blobs on struck coins as the metal shifted around during striking to fill in those gaps. (Sections that come off which are *along and connect to the outer rim* are called "die breaks" or "cuds.")

This 1955-S cent has three noticeable die chips. One is on the obverse found in the word LIBERTY between the "B" and "E" where it looks like a crude and incomplete letter "I" is now between them. These are known as **"B-I-E" cents** of which there are multiple dates and mintmarks known to exist for Lincoln cents. In addition, there are two minor reverse die chips; one on the left wheat stalk and one just below the right wheat stalk near the rim (between 4 and 5 o'clock). As with die cracks and cuds, a die chip's size and scope on a die can tend to enlarge through the duration of their use.

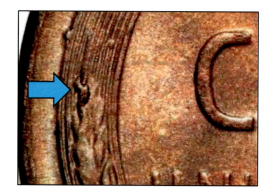

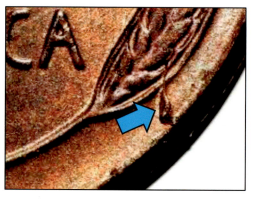

Die Cracks

1993 Lincoln Cent:
Large Y–shaped Obverse Die Crack

When a die with a crack strikes a planchet, the metal will fill in recessed areas of the crack just as it will for die chips and die breaks (a.k.a. cuds). As a result, the coin will feature raised lines where the crack(s) exists; these are known as **die cracks** which can be minor or extreme, and there can even be multiple cracks. If the die isn't replaced when cracks start, the die will continue to sustain further damage which could lead to it splitting, shattering, or even a complete die failure. This 1993 cent has a decent Y-shaped obverse die crack on the top of Lincoln's head. For many collectors, die cracks aren't very exciting and tend to carry little to no premium.

Roller Marks

1980-D Lincoln Cent: Roller Marks

Though some have theorized this 1980-D cent is an improper alloy mix, the streaks are too perfectly linear and uniform for me to accept that. Instead, I believe these are **roller marks** left by rollers which squeeze planchet metal to its proper thickness before coin blanks are punched out. Error expert Mike Diamond proposed stripes like this "may instead be a form of discoloration or staining" caused by rollers "that were dirty." Therefore it is possible that the rollers then "transferred their surface grime to the coin metal strip in a fashion similar to how ink is transferred to currency sheets in the intaglio inking process." This preparation error is not really considered collectible and many feel they lessen a coin's eye appeal, grade, and value. *(Mike Diamond's quotes used with his permission, sourced from "Different Causes of Stripes on Coins Not Fully Understood,"* Coin World, *Sept. 30, 2014)*

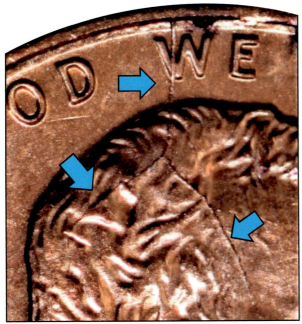

Zinc Cent Plating Blisters

Beginning in mid-1982, the Mint moved away from copper alloy cents and started using zinc planchets plated with a thin copper layer. Should the copper not bond properly (e.g. impurities), problems can arise. For example, heat generated from the striking process could excite/expand gasses forming bubble-like pockets; these are known as **plating blisters/bubbles**. (Plating blisters are similar to but not the same as occulated gas bubbles which form in solid-alloy coins.) Though technically these are considered Mint errors just as laminations are, there is no real premium because most collectors find them very unappealing. Only extreme examples have been known to carry a very modest price (about a few dollars), so you can say prices aren't *blistering* for this error type.

Plating blisters can vary in their shapes, sizes, and severity; some might only be on one side of a coin. Among the different appearances plating blisters can exhibit includes both **linear** and **circular blisters**. In the left column is a 1992 cent with linear blisters, while on the right is a 1982 cent with circular blisters. (It's also not uncommon for zinc cents to feature both kinds on the same coin.) Either way Mr. Lincoln is left with a *bubbly* personality.

1992 Lincoln Cent: Linear Plating Blisters

1982 Lincoln Cent: Circular Plating Blisters

Coin Trivia: Though the word/motto LIBERTY was required to appear on all U.S. coins under the Coinage Act of 1792, *there is no requirement for it to be printed on U.S. paper currency.*

Lathe Lines

1996-D Lincoln Cent

Abe is looking *groovy* here! Notice on the obverse close to the rim you see raised, circular lines similar to a vinyl record. *What causes them?* According to error researcher, columnist, and collector Mike Diamond, these concentric rings or **lathe lines** "are produced by a lathe which shapes the cone-shaped face of the unfinished working die. The cone is supposed to be polished smooth before hubbing." However, if polishing is omitted or inadequate, "the surface will remain covered by concentric lathe marks which will not be erased by subsequent hubbing" and will appear on struck coins *(Error-Ref.com)*. 1996-D cents are among the most common to find lathe lines. (Scarce; $10)

Coin Trivia: Did you know there is currently a genuine Lincoln cent on planet Mars? It is attached to the space rover Curiosity, *specifically to the Mars Hand Lens Imager (MAHLI). The coin's purpose is to provide an object of a known scale as small objects are photographed, like small rocks and soil.*
Curiosity *made its Mars landing on August 6, 2012 after an 8 and a half month journey.*

1994-P Washington Quarter: Obverse Rim Burr

This Washington quarter at first glance appears to have a stray piece of scrap metal struck into it. However, upon closer examination you can see it is actually a flap of metal from the coin itself; you can even see the exposed copper along the rim where it came from as well as copper on the flap. This error type is known as a **rim burr.** *How do these occur?* Basically a planchet's edge somehow becomes gouged by a machine part causing a portion of the metal to raise up; it is then rammed back into the planchet during a die strike. As to what machine part is likely the culprit for rim burrs, nationally-recognized error expert Mike Diamond believes based on similar coins he's studied with "identical-looking rim burrs in identical locations" that a "significant percentage" of these are generated "by the feeder finger immediately before the strike." *(Error-Ref.com)*

Rim burrs are sort of scarce but lack that "Wow!" appeal to them as other conspicuous errors do, so many don't usually sell for much. (And for those who collect rare coins/key dates, coins with rim burrs are considered "damaged" which often decreases their appeal and selling price). Then again this rim burr is considerably larger than most you will find, and the fact that part of it overlaps the date makes it more interesting. In my humble opinion, it is *burr*-fect! (Somewhat scarce; $20)

Close-up of the 1994 Quarter Rim Burr

Coin Trivia: In addition to the $1 bill and quarter dollar, George Washington is also featured on the Purple Heart – a military medal given to those wounded or killed during battle while serving in the U.S. armed forces.

Experimental Rinse

2001–P $1 Sacagawea:
Experimental Rinse with Anti–tarnishing Agent

Because a significant number of these developed unattractive spotting even before they reached the public (which greatly annoyed collectors), Mint officials experimented with an anti-tarnishing agent to try and make them more eye-pleasing. Though collectors and their reactions alone don't drive the Mint's policies, their input and the money they spend are not simply disregarded either. Collectibles like coins and stamps are enormous money makers for the government. *How?* Think of all the money spent on stamps by stamp collectors that won't ever be used for mailing, and all of the specially-minted coins purchased by coin collectors which are sold for much more than their metallic value yet never spent; it adds up pretty fast. And despite some coins being flops where the government lost money (e.g. Susan B. Anthony dollars), others brought in unprecedented profits like the incredibly popular 50 State Quarter series. Anyway, the result of this experimental rinse still left an ugly, dull, brown-ish color instead of a shiny golden look; it was abandoned soon after its initial run.

In terms of their utility, these "golden" dollars are simply an annoyance to most of the public. Other than being forced upon us when making change at rail station ticket kiosks in some cities, you hardly ever see them in circulation. Banks and businesses hate them. For collectors, aside from very high MS grades 67 and up, errors and trial test specimens like this one tend to have far greater premiums even in lower MS grades. Lastly, it should be noted that these can often be confused with toned or environmentally damaged $1 coins, so it is best to acquire certified examples. Approximately 2,500 of these were produced. (Scarce; $30; MS-66 by PCGS)

Below: The split-photo illustrates the difference in color and surface finish between a normal "Sac" (left) and the experimental rinse error (right).

Coin Trivia: To hype up the release of the new Sacagawea dollar, the U.S. Mint contracted with General Mills to place 5,500 of these new 2000-dated $1 coins in every 2000th box of Cheerios, which became known as "Cheerios Dollars." Some were found with a slightly different tail feather design, which have sold for thousands of dollars.

1971–D Lincoln Cent:
Struck on an Underweight Copper Planchet

Copper cents are supposed to weigh 3.11 grams, but this one is 2.2 grams, which is 1/3 less – a very significant weight reduction. *Why does it weigh less, and why does it look worn?* Though it resembles a split before strike, notice how smooth both sides are with neither illustrating evidence of splitting apart. The most likely explanation is that when this coin metal strip was being formed, it was squeezed a little too hard by the rolling presses. What resulted was either some or all of the metal sheet this coin came from wound up thinner than normal, referred to as a **rolled thin** planchet. Lacking 1/3 of its thickness also meant the dies were not calibrated to strike a planchet so much thinner, and as a result the dies did not fully reach the surface area of the planchet. What appears to be wear is merely the result of the thin planchet not filling in all the dies' devices. Grading these can seem to be somewhat subjective. (Scarce; $40; MS-64RD by ANACS)

Coin Trivia: In addition to the Sacagawea dollar promotion in 2000, all marked boxes of Cheerios had one of the first 10 million 2000-dated Lincoln cents that were minted inside each box. The packaging for these "Cheerios cents" is seen below.

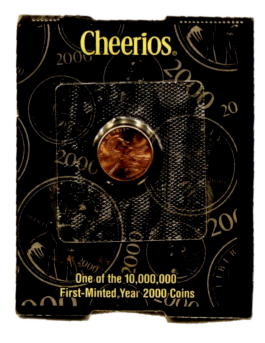 

Tapered Planchets

1955 Lincoln Cent:
Struck on a Tapered Planchet (2.2 Grams)

Looking similar in appearance to grease-filled dies and even weak strikes, the missing designs and details on this cent are due to being struck on a **tapered** planchet. This term is defined as a planchet that thins out at one end due to planchet metal being rolled improperly during the rolling process. As to its cause during the rolling process, error expert Mike Diamond asserts on *Error-Ref.com* that these errors "are derived from the leading or trailing end of the strip. The leading edge might be intentionally thinned for easier feeding into the rolling mill. Alternatively, the leading or trailing ends may be thinned due to decreased resistance to the pressure of the rollers; this would hinge on a failure of a mechanism that maintains the gap between the rollers."

Of course a thinner and uneven planchet means there will be a greater clearance/gap between the planchet and the dies upon impact for part of it, and is exactly why you see weaker and missing designs in the areas where the planchet is thinner; this includes the sharpness of the rims in those areas. Now you may have noticed that despite this cent and the 1971-D on the previous page are both equally underweight (2.2 grams), the degree of missing designs and their unevenness is very different. However, the 1971-D cent is not tapered (or is tapered but much less significantly) while this 1955 cent is tapered. Also, normally if you find a date that is tapered you will likely see several others with the same date. Lastly, don't always assume flat designs means tapering as illustrated on the Mercury dime below. (Somewhat scarce; $15)

This 1944 Mercury dime at first glance also appears to be struck on a tapered planchet (or possibly a rolled-thin planchet, or both). However generally tapered planchets have designs missing on both sides where the planchet is tapered; this dime only has designs missing on the reverse side. Therefore it's likely this was simply smoothed after it left the Mint (PMD).

There are many genuine error types which result in considerably weak designs on coins; some of them are on the last two pages. However the nickel on this page has a normal thickness and weight yet still has weak designs. *Why?* One reason could be that not enough ram pressure was applied as the dies struck the planchet, possibly due to a machine malfunction. A second reason could be that the die clearance was too great. What this means is that the dies – while fully engaged – were simply set too far away from the planchet to deliver a full impact. In either case, what results are coins with exceptionally **weak strikes**, and in some cases there is barely any design visible at all. For coins that have reeded edges (e.g. dimes, quarters, etc.), the reeding pattern should be considerably weak or missing entirely since it is the ram pressure that forces the planchet into the reeding pattern inside the collar. Weak strikes are referred to by some as "die trials" or "die adjustment" strikes, but since there is no way of proving those were the exact causes, those terms should be avoided.

Coin Trivia: Below are the original Jefferson nickel design submissions from Felix Schlag. His obverse and reverse concepts became the new nickel in 1938 featuring Thomas Jefferson and his Monticello estate. For the final revision, the angle of Monticello and fonts for the lettering and numbering were modified. (Photos courtesy of FelixSchlag.com)

Weak Strikes

1965 Jefferson Nickel: Weak Strike

At first it looks like something flattened it, but upon closer examination you can tell it is the result of a weak strike. This error type is scarcer for nickels than it is for cents, dimes, and quarters. (Scarce; $30; Ungraded by NGC)

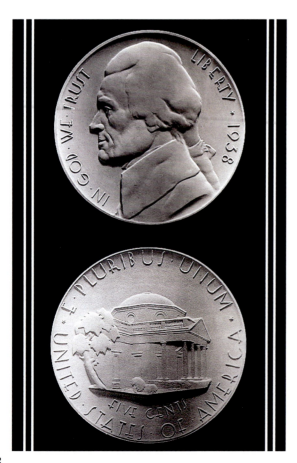

(19XX) Roosevelt Clad Dime: Weak Strike

Unlike the 1965 nickel, this dime has approximately 60% of its design missing from the result of a weak strike. A close look at the edge confirms it as there is virtually no reeding on its edges. However, it is not hard to file off the reeding or to squeeze a coin to the point of flattening its designs. *So, how can you tell a weak strike is genuine and wasn't altered by someone or something?*

Great question, easy answers: (1) Filing off the reeded edges will lessen the weight and diameter of the coin; and (2) flattening the coin by squeezing it or pressing it forcefully would expand the diameter, flatten the rims (which is a red flag), and could also cause designs to expand beyond normal size. (Scarce; $70)

1999 Connecticut State Quarter: Weak Strike

Roughly 85% of the design including a date is absent, yet on the reverse you can just make out the pattern of the Charter Oak tree. Since we know the Connecticut statehood coin was minted in 1999, we can therefore identify a date.

Like the dime on the left, many of the dings and scrapes you see on the planchet would normally disappear upon a forceful die strike, but due to a weak strike they remain; it also lacks its reeded edge for the same reason. Some people even collect the State Quarter series through error types including weak strikes like this one. (Scarce; $110)

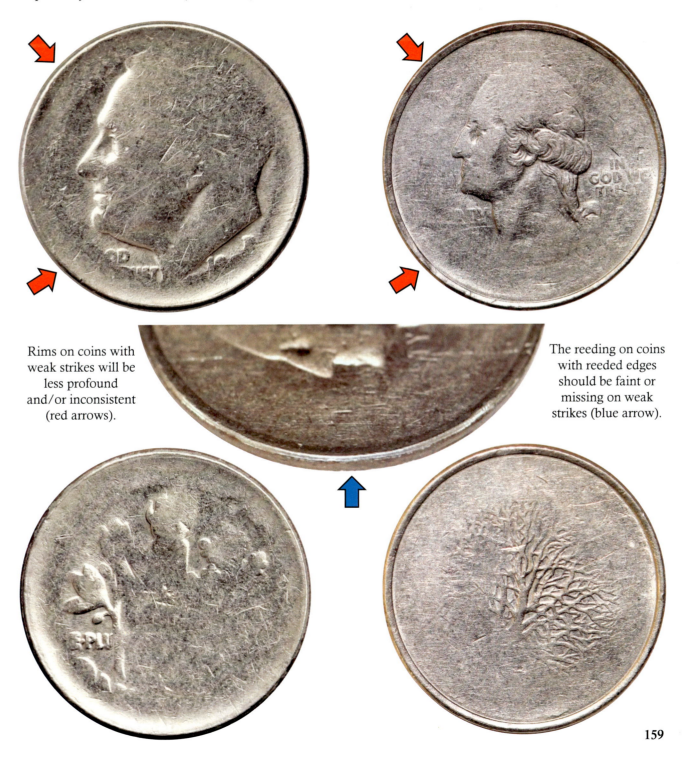

Rims on coins with weak strikes will be less profound and/or inconsistent (red arrows).

The reeding on coins with reeded edges should be faint or missing on weak strikes (blue arrow).

Lincoln Cents: How to Tell a Weak Strike from a "Greaser"

196X Copper Lincoln Cent: Weak Strike or "Greaser?"

American 1 cent coins don't have edge reeding (though some early large and half cents have edge lettering). Since cents don't have edge reeding, it can be difficult to distinguish a weak strike from a grease strike-through error if both sides have roughly the same degree of missing designs. For example, above is a 196X copper cent and below is an undated copper-plated zinc cent which both have similar degrees of missing designs on each side. Can you tell which is the weak strike and which is the greaser based on these photos?

Answer: The weak strike is above and the "greaser" is below. *How can you tell?* Since a weak strike involves much weaker striking pressure, the rim should not be very pronounced. Observe above how the rim formation looks weak and even incomplete on the 196X copper cent, yet the copper-plated zinc cent below has a rim that is well-defined. (196X is very scarce; $70. The zinc cent missing this much detail is also very scarce; $60.)

Undated Copper-plated Zinc Lincoln Cent: Weak Strike or "Greaser?"

Severe Circulation Wear vs. Weak Strikes

You might think that both of these coins are the result of a weak strike. Though not the most popular errors due to having scant details, some collectors will pay big bucks for genuine weak strikes, especially on silver coins. In fact this dateless Peace dollar (left) would likely sell for over $1,000. Unfortunately the worn designs on the Peace dollar below are due to severe circulation wear, but the clad Roosevelt dime (right) is a weak strike. *How can you tell the difference when their worn look is so similar?*

The answer lies on a coin's rim. Planchets have a raised rim due to being squeezed in an upsetting mill forcing the metal along the perimeter to shift upward on both sides. A coin resulting from a weak strike will still have that solid rim on it even if designs are faint (unless the coin was struck on a blank with no rims, which can happen occasionally). Notice the dime has raised rim formations – a good sign it is a weak strike (and don't forget to check the edges and weight to confirm it).

In contrast, a coin which was passed around for multiple decades will show evidence of **circulation wear.** Areas with the highest relief on a coin normally wear down first. As the coin continues to pass through thousands and thousands of hands, new areas become the high points which wear down along with the rims and so on. Because the coin is actually being flattened by repeated contact, it is normal for severely-worn coins to feel considerably thinner and become wider in diameter yet the weight might be unaffected. (It's more common on older silver and copper coins which were made of softer metals than on modern coinage.) The Peace dollar below lacks any semblance of a raised rim on either side and is a victim of hyper circulation wear. This one is so worn that you can just barely make out the top of the eagle on the reverse. Believe it or not, some people actually collect severely worn coins for different series and denominations and compete with others' collections of them.

(No Date) Peace Dollar: Severe Circulation Wear

Flattened Rims

(No Date) Clad Roosevelt Dime: Weak Strike

Rims Present

Lamination Errors

Any time contents for a product have to be mixed together, there is always a chance that problems can arise with the overall quality of a finished product; that also includes coin production. Whether it's too much of an ingredient, not enough of another, the ingredients weren't thoroughly mixed, some foreign matter/impurity contaminated the mix, or an ingredient wasn't added, the finished product unfortunately can become conspicuously corrupted and even downright damaged.

With coins, improper mixes and contaminants can prevent proper bonding of the metals which can cause flaking or result in entire sections coming detached from the planchet. Should these occur, these are known as **lamination errors** (though technically it's really a "delamination" error). Lamination errors are typically found on alloy coins like copper cents, nickels, and 90% silver coinage. Also, it's not uncommon to find laminations on only one side of a coin. Since 1983, the only alloy coin minted for circulation is the nickel, but major laminations on modern nickels are pretty scarce. And don't forget, lamination errors on alloy coins are *not* the same as clad layer separations on clad coins.

1944-P Jefferson
"War" Nickel: Obverse Lamination

One series where it isn't difficult to find laminations great and small is the Jefferson nickel series, specifically on 35% silver Jefferson "War" nickels from 1942-1945. As nickel was needed for war time use during World War Two, the nickel's composition changed. Nickel was removed and substituted with manganese and silver. The Mint during this period was much more focused on keeping up production and less on the actual quality of the coins being minted, and thus lamination errors on war nickels are plentiful even on MS examples like this 1944-P. This coin is also a good example illustrating how laminations can be limited to just one side; notice the reverse of the nickel on the right shows no evidence of any laminations or cracking anywhere. (Somewhat common on war nickels; $25 for MS grades.)

Close-up of some of the obverse laminations on the 1944-P nickel, some of which have folded over after it was struck by the dies.

1959–D Lincoln Cent:
Obverse Lamination with Detached Fragment

What is neat here is that the detached area is small yet contains the entire date and mintmark. It's also thin enough where you still see the date showing on both sides of the fragment and on the planchet itself. (Very scarce with a fragment this small with a full date; $150)

1962–D Roosevelt Dime:
Obverse Lamination with Detached Fragment

Similar to the 1959-D cent, what is especially cool is that almost the entire motto of IN GOD WE TRUST has separated on this toned 90% silver dime. It's not often you have the entire detached piece with the coin. (Very scarce; $150)

Coin Trivia: Upon the Roosevelt dime's release in 1946, a few conspiracy theorists speculated that the initials "JS" were placed on the dime by communist infiltrators at the Mint to represent those of Soviet leader, Josef Stalin. They're actually the initial's of the dime's designer, John Sinnock.

1921 Peace $1: Cracked Planchet

As with laminations, improper mixtures and impurities in alloy coining metals can also lead to **cracked planchets**, however it can be difficult to determine if a crack occurred before or after strike. Though many cracks are small, the one on this 1921 Peace dollar is considerably large. (Very scarce this large on dollar coins; $300; MS-64 by PCGS. The coin was photographed by me but is part of a friend's collection who wishes at this time to remain anonymous.)

Obverse Close-up

Reverse Close-up

Planchet Crack Vs. Die Crack

A coin with a planchet crack reflects a *planchet* that is defective due to cracking either before or after striking, whereas a coin with a die crack reflects a planchet struck from a defective/cracked *die*. That being said, it is possible for a coin to have both a planchet crack and a die crack.

164

Broken Planchets

1963 Lincoln Cent: Broken Planchet

As seen on the previous page, planchet cracks can be pretty significant. In fact they can be so substantial that they might span from rim to rim. Should the entire cracked region fully detatch from a planchet as it did on this 1963 cent, it is referred to as a **broken planchet**. Beware of both counterfeits and altered coins that can appear as genuine broken planchet errors. (Very scarce; $125.)

Broken Planchet Imposters

There are several great websites where you can find genuine errors for sale. Among my favorites are Fred Weinberg's site (*FredWeinberg.com*) and Jon Sullivan's site (*SullivanNumismatics.com*), as well as Heritage Auctions (*HA.com*), Stacks and Bowers (*StacksBowers.com*) and Great Collections (*GreatCollections.com*). Though you can also find some great errors on other popular online sites, at times I feel the number of altered, counterfeit, and damaged coins they have listed for sale can outnumber those which are genuine, undamaged errors. One particular example includes the 1967 quarter to your right which was listed as a "Broken Planchet Error." However, genuine broken planchet errors should not have any bending or evidence of tool marks. Unlike the 1963 cent above, the two pieces of this 1967 quarter don't have a flush fit anymore; the most likely cause was being cut by a pair of metal shears.

Split Planchet Errors

Just as improper mixes/bonding can cause flaking or detachment of entire fragments from *part* of the planchet, it can also cause the *entire* planchet to split apart (top row). Obviously split planchets become much lighter with some being half their normal weight or less. Splitting in two (or more) pieces can occur either before or after striking, and often these are mistakenly overlooked as post-Mint damaged coins. Many can appear "broken" or "scratched" (and thus deemed "worthless") to the uninformed collector, but some can be pretty valuable depending on their date and overall condition.

Split *Before* Strike

Is there a way to tell if the coin split before or after striking? Actually, yes, there is. Should the planchet split apart and then become struck with coin dies, these become known as **split before strike (SBS)** errors. On both sides there will be evidence of direct die strikes but will generally look weak and/or have some designs missing. The side which has a more rough looking texture is the side where the split came apart. Notice the 1960 Lincoln cent (center row) has the rough texture on the reverse, whereas the 1954 Jefferson nickel (bottom row) has the rough surface on the obverse.

1 Cent 95% Copper Unstruck Split Planchet
On the right, striations from separation are clearly visible and illustrate why the pattern on struck split planchets look as they do.
1.7 grams (Scarce; $30)

1960 Lincoln Cent: Split Before Strike
Observe how you can see the upside-down, incused (i.e. sunken in) bust of Abraham Lincoln on the reverse due to its thin nature. 1.7 grams. (Scarce; $35)

1958-D Jefferson Nickel: Split Before Strike
At 2.5 grams, this nickel is exactly half the weight it should be. (Scarce; $100)

Split *After* Strike (Vs. Split *Before* Strike)

In contrast to a split before strike, a **split after strike (SAS)** comes apart after the coin was struck and usually occurs for the exact same reasons – bad mixtures, impurities in the metals, etc. – that prohibits bonding of the metals within the coin. It's easier identifying SAS errors because generally they have one side with strong details (top left) while the other simply has a textured appearance (top right); of course, this also depends on the level of circulation wear or damage a coin has.

At times a phantom, reversed image from one or even both sides can appear on the textured side. Can you spot the phantom, reversed image of Lincoln on the textured side on the top right? On the other hand, split before strikes have some degree of designs on both sides (bottom left/right), though they usually aren't nearly as sharp as what is normally seen on the non-textured side of a split after strike. Can you see the differences between both error types on the two coins below?

1936 Lincoln Cent: Split After Strike
(Scarce; $40)

On split-after-strike coins only one side has designs while the other has textured striations just like you see on the 1936 cent above.

1961 Lincoln Cent: Split Before Strike

Split-before-strike coins have areas of weakness on rims and designs on both sides with one side having some textured striations.

1899 Liberty Head Nickel: Split After Strike

Lady Liberty had a complete split here sometime after her experience in the striking chamber. Despite a little circulation wear, she is a very nice example free from any problems like unattractive toning or scratches. *How do we know this is a nickel? Because the "V" on the reverse is the Roman numeral for "5."*

Notice the term **mated pair** on the label; this signifies both halves came from the exact same coin, but it can also mean any two (or more) separate coins struck together in the chamber as well. In either case, mated pairs are rare and more desirable, and buying them as a certified set is highly recommended as some dealers – knowingly or unknowingly – try to sell pairs as mated pairs when they clearly are not from the exact same coin. (Scarce; $400 for the pair; VF-35 for both coins by PCGS)

1899	Mint Error	5C
PCGS VF35		
100% Split Planchet Obv		
Mated Pair-Coin 1		
E11111.35/28646255		

1899	Mint Error	5C
PCGS VF35		
100% Split Planchet Rev		
Mated Pair-Coin 2		
E11111.35/28646256		

Coin #1

Coin #2

Clipped Planchets

Planchet Strip with Punched Holes (i.e. Webbing Strip)

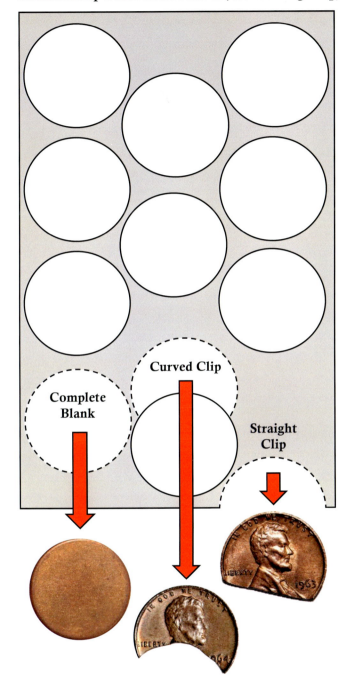

Once the Mint is in possession of the long sheets of metal called planchet strips, the next step is to feed them into the blanking dies to produce blanks. If the metal is not fed in far enough after the process begins, the punches could overlap a previously-punched hole on the strip. The resulting curved planchets become known as **curved clips** which sometimes even wind up being struck by the dies. In contrast, **straight clips** (below) are planchets likely punched over the edge of a planchet strip, though they are not always perfectly straight. Then there are **ragged clips** which have – you guessed it – ragged-looking edges which likely arise from the ends of strips that were not properly trimmed or possibly from the blanking dies striking areas containing cracks within the strip. Other clips include elliptical, bowtie, corner, assay (triangular-shaped), and incomplete clips to name a few. In fact, some coins can have multiple and/or different clips. Occasionally there is more of the planchet missing than what's left remaining of the coin itself.

Like all errors, these are sometimes faked. One method includes using metal shears to cut them. Look for raised metal along the end of the clip, bending, and even scrapes from the shears to indicate tampering as these should generally lay flat. You should also see the correct metal flow towards the clip.

Straight Clips

1963 Lincoln Cent: 25% Straight Clip

Abe is sporting a roughly 25% loss in what may have been punched out at the end of the planchet strip. (Scarce; $35)

Coin Trivia: 1909 is not just the first year Lincoln appeared on our 1 cent coin; it's also the first time the motto IN GOD WE TRUST appeared on a 1 cent coin.

169

1967 Washington Quarter: 26% Straight Clip

There have been several professional grading services that have come and gone through the years. Some of these currently defunct companies have included Accugrade (ACG), Star Grading Service (SGS), and Photo-certified Coin Institute (PCI). While you can always find people who aren't happy with any grading service, for whatever reason these companies just couldn't stand the test of time. I have heard both good and bad things from people who currently own or used to own coins housed in their holders. For example, some who own coins in PCI holders said they were correct in how the coin was graded, while others have said they always overgraded coins. Regardless, in my opinion so long as you treat every coin as if it were raw – including those in slabs – and you learned how to examine them properly, it shouldn't matter what a label says.

The issue with this 1967 quarter is a little different. It was submitted to PCI in 2002 by a friend of mine, John Amirault, who believed it had a genuine straight clip error and was hoping to get it certified and slabbed. However, PCI's Mint error experts denied encapsulation and determined the coin had been "cut in two" after it was minted (see their rejection notice below) and thus was considered damaged. Now I know no one is perfect and that even experts can make mistakes once in a while, but in my opinion this one is an easy call. I can't imagine a highly-trained Mint error specialist would get this one wrong. John posted this coin on my Facebook page, "Joe Cronin's Mint Errors Explained," and I offered to examine it for him. I found that though not all clips have the Blakesley effect, this one does for sure. Also, not only is there no evidence of tool marks anywhere on the coin but the pattern on the clipped edge is consistent with this error type; it's a genuine straight clip error, and a nice one at that. Fortunately John didn't get rid of the coin or the rejection notice which now sit proudly in his error collection. (Scarce; $90)

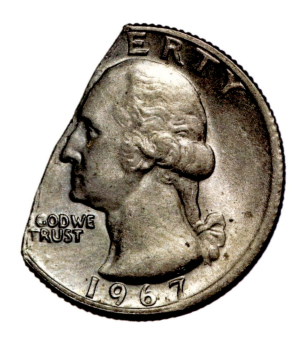

This quarter has 26% of its weight missing, thus it is a 26% straight clip.

Edge View of the Straight Clip

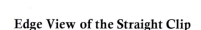

PCI Confidential Grader's Report

Customer Name *Amirault* Date **7-26-02**

While we strive to encapsulate each coin that we receive, there are instances where we are not able to do so. Also, some coins are encapsulated without the notation requested or with a different notation on the label. Below is a listing of the coins that were sent in that were either not holder or received a different notation on the label and the reasons fro the change.

Coin Description	Explanation of Changes or Non Encapsulation	PCI Grade	Other Comments
1.			
2. 1967-1 Qtr –	This Coin HAS BEEN Cut inTwo – NoT A Mint eRRoR!		
3.			

Curved Clips

1989-P Jefferson Nickel: 35% Curved Clip

This is an uncommonly large curved clip for any denomination, but it is certainly nowhere near the largest. Clips are much more desirable if a full date is visible like this nickel below. (Scarce; $50)

(No Date) Clad Washington Quarter: 47% Curved Clip and Broadstruck on a Type 1 Blank

What a beautiful triple error loaded with a gleaming luster. It's also a good example illustrating not all curved clips exhibit a perfect spherical shape. I must confess that this is the only 13.25 cent piece in my entire collection. (Scarce; $100; MS-64 by PCGS)

Coin Trivia: Thomas Jefferson is also featured on America's first gold commemorative; it's a $1 gold piece commemorating the Louisiana Purchase in 1803. (Photo courtesy of Heritage Auctions/HA.com)

1946 Lincoln Cent:
14% Elliptical Clip (2.7 grams)

No, this is not an error coin produced on those exercise machines simulating cross-country skiing. An **elliptical clip** occurs when a previously punched-out blank fails to detach completely from its hole in the planchet strip; this leaves what some error collectors refer to as a "hanging blank" (presumably a reference from the infamous "hanging chads" on Palm Beach, Florida ballots that had to be recounted during the 2000 presidential election). However, if the planchet strip did not advance far enough the blanking dies would cut through that "hanging blank" albeit misaligned. What results is an oval-shaped blank known as an elliptical clip; its mate is referred to as a crescent clip (see the purple-shaded areas below).

Like all error coins, elliptical clips with full dates are more in demand than those with partially or completely missing dates, but those which are struck on football-shaped planchets are perhaps the most desired and expensive. This 1946 cent on the top row weighs in at 2.7 grams which is about 14% less than it should weigh at 3.11 grams. The photos below should provide you with a better understanding of just how much of the planchet is missing.

Be sure to check the edges for signs of cutting or other tool marks as well as bending on the coin to ensure it hasn't been altered. Also, though this coin does exhibit what is known as the **Blakesley Effect** where the rim opposite of a clip will appear flat and weakly-formed, not all clips will exhibit these characteristics. (Scarce; $90)

(No Date) Lincoln Cent: Struck on a
Clad Dime 65% Elliptical Clip (0.8 Grams)

Hut…Hut…Hike! And by "Hike!" I mean hike up the price of course for this totally astounding double error. Symmetrical football-shaped errors are super rare, but are nearly impossible to find on wrong planchets/off-metals. Whoever the seller was

that decided to *hand-off* this coin to Heritage Auctions for their September 2013 auction was likely pleased with the people who *rushed* in to bid; the final bid went for $2,115. That price is "Good!" (Yes, my hands are straight up in the air.) Graded MS-66 by PCGS. *(Photos courtesy of Heritage Auctions/HA.com)*

This coin weighs 65% less than a normal clad dime, thus it's a 65% clip.

Close-up of the Obverse Perimeter

1960 Lincoln Cent: 35% Ragged Clip

Normally when you hear or see the term "ragged," one usually associates it to mean an object that has become "very worn out" like an old, faded, twenty-year-old T-shirt your husband refuses to part with (for which there is always a very good reason!). Clearly this coin is not worn at all and in fact is consistent with being uncirculated due to its crisp and sharp details in conjunction with a powerful Mint luster. In numismatics "ragged" does not mean "worn" but instead refers to a planchet missing metal that possesses a jagged, frayed, or torn appearance. Unlike strait or curved clips which normally appear more uniform and clean cut, many ragged clips appear as if a snaggletoothed person or creature took a bite out of it just as this one does.

What causes a ragged clip? Some experts believe these are from the end of coin metal strips that were improperly trimmed or not trimmed at all; they were then punched out as incomplete planchets with ragged edges. Other possible factors could include the presence of cracks, fissures, or pockets of improper mixtures or impurities within the metal strip. It could even be a combination of these and/or other factors.

How do you know it is a 35% clip? How can you be so precise? Because you can tell by its weight. This coin weighs in at 2.03 grams, and a standard 95% copper small cent planchet weighs 3.11 grams. Simple math calculates it's only 65% of what it should weigh (2.03 divided by 3.11 is 65%), so therefore it is a 35% ragged clip.

All clip types are popular errors, especially those with full dates. But inspect these very carefully because you'll come across several which have been altered to appear as genuine clips. Ragged clips can also be counterfeited as we shall see with some 90% silver blanks later on in the book. (Scarce; $250)

Edge View

Incomplete Clips/Punches

The purpose of a blanking die is to punch out coin blanks from the planchet strips, and it's those punched-out round discs that will eventually be struck as coins. But for some reason the blanking dies don't always don't go through the planchet strip far enough for the blanks to separate. (It's similar to cutting through your chocolate chip cookie dough with a cut-out mold, but you didn't go down far enough through the dough.) Though not going deep enough into the planchet strip, often the blanking dies still leave evidence of a curved, "incomplete" impression of the actual blanking die. As the strip continues to feed into the blanking press and advance, the next successive die strike just might make it through. You would then wind up with a blank which has an off-center, curved, and incomplete punch on it. These can subsequently be struck by coin dies which may not completely eradicate the impression left by the markings of the incomplete clip. Coins displaying such markings, including the featured 1972 Ike dollar on the right (which also has dual curved slips), are referred to as **incomplete clips (a.k.a. incomplete punches)**.

Errors such as these are pretty rare yet are affordable on modern, lower denominations. Even as of this writing there are a few certified cents and nickels which can be purchased for under $300. Of course on half dollars, dollar coins, discontinued series, and discontinued denominations, prices can go into the thousands. For example, this 1972 Ike graded MS-63 by PCGS sold for $1,495 at Heritage Auctions in 2010. One key diagnostic to look for on this error type is that the punch is visible on both sides as well as on the edges. Don't confuse incomplete punch errors with the circular scarring pattern found on coins damaged by coin crimping machines as seen below.

<u>Below</u>: Damage caused by crimpers which seal the ends of coin rolls can often leave circular marks similar to incomplete punch errors.

1972   Mint Error $1
PCGS MS63
Incomplete Punch Plan
+ 3% Double Clip Plan
E87409.63/13048579

Eisenhower photos courtesy of Heritage Auctions / HA.com

Ragged Fissures

1959 & 1961 Lincoln Cents: Ragged Fissures

Similar in appearance to ragged clips like the 1960 cent on the previous page, the two Lincoln cents featured here are examples of **ragged fissures.** *What is a fissure?* In relation to numismatics, fissures are long openings or cracks in coin metal caused when pressure/tension is applied to planchet metal. If a particular area of the planchet metal is brittle and/or contains impurities, the stress and pressure from the rollers pressing the metal to its desired thickness can cause those brittle areas to crack, split, and tear creating fissures. What happens next according to *Error-Ref.com* is that when the "blanking die slices through one end of a fissure, the resulting blank will contain that fissure." Both of these cents are great examples of what ragged fissures look like when struck by dies. (Scarce; $65 each)

Coin Trivia: According to superstition, it is considered good luck to pick up a cent or other coin from the ground if it is facing heads up, and bad luck if it is tails up. However, it is believed karma will reward you if you turn over a coin facing tails up so the next person who finds it can pick it up heads up.

Ragged Perforations (i.e. "Blow Holes)

1959 Lincoln Cent: Ragged Perforation (Blow Hole)

Hole-y cow! Did someone drive a flat head screwdriver through this cent? No, but people do some bizarre things to coins. What we have here is a **ragged perforation** or "**blow hole**" error. Despite what some might imply by the name, a blow hole is not caused by a forceful burst of air which blew out weak areas of the planchet metal. The cause of this error type is the same as those ragged fissures on the previous page: Immense pressure was applied by the rollers pressing the planchet metal to its desired thickness can cause brittle areas to crack, split, and tear. In this case, it literally left a hole and was then struck by the dies. According to the website *Error-ref.com,* these holes/openings that can appear "are usually characterized by an edge that is beveled on both faces," which you definitely see here. Ragged perforations are incredibly rare for all denominations yet are still relatively affordable. (Very rare; $175)

Coin Trivia: If you ever find a symmetrically-rounded hole in a copper cent, it's possible it was once used as a washer for a screw. Copper is a softer metal and copper cents were at times cheaper to use than buying actual washers. This 1959-D Lincoln cent with a rusted screw through it was found metal detecting. (Thank you, Mr. Dwayne Kelly, for this cool piece.)

Strike Clips

(No Date) Zinc Lincoln Cent: Two 95% Off-center Strikes (Saddle-struck) with One Strike Clip

Normally when you hear or see the word "clip" it refers to an error resulting from a misfed planchet strip into the blanking press. As the blanking dies slice through and overlap previously punched-out holes, cut through the ends of the strip, or cut through cracks or fissures, what results are incomplete blanks featuring curved, straight, or other clips.

As for the coin on right, the cause of the small, arched strike clip is quite different from the curved clip on the bottom left. *How are they different?* Whereas curved and other clips are formed as blanks are punched out of the planchet strips, **strike clips** like this one are created as a result of the die-striking action. Basically, the rounded outer perimeter of the die rammed this off-center planchet and literally sheared off a portion of the planchet's rim; the other strike featuring minimal designs managed to remain attached, though it is noticeably thinner than the rest of the planchet. Because zinc is a much softer metal than copper, nickel, and clad coinage, you will most likely see strike clips on zinc cents rather than on copper cents or other denominations.

How can you tell if a rounded clip on a zinc cent is a strike clip or a curved clip? Perhaps the best indicator is to look at the edge of the clip. Notice on this coin you can see the edges are gray on the missing area (red arrows). *O.K. What does that tell you?* Since the gray is showing, that's a good indication it is a strike clip and not a curved clip. *Why is that?* Because zinc cent planchets are copper-plated after blanks are punched out and before die striking. If the clip was caused during the blanking process, the edge of the clip should also be copper-plated (bottom left, green arrow). Since the gray-colored zinc is showing, we can deduce it came off during the die-striking action, thus it is likely a strike clip and not a curved clip. This coin is also considered a saddle strike error because it received "two simultaneous off-center strikes from two adjacent die pairings," (*Error-Ref.com*) even though one of the two strikes became detatched. (Very scarce but not highly sought after; $25)

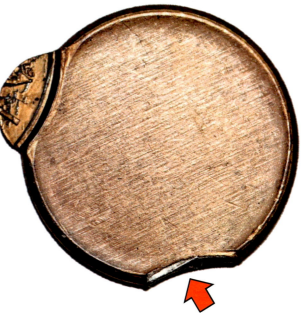

Below: Strike clips are caused by the die-striking action, unlike other clips caused during the blanking stage. Since zinc cents are plated with copper before striking, the edges on strike clips should be gray in color due to the zinc core being exposed. Clips which occurred before plating should have copper-plated edges like the 1985-D cent on the bottom left.

Above: Unlike strike clips, this curved clip error occurred during the blanking phase, not the die-striking phase.

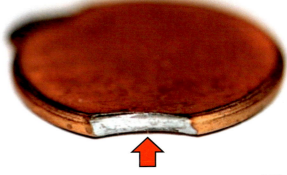

Elliptical Strike Clips

1983 Lincoln Cent: Elliptical Strike Clip
Struck Off-center with a Uniface Reverse

On the previous page (and again on the bottom right), the strike clip shows a curved portion of the planchet missing (red arrow). Again, this error was not preexisting before it entered the striking chamber; it was caused by the die-striking action in the striking chamber. Notice the other off-center strike, referred by some error experts as a "tongue," remains attached (green arrow); this phenomenon is not uncommon. Anyway, presumably like many of you I often wonder where the detached portions from these strike clips wind up and what they look like. If you look at the left column, you should have a good understanding of how a surviving detached tongue can appear. (It is not from the strike clip below, but if so it would make it an incredible find as a mated pair.)

This 1983 cent is technically a detached tongue from an off-center uniface elliptical strike clip (i.e. another planchet blocked the reverse of this coin from receiving a direct strike from the reverse die, thus no designs are showing); it then separated from the planchet due to the force of the die strike. What makes this particularly neat is that the only thing visible is something most error collectors want on a coin more than anything else: A full and complete date and mintmark area to identify it's origin. Perhaps it was found in a Mint bag of 1983 cents and its mate could have been in there with it. Who knows?

It is important to note that many collectors and even some grading companies refer to the detached portions of strike clips as "struck fragments," but technically this coin and others like it are not. *Well, if it is only a small portion of the coin, and it was die struck, why shouldn't it be attributed as a "struck fragment?"* Because in numismatics, the term "fragment" implies that it was a small piece of coin metal *before* it entered the striking chamber. If it was a normal planchet right *before* striking and then fragmented *as a result of* the die-striking action, it is not really a "struck fragment," which are worth considerably more money. It also somewhat resembles an elliptical clip caused by a misfed planchet strip during the blanking stage. However, notice there is evidence of a raised rim on the obverse, and a chunk of metal this size and shape likely wouldn't be big enough to be compressed in the upsetting mill to receive a raised rim on any part of it. (Rare; $90)

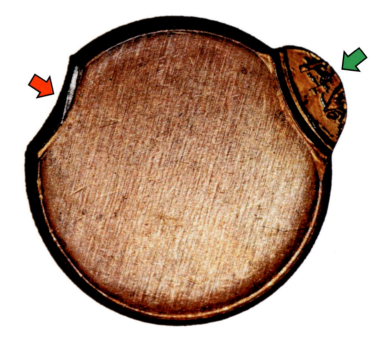

Slag Inclusions

1944-D Lincoln Cent & 1945-P
Jefferson War Nickel: Slag (Iron) Inclusions

Ores are naturally-occurring solid material deposits which can be mined and from which metals and other minerals can be extracted. Ores used to produce coining metals (e.g. silver, copper, nickel, etc.) are melted down to a liquid state in a process known as **smelting,** which is done mainly to both make it easier to pour into forms/molds and to remove impurities and contaminants known as **slag.** *What does slag consist of?* It can include anything from metal oxides to silicone dioxide or even metal sulfides and elemental metals like

iron. Normally slag floats to the top of the molten mixture and is skimmed off, mainly because it can corrupt the integrity of metals leading to improper bonding, laminations, or visible inclusions like these two coins below. On both the reverse of the wheat cent and the obverse of the silver war nickel, the slag inclusions are iron deposits (which can be magnetic if enough is present). It is difficult to find significant slag inclusions while coin roll hunting, but despite being rare they're normally not expensive; I bought these for $5 each. However, those on silver halves and dollars can be over $40.

Notice how the slag impurities caused laminations to form on the planchet.

179

Die Clashes

Without a planchet in the striking chamber, the dies can actually wind up striking each other depending on the degree of spacing between the dies as they engage, known as **die clearance**. If they do make direct contact, what can result is the partial transfer of designs from an obverse die to the reverse die and vice versa. The extent as to how much design is transferred – if at all – can vary greatly even within the same denomination, series, and sets of die pairings.

The result of a planchet struck with **clashed dies** or **die clashes** is a coin showing both a normal design as well as reversed markings from the opposite die all on the same side. Some die clashes can be very strong or faint, and often they are more prominent on one side than the other. They can also appear on only a small area of one or both sides. Normally coins with more prominent clashes are more valuable than others with weaker clashes. Some coins even feature multiple clashes on both sides, and there's even something called a counterclash (more on that a little later). Those featuring fully clashed dates are super rare and can significantly jump in price for what is traditionally a very inexpensive error type that most collectors can afford. Of course, as with most errors those struck on higher denominations (quarters and up) can normally fetch higher premiums when they become available.

When significant clashes are discovered at the Mint, at times press operators have attempted to remove clash marks by polishing off or **abrading** affected areas on a clashed die. However, in doing so workers run the risk of accidentally removing some of the designs and also leaving the telltale signs of very fine linear scratches which can often be seen on struck coins.

Below is an unusually strong die clash on a Jefferson nickel. Both Jefferson's reversed profile and a reversed Monticello can be made out on their opposite sides. Die clashes on this series aren't super rare, but they are seldom seen this significant on both sides. (Very scarce; $50)

 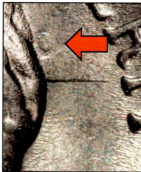

<u>Above</u>: Both the "M" and the last "O" in MONTICELLO are visible on the obverse despite being reverse markings

Jefferson Nickel Die Clash Overlay

1952-D Lincoln Wheat Cent: Clashed Dies

Gleaming with Mint luster and sharp details, the reverse side of this cent in particular has the strongest clash marks I have ever seen to date on a "Wheatie." In fact it is so defined you can almost make out Lincoln's entire profile including his brow, nose and lips.

The obverse side has considerably weaker clashing. If you look behind Lincoln's head, you can just make out part of the "C" in CENT (blue arrow), and from the bottom of his Adam's apple to the top of his bowtie you can see part of the "N" in CENT (green arrow). A true gem! (Very scarce with strong profile clashes; $80)

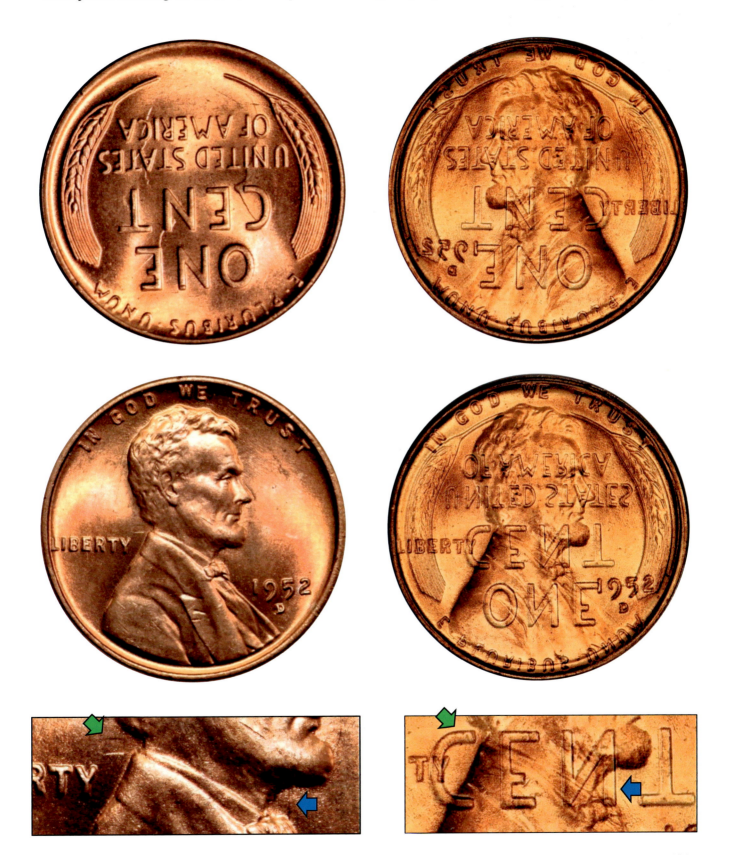

1967 Lincoln Memorial
"Prisoner" Cent: Die Clashes (Severe)

In general, die clashes on both Lincoln Memorial cents and Lincoln Shield cents exhibit stronger clashing on the obverse side than the reverse side. (Many Memorial cent die clashes also tend to have a slight counterclockwise rotation as well.) Some collectors refer to Memorial cent die clashes as "jailed Lincoln" or "Prisoner" cents due to the clashed Memorial columns appearing as jail bars on either side of Lincoln's face. (Interestingly, strong clashes on Shield cents yield a similar jail bar pattern to clashed Memorial cents as you'll see on the next page.)

A cent clashed die is one of the few modestly scarce error coins that some people have managed to find while coin roll hunting, but normally those are people who have usually searched thousands and thousands of coins to find just one. However someone did manage to discover this one, which has incredible clashing so severe you can make out part of the "O" and "N" in the word ONE behind Lincoln's head, the "RTY" of LIBERTY along the Memorial columns, and even a good portion of the date along the top corner of the Memorial. (Visible dates on coins with clashes are very rare; $125)

"ON" of ONE

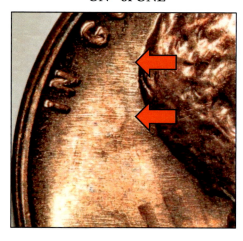

"RTY" of LIBERTY

"196" of 1967

2017-P Lincoln Shield Cent: Clashed Dies

When the Mint stopped shipping out coins in those small cloth bags (and switched to ballistic bags) in 2002, the chances of finding significant errors dropped exponentially. Remember that even though we love errors, Mint officials are tasked with the responsibility of making coins as perfect and uniform as possible. Today's technology not only helps prevent some error types from ever occurring again, but also makes it easier to screen and intercept those which are still possible. Among those errors which can still happen and sneak out in rolls are noteworthy clashed die coins including this 2017-P Lincoln Shield cent. I have seen several die clashes on Shield cents, but not many are this prominent. Like the Lincoln Memorial cents, clashing is much more noticeable on the obverse than the reverse. Interestingly, despite the reverse design change starting in 2010, both the Memorial and Shield cents yield clashing patterns which resemble jail bars in front of and behind Lincoln's face. He may have *freed a lot of people*, but he's still a "prisoner" on the Shield cent. Several dates with clashes exist on Shield cents. (Scarce; $20)

Both Lincoln Memorial cents and Lincoln Shield cents exhibit "jail bars" as a result of coins struck with clashed dies. It's almost like it was intentional to have the same effect from two different reverse designs.

Shield Cent Close-up

Memorial Cent Close-up

Clashes found under the Chief's chin.

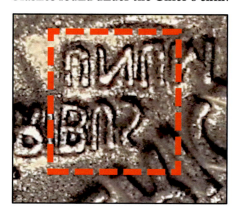

1913 Buffalo Nickel (Type 2): Clashed Dies

Clashes on Buffalo nickels aren't uncommon, and they vary in terms of how severe they are and where they show up. (This one appears to have at least two sets of clashes.) Common areas of clashing are under the Chief's chin (clash of E PLURIBUS UNUM; red arrows), behind the Chief's head (clash of the Buffalo's hump; blue arrow), and above the Buffalo's lower back and under E PLURIBUS UNUM (clash of the Chief's neck and chin; green arrows). Numerous dates exist with strong clashing. (Not uncommon; $60)

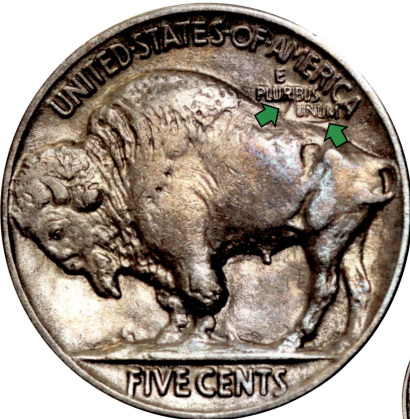

Buffalo Nickel Die Clash Overlay

Coin Trivia: The website MadDieClashes.com is an excellent resource to see dozens and dozens of different die clashes on various denominations.

2016 $1 American Silver Eagle: Clashed Dies

Bullion is a term for gold, silver, or other precious metal in the form of bars or coins produced for investors and collectors – not for circulation. One of the most affordable and popular U.S. bullion coins is the 1 ounce American Silver Eagle (ASE). Because the production and inspection of all U.S. bullion coins is vastly more controlled, significant errors on them are almost unheard of. Below is a 2016 ASE with what is believed to be the strongest die clash on any U.S. bullion coin. (At least one other 2016 was certified and graded MS69, also by NGC.) Though a handful of 2017 ASEs with clashed dies also exist, the clashing on the 2016 is much more dramatic. (Very Rare; $300; MS-67 by NGC).

(Left) Clashing of the reverse designs is so clear on the obverse that you can actually see individual barbs on the feathers' vanes on both sides of Lady Liberty.

(Below) Can you make out the upside-down "BUS" in E PLURIBUS UNUM?

(Right) Designs from Lady Liberty's dress on the obverse are very clear on the reverse side on either side of the Eagle's head. Like many die clash errors, the degree of designs transferred on one side can be much weaker or stronger than those on the other.

Coin Trivia: Production of the American Silver Eagle began in 1986. It is one of the few U.S. bullion coins that can be used to fund Individual Retirement Account investments (IRAs).

1981-P Roosevelt Dime:
Clashed Dies with Type 1 Counterclashes

Die clashes on modern coins are scarce, but finding a coin with two or multiple clashes is even scarcer. In the words of error specialist Mike Diamond, a premier numismatic researcher, collector, and author of the "Collectors' Clearinghouse" column in *Coin World* for over ten years, he concluded that on this dime "…there are two clashes, both equally strong where one would naturally have to be misaligned. During the second clash, the first set of clash marks transferred back to the die they were derived from producing Type I counterclashes on both faces. They're most easily seen on the reverse, where you have, for example, a raised extra olive and a raised extra oak leaf. Type I counterclashes are quite rare in my experience." *But*

what is a Type I counterclash? Well, these occur when a second clash transfers the initial die clash's markings back to the original die; thus a counterclash should have a minimum of two sets of clash marks with one in a slightly different position. (See the close-up photos on the bottom row.)

This is a remarkable coin, and if you look closely enough, you can make out the top of a doubled number "1" from the date and "D" from "GOD" – which are obverse features – right under the letter "F" from "OF" on the reverse, and also part of a doubled "O" from "ONE" – a reverse feature – between the "T" and "Y" in LIBERTY on the obverse. Despite what the fashion police say, this coin is en vogue and sports *clashing* quite well. (Very scarce with Type I counterclashes; $75)

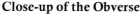

Close-up of the Obverse

Close-up of the Reverse

1979-D Susan B. Anthony Dollar (SBA): Severe Misaligned Die Strike with Multiple Die Clashes & Multiple Type 1 Counterclashes

This Susan B. Anthony dollar is not only a superb example of a misaligned die (and was featured earlier in that section) but it also features multiple (four) die clashes on both sides and strong, multiple Type 1 counterclashes on the obverse. While the reverse boasts bold clashes including her hair, bun, nose, and lips, the obverse shows clashes of Earth above her right shoulder and wing tips to the right of her brow. The obverse also has softer yet very visible counterclashes of her profile in front of her face. According to Mike Diamond, he states "this is the first case of multiple Type 1 counterclashes I've come across" and even featured this SBA error coin in his "Collectors' Clearinghouse" column in *Coin World*. (Rare error combination; $300; MS-64 by ANACS)

Profile Counterclashes of Her Nose, Lips, and Brow on the Obverse

Multiple Clashes of Her Nose, Lips, and Brow on the Reverse

1937-D "3 Legs" Buffalo/Indian Head Nickel: Intentional Die Abrasion to Correct Clashed Dies

In 1937, workers at the Denver Mint noticed die clashes on some Buffalo nickels upon a routine inspection. Using an emery stick, a worker began polishing off the clashes to repair the damaged die. Unbeknownst to him, he also subsequently created one of the most popular U.S. coin oddities of all time. *How? Why?* Because he overpolished the area of the front right leg which caused it to simply disappear. Hence the "3 Legs" Buffalo nickel was born due to his intentional abrading of the die. (This mistake was also soon detected and the die was replaced). Even collectors who normally shy away from Mint errors and die varieties seem to make an exception for this well-known coin.

So is this considered a die variety or a Mint error? There is considerable debate on which category it is even among numismatic experts. There are some who feel that any flaw on a die which then strikes those flaws on to coins, regardless of how the die's flaw was caused, equates to a die variety. Others feel this particular circumstance is a die variety only because the original Mint error – the clashed dies – were removed via overpolishing. In doing so the leg design was removed due to human error. (Note that repunched mintmarks on dies, also a result of human error, are considered die varieties and not Mint errors.) Then there are those who feel die abrasions – the polishing off of imperfections on a die (yet can result in visible, fine scratches) – are considered Mint errors even if the abrasions to remove clashed dies are intentional like this nickel. *OK, so is the 1937-D "3 Legs" a die variety or a Mint error?* I guess that depends on the expert you ask. None of the major grading companies list is as a Mint error, but are they correct? (Rare; $850; AU-55 by PCGS w/ CAC. Beware as these are very often altered and counterfeited.)

1937-D Missing the Front Right Leg

Normal 1937-D

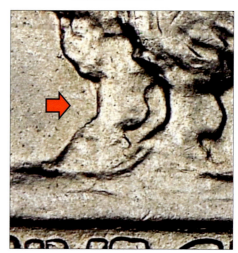

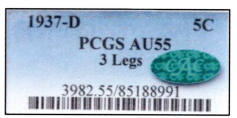

Cuds (i.e. Major Die Breaks)

Because dies are under significant pressure from repeated strikes, they can weaken in strength over time resulting in impairment. On top of that dies can also accidentally hit each other if no planchet is in the chamber, can strike a foreign object (e.g. a screw from a machine part), or they may not have been properly prepared (e.g. not properly annealed or contains impurities) which can also lead to damage. Forms of damage and die errors like clashing, cracking, shattering, or even sections of a die breaking off are known as **die stages.**

Featured here are die stages called **cuds**. *What is a cud?* A cud is a coin struck from a die where a section broke and fell off along the rim or "shank" of the die (known as a **die break**). Cuds will feature raised blobs

of metal around the rim (red arrow) in areas where the die section broke off. (Pieces not connected to the rim which break off are called **die chips**). As the striking process continues, the die break and subsequent cuds get progressively larger until the broken die is replaced. On the exact opposite side of the cud usually coin metal will be "missing" as it shifted to fill in the die break. Areas that normally have struck designs opposite the cud will often appear weak or may even be missing completely (green arrow).

There is some disagreement as to whether or not cuds (and other die stages) are rightly considered Mint errors or die varieties. In my opinion, cuds are Mint errors because the flaw on the die which struck this coin was certainly not there before it struck the first planchet.

1987
Lincoln Cent: Cud
(Scarce; $135;
MS-65RD
by NGC)

1970-D
Jefferson Nickel: Cud
(Scarce; $95)

189

Shattered Dies

2007-P Roosevelt Dime: Shattered Obverse Die

Striking planchets with multiple tons of pressure at a rate of around 720 per minute is quite taxing on coin dies. If a steel die has impurities and/or wasn't properly annealed it can eventually succumb to the constant pressure and start to crack. Damage/cracks can also result from coin dies smashing into each other should a planchet not be in the striking chamber. Each successive strike can continue adding trauma to the die(s) where it can start to crack in other areas, split, shatter, or even break off in sections. Oftentimes the progression and growth of the crack/split can be seen on coins struck by the same die over time depending at what point striking occurred (similar to cuds). Obviously a much smaller crack would have occurred at an earlier stage in the die's usage and a larger one at a later stage. Until a shattered die is replaced, damage to it will continue to worsen.

Featured here is a dime struck with a massive shattered obverse die with many cracks and splits; the reverse die was undamaged. There are other dimes struck from this exact die that are known, both at this stage and earlier stages with much less damage. There are also other years with shattered obverse dies from this series (including 2006 and 2001) that look incredibly similar both in the location and nature of the cracks and splits. What a truly remarkable and rare die stage error with strong MS luster. (Rare; $175)

Close-up of the Obverse Shattered Die

190

Strike-through Errors

A **Strike-through error** is a coin that had some type of foreign object rammed into the planchet during a die strike. The debris will often exhibit its contours on the planchet (depending on the object's hardness) leaving a divot/recession, and consequently the blocked areas of the die faces will leave weaker – if any – details on affected areas of the coin; it can also affect the other side leaving weak or missing details opposite the struck-through debris.

Occasionally a specific object's impression can be identified, some of which can be quite amusing. For example, things like paper clips, spring coils, clothing buttons, staples, and even pieces of cloth have had their patterns rammed into coins. *How did these objects manage to get into the coining press?* The answer is simple: If something enters a facility where a product is made, there is the potential for it to come into contact with the product at some point in the production process. Just as a server's Band-Aid can fall off into your Caesar salad at a restaurant, a paper clip or broken machine part can wind up in a coining press. Other objects rammed into coins which are less amusing but still interesting include built up and dried grease, fragments of planchets or struck coins, and even complete planchets or struck coins which can leave mirrored, incused designs on the other planchet they were smashed into (i.e. brockages).

Among the most desired and expensive of all strike-throughs are coins where foreign objects were not only struck into the planchets, but those objects remain bonded to the coins; these are referred to as **retained strike-throughs.** Objects which can be identified generally sell for more than those which can not, especially if the object itself is still fully intact (e.g. an entire staple is embedded into the planchet rather than only a fraction of it). Two of the most dramatic retained strike-throughs I have ever seen are both on 1967 Lincoln cents. For both coins, a screw was rammed into each planchet and bonded to it creating absolutely astounding errors. (One of them will be featured soon.)

Be aware that there is no shortage of altered coins for sale being marketed as authentic retained strike-through errors, including coins with staples or paperclips hammered into or even glued onto them. One way to tell a retained strike-through is genuine is to check if the contours of the embedded object match and line up with the rest of the contours on the designs of the coin; raised design/rims also shouldn't be flattened on either side.

1972 Jefferson Nickel:
Struck-through a Foreign Object

Most strike-throughs do not have the object retained, and more often than not exactly what was struck into them remains unknown (but it's always fun to theorize). As you probably predicted by now, if it can't be determined what the object is the coin will likely sell for considerably less money than one leaving a definitive, recognizable pattern (e.g. a paperclip). For example, observe the 1972 nickel on the right which has a strike-through area taking up over 1/3 of the obverse side. What do you think was struck into it?

Could it be a crumpled-up gum wrapper? Possibly a metal fragment? Maybe even a used facial tissue? (Gross!)

My guess based on its appearance is that it's from a planchet fragment or other scrap metal piece, but no one can say for sure. Some have told me it is from a section of cloth left behind which are used to wipe down Mint equipment, but almost always there is evidence of a weave pattern which this coin lacks. Whatever the foreign object was, this nickel is definitely a genuine strike-through Mint error. (Scarce; $30)

Exactly what was rammed into the obverse side of this Jefferson nickel remains a mystery.

Sometimes laminations like this silver dime fragment can wind up in the press and struck into planchets leaving similar impressions as seen on the nickel above.

Struck-through Grease ("Greasers")

Since Mint machinery involves moving parts, grease is needed to lubricate them. Over time dust and dirt can stick to greasy parts and start to thicken into a paste and even harden over time. If greasy goop works its way to the faces of coin dies it can fill in recessed design areas. Should this happen, clogged portions of the die(s) might not transfer their markings and appear as "missing" on struck coins or may appear weaker than normal. Coins of this nature caused by a build-up of grease on coin die faces are known as **grease strike-throughs** or "**greasers**."

1943 "Ghost 4" Lincoln Cent: Grease-filled Die

In this case, machine grease filled in the "4" on the coin's obverse die and so it barely appears as a "ghostly" numeral on this "steelie." The dark shaded areas around the date are also likely grease struck into the coin. However, the only thing scary about "Ghost 4" steel cents is usually the price some dealers ask for them! (Somewhat scarce; $4 for MS grades)

1974-D Kennedy Half Dollar: Struck-through Grease

There is just enough of the date to see it, but design details are weak overall on both sides of this JFK half dollar. I'm open to the possibility this is a weak strike and not a "greaser," but because I can't see the edges while JFK rests in this old ANACS holder, I can't say for sure; it would be worth around $100 more if it is. (Scarce; $50; MS-60 by ANACS.)

"Ghost" 4

Normal 4

A Comparison of Two Different Grease Strike-throughs on Zinc Lincoln Cents

Not only can missing details from grease-clogged dies be restricted to one letter/number,
one side, or vary from one side to the other, they can also be equally extreme on both sides.

1996-D Lincoln Cent: Major Grease Strike-through (Dual Sided)
This greaser is a bit more extreme than most other grease strike-throughs. ($10)

(No Date) Zinc Lincoln Cent: Severe Grease Strike-through (Dual Sided)
In contrast to the coin above, this dateless zinc cent below has a grease strike-through
so severe that it almost appears as an unstruck planchet. (Rare this severe; $60)

Though resembling weak strike errors, the strong rims on both of these cents suggests
the strike pressure was normal; the likely culprit was a heavily grease-filled set of dies.

Struck-through a Dropped Letter/Number

2006-D North Dakota State Quarter: Obverse Dropped Letter "Y"

This is a truly odd and freakish error type that leaves many initial onlookers and inexperienced collectors very skeptical at what they see. *How on God's green Earth does a letter "Y" just randomly appear on a coin? Did part of the die break off where the "Y" in LIBERTY is and then got struck into this coin?* No, it didn't, and despite the peculiar nature of this error type it is actually one of the easiest to explain and understand its causes.

Just as junk and crud can build up and clog portions of recessed die faces during striking, that gunk can also harden, fall off the die face, and land on planchets in the striking chamber. The next successive strike would then ram that crud right into the planchet; it could even remain bonded/retained to the coin, but normally it just leaves an impression. The fallen or "dropped" debris can be from anywhere it filled in on the die – even individual letters or numbers from the recessed die marking(s) it clogged. For example, it can take the form of a "G" in GOD from the motto IN GOD WE TRUST or a "2" from a 2002 date. Strike-through errors such as these are often referred to as **dropped letters/numbers** (or **struck-through dropped filling** if no specific or "isolated element" is present like a number or letter, according to *Error-Ref.com*). For reasons I can't explain, I have seen more dropped fillings on the Statehood Quarter Series than on other modern denominations. (Rare; $350; MS-65 by PCGS)

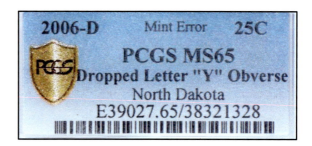

Close-up of the Dropped "Y" from LIBERTY

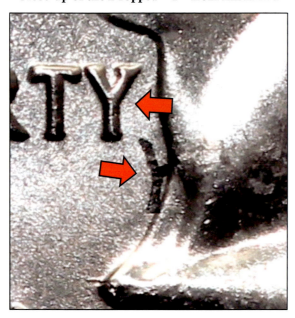

Close-up of the Cloth's Crisscross Weave Pattern

1968-D Lincoln Cent:
Obverse Struck-through Cloth

Just as we like to keep our work areas clean, so do employees at the Mint. All forms of equipment, especially anything involving moving machine parts that require lubrication, will start to become messy very quickly if they aren't cleaned regularly. Grease, dust, and other debris can build up over time clogging dies and machine parts. One of the tools used to clean Mint machinery in the past (and possibly still used today) were cloth rags to wipe things down.

OK, but how would a cloth rag wind up inside the striking chamber of a coining press? One theory I find reasonable is that rather than a rag simply being left in the coining press (which could also happen theoretically), perhaps a section of the cloth snagged and caught on part of the machinery during the cleaning process and ripped completely off. The torn section then remained in the equipment until it was jarred loose and eventually landed in the striking chamber. Then came a die strike with dozens of tons of pressure which rammed the cloth's weave pattern into an unsuspecting planchet, and Voila! You have a cloth strike-through!

Like other error types, certain characteristics make one more desirable than another. For example, those which are struck-through fully and show a very strong weave pattern seem to sell at higher prices, and even more so if it's on the obverse; a readable date like this one is even better. (Readable dates on this error type are rare when the area of the date is affected.) Those struck on type coins like war nickels, steel cents, and bicentennials can sell for well over $1,000. Discontinued series (e.g. Buffalo nickels), proof coins, larger denominations, and silver/gold coin cloth strike-throughs can go even higher.

Although you would think this error type would be very difficult to forge on your own, Mike Diamond attests he has seen examples where someone chemically altered coins by using "bits of cloth that have been soaked in acid or some other corrosive solution" which then "gradually etch a sunken grid pattern into the coin's surface that can fool the unwary collector." He goes on to say that you can differentiate genuine cloth strike-throughs because "the weave weakens or vanishes over the high relief areas — not so with an acid-etched coin. Genuine examples of the error will also usually show an elevated 'wire' rim where the cloth overlaps the rim." In fact, you can actually see the "wire rim" on this coin that Mike refers to. (Very scarce; $500; MS-64BN by NGC. *Mike's comments retrieved from his Collectors Clearinghouse column in the May 4th, 2012 edition of* Coin World *titled "Cloth a Familiar Cause of Interesting 'Struck-through.'")*

1985 Lincoln Cent:
Broadstruck with Clashed Dies and
Struck-through & Retained Zinc Fragments

What might first come across as just another zinc cent broadstrike is actually quite a fascinating error coin. First, both in front of and behind Lincoln's head are visible die clashes of the Memorial columns. Second, what you don't normally see are zinc fragments from other planchets struck into and retained on a coin.

Look at the reverse side of this cent, in particular the area on the right side of the Lincoln Memorial. Observe the raised areas of gray metal embedded into the coin (green arrows) as well as indented areas where the fragments were struck into it but did not retain (red arrows). If you only glance at it quickly, you might mistake the gray area for missing copper plating as a result of the broadstrike. However it is actually zinc from another planchet pressed into this coin, possibly from what was left of a mangled and detached die cap floor (bottom right) that remained on the reverse die or fell off and landed on this planchet right before striking. (Very scarce; MS-64RB; $100)

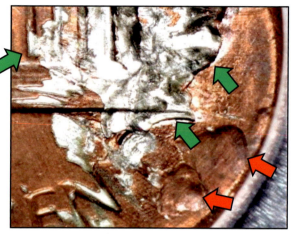

Below is what remains of a zinc cent die cap floor. It's likely what is retained on the back of this 1985 cent.

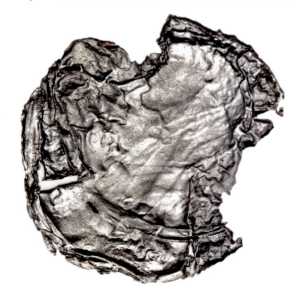

1959-D Lincoln Cent:
Reverse Retained Grease Strike-through

The reverse of this 1959-D cent features some hardened grease that was struck into it and retained on the lower third of this coin. Because grease clogged part of the reverse die, it left both some weak lettering and indentations on the planchet; you can also make out areas where struck-in grease didn't retain (red arrows).

Most "greasers" and other strike-throughs do not have the grease/foreign object remaining on the coin, but this one has a significant amount of hardened grease that bonded to it. What many might write off as post-Mint crud is actually a very neat and rare find. As to its value, there really aren't recorded sales to give a more confident estimate, so I would guess this Mint State coin is worth around $20 since it isn't a popular error type.

Coin Trivia: Did you know that Abraham Lincoln is also on a half dollar? In 1918, a silver commemorative was released celebrating the centennial of Illinois' admittance into the Union in 1818. (Photos courtesy of Heritage Auctions/HA.com)

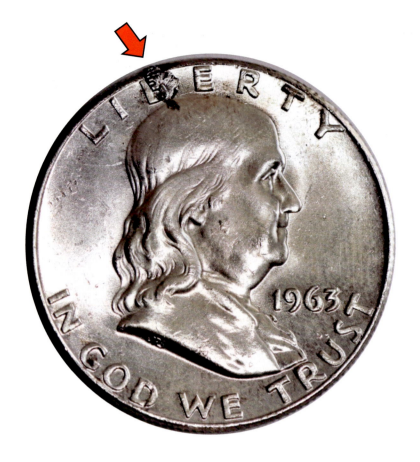

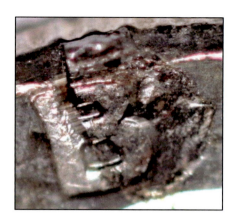

1963 Benjamin Franklin Half Dollar: Struck-through & Retained Magnetic Metal Fragment

Other than 1943 steel cents, U.S. coins aren't made of magnetic metals. However, slag which can contain iron – which is magnetic – is found in metallic ores including copper, nickel, gold, and silver that are (or were) used to produce coins. Slag impurities normally rise to the surface as metal ingots are melted, which are then scooped out before being poured into forms used to produce planchet strips. But just as egg farmers can't catch every bad egg, smelters can't possibly filter out every mass of slag. As we've seen earlier, they can wind up on struck coins and can cause laminations.

As for this coin I'm not certain the embedded fragment is slag despite being magnetic. *Why?* Slag is often much harder than coining metals and tends to reject shifting into a die's devices. In other words, you normally don't see struck designs on slag fragments. Also, the fragment doesn't appear to be flush with the coin's surface and is raised above it slightly. This leads me to believe it wasn't on the planchet to start with. *Then where did this fragment come from?* Who knows? It could be anything from a broken piece from a machine part to something transferred inadvertently by a press operator. Whatever it is, it's fitting for Ben's *magnetic* personality as a ladies' man. (Rare; $200)

1964-D Jefferson Nickel: Struck-through and Retained Staple (Dual Brush Bristle)

Just like rocks can get embedded into the bottom of your shoe, staple-like wires from a dual bristle brush used to clean the coining press can sometimes wind up making their home struck into coins. *How can you tell it wasn't added after it left the Mint?* Notice in the close-up photo below how the obverse designs and contours are actually formed and struck into the staple which flows with the designs and contours on the planchet. A staple hammered in after minting would not feature these and might display flattened details on both sides (especially around the object itself).

What makes this retained strike-through even more special is that it is: (a) an identifiable vs. an unknown object; (b) struck into the obverse rather than the reverse; (c) exclusively struck into the bust of this coin; and (d) perfectly centered. Each of these factors not only enhances eye appeal but normally garners much higher premiums than those which do not. This is a very fitting error for someone whose Revolutionary writings became a *staple* of American liberty. (Very rare; $975; AU-55 by PCGS)

Close-up of the Genuine Retained Staple

There are many coins which were altered intentionally by gluing or squeezing staples on to coins to try and rip off error collectors.

Notice on the genuine retained staple above that the contours of the staple flow with the contours of the coin, while below the staple is flattened uniformly. No raised or recessed designs of Lincoln's bust appear anywhere.

Close-up of an Embedded Staple via a Vise Job

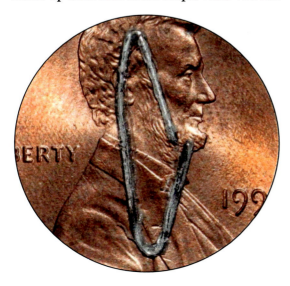

Coin Trivia: To "nickel and dime" someone means to repeatedly charge small fees over time where it eventually adds up to a substantial sum of money.

199

1967   Mint Error   1C
PCGS MS64RD
Magnetic Screw Struck
And Bonded onto Coin
E2902.64/34128957

Struck 50 years ago!!

*Photos of the 1967 cent courtesy of
Fred Weinberg and FredWeinberg.com*

1967 Lincoln Cent: Broadstruck with a Magnetic Screw Attached and Bonded to the Coin

Going to national coin shows in places like Baltimore, Pittsburgh, Chicago, and the Florida United Numismatists (FUN) show in Orlando are quite the experiences. It is at these shows – if you can make it to them – where you can actually meet many of the major Mint error dealers and writers in person and get to see some of the most incredible errors in their inventories and collections. Mint error expert, dealer, writer, and PCGS authenticator, Fred Weinberg, never seems to disappoint with what he brings to these shows. Among one of his most bizarre acquisitions he brought is this 1967 cent – one of two he had – that was struck with a screw and wound up bonding to each coin. (The other coin had a longer screw bonded to it.) Although I know he has since sold this particular coin, I am not sure of the final sale price though he did have it listed on his site for around $12,000 at one time. (MS-64RD by PCGS)

Here is a 2.8 gram screw that was struck by Lincoln cent dies but is not bonded to a planchet. No date or mintmark is visible on this "coin." (MS-64+ by PCGS.

PCGS© Used by permission at PCGS.com/ CoinFacts

$5 photos courtesy of Stacks & Bowers® at StacksBowers.com

$5 1988 A Federal Reserve Note (NY): Obstructed Printing with Retained Tape and Brown Paper

Paper currency errors are not "Mint" errors since currency (i.e. paper money) is not minted; it's printed. However they can and do wind up with various errors at times, including retained errors just as coins have them. This $5 bill wound up with a small piece of what looks like masking tape, or possibly some kind of medical tape, that stuck to a brown piece of paper and landed on a sheet of currency paper. The printing rollers then pressed and printed over this obstruction which left it bonded to the bill. Since the printing for currency is done in three stages rather than all at once, it explains why part of the printing is under the obstruction yet the serial number, Federal Reserve seal, and Federal Reserve district number (2) are on top of the obstruction. This error was sold in a Stacks & Bowers Auction in 2018 for $4,080. Graded 63 Choice Uncirculated Net by PMG.

$20 1996 Federal Reserve Note: Obstructed Printing with Retained "Del Monte" Sticker

Reportedly an Ohio college student received this "Del Monte Note" from an ATM in 2004 and sold it on EBay for around $10,000. But at a Heritage Auctions offering in 2006 it sold for a whopping $25,300. Some people feel its placement was done intentionally at the Bureau of Engraving and Printing, but regardless it's one of the most humorous retained objects on any coin or bill. Graded 63-PPQ Choice New by PCGS.

$20 photos courtesy of Heritage Auctions/HA.com

Bonded Coins

19XX-P Roosevelt Dimes: Obverse Die Cap / Two Coin Multi-struck Bonded Set

A Roosevelt dime is currently the smallest-sized U.S. coin intended for circulation, but these broadstruck and multi-struck 19XX-P dimes – which were struck and bonded to each other – are now almost as large as a half dollar. The term **bonded coin** refers to a coin that adheres securely to another coin/planchet as a result of being struck together. *But how do they wind up being stuck to each other?* Heat generated by the striking action, along with the flow of the metal as it expands and the multiple tons of force, can all contribute to coins becoming stuck together as one piece. This beauty sold at a Stacks & Bowers auction in 2014 for a bargain price of $1,410.

1979-D Lincoln Cents: Obverse Die Cap Bonded Pile-up

Reminiscent of something you'd see at a 19th century travelling freak show, this error type is known as a multiple coin **pile-up** for obvious reasons. At some point a planchet stuck to the die (in this case, the anvil die) and remained there with each successive planchet ramming into and bonding to the coin before it. *How many coins are bonded here?* Well if you consider this "coin" weighs 105 grams (or 3.7 ounces), and a normal copper cent weighs 3.11 grams, that means there are 33.76 coins in this pile-up (assuming all the planchets are complete and at a standard weight). I'm not sure exactly how this absolute monster of an error and a freak among freaks made it out of the Denver Mint as all errors are supposed to be destroyed and recycled when discovered. Fortunately a kind soul spared this coin and it made its way to an appreciative collector somewhere. This error type is super rare for all denominations and are seldom on the market for sale. This one sold for $11,162.50 at a Stacks & Bowers auction in 2012.

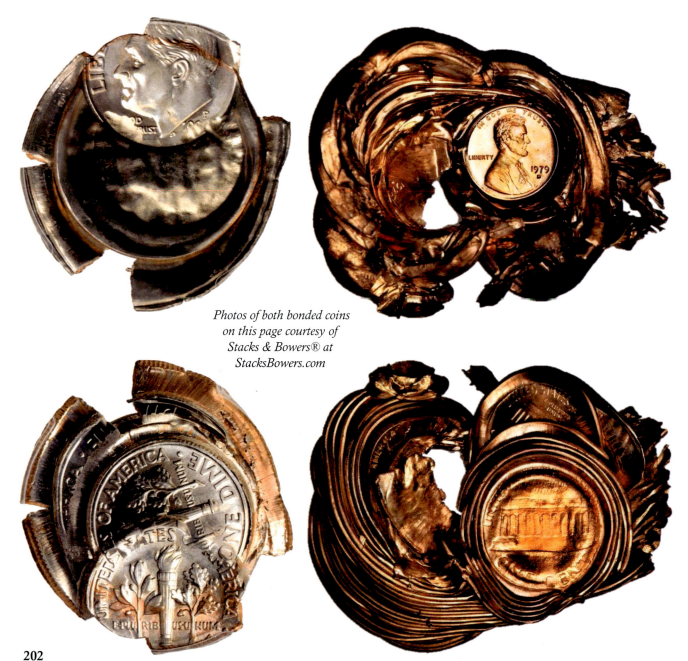

Photos of both bonded coins on this page courtesy of Stacks & Bowers® at StacksBowers.com

Rolled-in and Retained Objects

Along with slag, sometimes a foreign object can be embedded in planchet metal even before blanks are punched out. For example, the three copper cents below all have foreign metal flakes that bonded to them. Though some people might call these "strike-throughs," in my opinion that term is factually incorrect. *Why is that?* Because their long, linear pattern suggests those flakes were "rolled" into/on the planchet strips during the rolling phase – not "struck" into the planchet during the die-striking action. Therefore, I believe a more accurate term is **rolled-in**, not "struck-through." *O.K.,*

but how did those flakes get on the planchet strips? Perhaps workers making these metal sheets had flakes from various coining metals on their clothes, gloves, or tools and they fell off and landed on the copper cent strips. But what I do know is however it happened, the results are cool Lincoln cent errors! Metal scanning of the affected areas turned up gold particles (1912-S), nickel particles (1909 VDB), and though it didn't register, it is likely silver, aluminum or tin (1919). Who knew Lincoln was so *flaky?* (Rare; $60 each)

1909 VDB Lincoln Cent: Rolled-in Nickel Flakes

1919 Lincoln Cent: Undetermined Rolled-in Metal Flakes

1912-S Lincoln Cent: Rolled-in Gold Flakes

Since the San Francisco Mint was producing gold coins at the time, it is plausible there was some degree of transfer of gold flakes on to the planchet strip before the rollers went into action.

Close-up of a Portion of the Rolled-in Gold Flakes on the 1912-S Lincoln Cent

Coin Trivia: The original building where the San Francisco Mint first operated was the only financial establishment still standing and/or left operational after the devastating 1906 earthquake and fire.

203

Die Caps

Every so often a struck coin can wind up adhering to a coin die (usually the obverse die) and actually becomes the die itself striking incoming planchets. Should this happen, planchets/coins that stick to a die are called **die caps**. Coins that stick to the reverse die, which is most often the anvil die, are called **reverse die caps**. *Why are they called "caps?"* Because they resemble a bottle cap, silly!

The longer die caps remain on a die, the more stretched and distorted designs will become on the side making direct contact with incoming planchets. Also, the outer edges of the coin will continue to rise up and hug the neck of the die forming what are known as **cap walls**. In a matter of time the shape of the die cap can look more like a thimble or shot glass, and the metal stuck to the face of the die – called the **cap floor** – continues to get thinner (and even crinkle up) until it detaches from the walls and/or falls off the die.

Incoming planchets struck with die caps will have the cap's designs hammered into them leaving reversed, mirrored designs known as brockages. Of course, as the die cap continues to become distorted, so will the appearance of brockages. Like most other errors, severe errors like deep die caps on higher denominations (e.g. half dollars and dollars), older gold/silver circulated coinage, type coins, and very recent strikes are incredibly rare and can sell for thousands of dollars.

1998 Lincoln Cent: Double-struck Reverse Die Cap (or Centered Double-strike and Broadstruck with a Full Indent on the 2nd Strike)

Though not indicated on the label, this 1998 Lincoln cent is a reverse die cap that was struck outside the collar and so is also broadstruck. (Remember, previously I mentioned TPGs are most likely to make mistakes on labels for Mint errors whether it's due to laziness, sloppiness, or possibly even ignorance. Though people do make mistakes, incorrect information on slab labels can certainly cost sellers money which could be quite significant.) Notice how only the designs on the obverse are greatly distorted; this is because the reverse side remained anchored to the reverse die while the obverse side is what was making contact with newly arriving planchets.

You should be able to see the deep indent from at least one cent planchet that was rammed into Abe's bust virtually doubling his profile. It also formed a bowl-like shape and stretched the thin copper plating exposing the zinc's gray color. The reverse side started to wrap around the reverse die yet maintained the integrity of its details. None of the reverse lettering or the Memorial became distorted despite a severe broadening of its diameter. The copper layer also started wrinkling and folding up in spots revealing its gleaming gray core. This is a perfect example of what some would see as a damaged coin yet is a beautiful Mint error. It's also a good example of an incomplete label description. (Scarce; $250; MS-66RD by NGC)

Coin Trivia: The motto E PLURIBUS UNUM on U.S coins is a Latin, thirteen-letter phrase translated as "Out of many, one." This is symbolic of how there were thirteen colonies that came together to form one nation.

1998 1C MULTI STRUCK
W/100% OBVERSE INDENT
MINT ERROR MS 66 RD
2072944-005

NUMISMATIC GUARANTY CORPORATION

1981-P Jefferson Nickel: Obverse Die Cap with a Full Obverse Brockage on the Reverse Face

The nickel featured here managed to stick to the obverse die and remained there for a series of additional strikes. It proceeded to work its way up the die's neck and explains why it looks like a very small deep-dish pizza pan. The cap walls are reasonably high with the obverse designs, date, mintmark, and lettering displaying incredibly sharp and crisp details. The reverse side features a full brockage of the obverse design with most of Jefferson's bust. At least for me, what is particularly remarkable about the brockage is that Jefferson's distorted image now strongly resembles the design – and faces the same direction – as the Indian Chief on a Buffalo nickel. I acquired this coin from an online auction and thought at first it would be a great piece for my error collection, but then I looked a little closer and saw some problems. *What's wrong with it exactly?*

To my disappointment, upon closer inspection I saw hundreds of fine hairline scratches (red arrows) all throughout the fields and on the raised designs. There's no denying the coin has been cleaned harshly and improperly, possibly by being wiped with a cloth or paper towel. There are also some areas of pitting/corrosion (green arrows), possibly the remains of permanent damage caused by PVC film that may have once plagued this coin. This would be a $650 coin if not for the damage that ruined a great error.

Die Cap Floors

Again, a **die cap floor** is the remaining flat portion of a die cap which was stuck to the face of a die. Cap floors become progressively thinner with repeated strikes and often take on the appearance of crumpled pieces of paper. At times the cap walls which ride up the die's neck give way and detach from the planchet leaving just the cap's floor (a.k.a. base) as seen here.

1989 Lincoln Cent:
Die Cap Floor

1989 (.17 Grams) and 1997 (.14 Grams) Lincoln Cents: Multi-struck Die Cap Floors/Bases

Both the 1989 and 1997 cents are a mere fraction of their original weight (2.5 grams for zinc planchets) as they eventually broke off from the rest of their respective planchets. Notice that these two coins also shifted position along the face of the die a few times (e.g. more than one date, motto, etc.). Incused images of Mr. Lincoln and other designs and lettering are also present on both coins on the gray-colored zinc side. (Rare; $300 each; the 1989 is graded MS-65 by NGC)

1997 Lincoln Cent:
Die Cap Floor

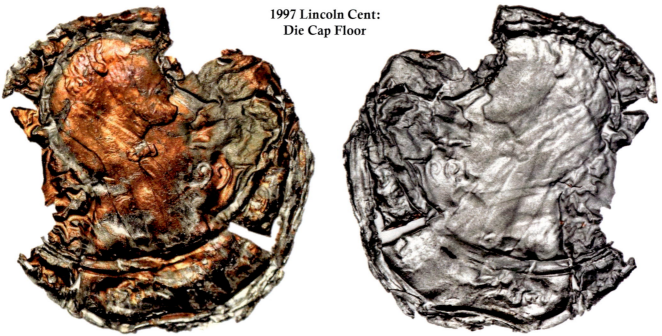

Struck Through a Late Stage Obverse Die Cap

1996 Lincoln Cent and a 1998-P Roosevelt Dime: Struck-through a Late Stage Obverse Die Cap

As for the coins featured here, the die caps which struck them were on so long that (a) they became so thin that most of the designs on the cap floor disappeared and (b) the cap floors sunk in to the recessed areas of the obverse dies. At this point struck coins will feature raised obverse designs again that are struck through the ultra-thin die caps, but they appear mushy as the faces of the

obverse dies were still blocked. Coins like these are referred to as **struck-through late stage die caps** once the die's designs start to show through the thin floor of a die cap. In fact, you can just barely make out the date and mintmark on the dime, and the date plus IN GOD WE TRUST on the cent. Note both reverse sides are unaffected because the reverse dies made an unobstructed, direct die strike. (1996 1c; Scarce; $20; 1998 10c; Scarce; $50)

**1996 Lincoln Cent:
Struck-through a Capped Die**

**1998-P Roosevelt Dime:
Struck-through a Capped Die**

1964-D Lincoln Cent: Struck Through a Late Stage Shifted Obverse Die Cap

As mentioned previously, a coin stuck to a die that strikes incoming planchets is called a die cap, and the cap floor gets gradually thinner as it strikes more planchets. However it was also stated that designs should be raised, not sunken into the coin (a.k.a. **incused**) for late stage die caps. *So why on this coin are there both raised and incused designs and details? Is it counterfeit, altered, or genuine? How can you tell?*

Well, for starters the coin is the standard weight of 3.11 grams for a copper Lincoln cent, has the correct relief (the degree to which it has a 3-D effect of raised designs) and other diagnostics indicating it came from the U.S. Mint. It also was not altered as the diameter is standard, the rims and the reverse side are not corrupted, and there is no sign of a vise or "squeeze" job. *Now that we know it is not counterfeit nor altered, exactly how can the appearance of incused yet correct-facing multiple designs/details on this coin be explained?*

Being a late stage die cap, the cap floor is unbelievably thin. However, it is not all the same thickness because part of the metal has recessed into the obverse die's designs. Should you remove the die cap and observe it from the inside, you will notice metal which has filled in the die's date, mintmark, bust, and lettering are thicker than metal touching areas with no designs/details known as the "fields." (The best way to explain it is that it resembles a plastic child-proof power outlet plug; evenly flat on the outside, and the other side has two prongs sticking out that fill in the vertical openings on the outlet).

Should the cap floor then shift in position for additional die strikes, those thicker areas like dates and lettering will become pressed through the cap floor and *into* incoming planchets as incused rather than raised designs, though still facing the correct way. As for the coin on your left, there were at least three times the cap floor shifted along the die – being struck each time it shifted – before the cap floor detached. This is perhaps one of the more complicated errors to explain to others, and despite many claiming it is fake or altered (including myself at first!), it is a genuine, undeniably odd, and rare error type. (Very rare; $400.)

Despite the fact that the collar in a coin's striking chamber is meant for only one planchet, at times a second planchet – either a complete or split planchet – has accompanied the other in there. Should they be stacked up perfectly, squarely, and simultaneously inside that collar when the dies strike, the end product will be two coins – one with only an obverse strike and the other with only a reverse strike. An error of this nature is called a **full uniface strike** or **full indent,** meaning it has only "one side" due to the additional planchet fully blocking a direct die strike from the opposite die. (If a blank planchet only covers part of the other planchet when struck, those are known as partial indents, including my 1998-P dime featured later).

Genuine full uniface strikes are rare as opposed to many altered coins I see where someone ground down or buffed out one side and made it both featureless and flat. However, usually you can see grinding or filing marks on the "unstruck" side and the planchet will weigh noticeably less. Also, if only the struck side has a full rim and the uniface side does not, that strongly suggests a coin was altered.

There are quite a few dates I've seen from the 1950s through the 1970s featuring this exact error type on Lincoln cents. It's one of many error types where it's fun to build a short set with sequential dates and is affordable even on a modest budget. Beware of altered coins which were ground down that can mimic genuine full uniface coins.

1961 Lincoln Cent: Full Uniface Reverse

This beautiful example shows how designs from both sides can transfer through one planchet and on to another when stacked on top of each other and the dies strike. Can you make out the ghostly images of an upside-down Lincoln Memorial and the mirrored profile of President Lincoln on your left? This should give you a sense of just how much force is applied when planchets are struck, which is dozens of tons of pressure varying with the denomination. Presumably this coin's mate – a struck reverse side – is hopefully part of someone's collection. Note how NGC explained *how* the error occurred on the label rather than state *what* the error is. (Rare; $90; MS-64RB by NGC)

1961 1C
MINT ERROR MS 64 RB
OBVERSE HALF OF TWO
PLANCHETS STRUCK TOGETHER
4930241-002

NUMISMATIC GUARANTY CORPORATION

2003-D Roosevelt Dime:
Full Uniface Strike/Full Reverse Indent

Like the cent on the previous page, this 2003-D Roosevelt dime exhibits very bold and ghostly design transfers from both dies on its uniface side. Taken from two different angles, the unstruck side clearly shows fuzzy, mirrored design features of both the oak leaves, olive branches, and lit torch from the reverse and Roosevelt's head from the obverse. The label's description is the same as the cent as well. (Rare; $300; MS-64 by NGC)

2003 D 10C
OBVERSE HALF OF TWO
COINS STRUCK TOGETHER
MINT ERROR MS 64
4425924-004

NUMISMATIC GUARANTY CORPORATION

2003-D (Obverse)

2003-D (Reverse Angle 1 Showing Roosevelt's Head)

Roosevelt Dime Reverse (for Comparison)

2003-D (Reverse Angle 2 Showing Torch/Leaves)

Coin Trivia: According to the U.S. Bureau of Labor Statistics, when the Roosevelt dime debuted in 1946 a dime had the same buying power as $1.45 in 2021

2000-P Roosevelt Dime:
Reverse Indent from a 15% Curved Clip Blank/Planchet, Struck Together In-collar

Similar to the 2003-D full reverse indent on the previous page, this 2000-P Roosevelt dime instead had a curved clip blank or planchet resting directly below it when it was struck in the collar. Though it might appear altered, the weight is good, the rims are still intact, the natural luster is there, and it has the same little nicks and marks you find on unstruck blanks and planchets; this is definitely genuine and was not tooled or filed off.

Only about 15% of the reverse design on this coin is present. This means that somewhere there has to be a 15% curved clip planchet with the other 85% of this reverse design and an unstruck obverse on the other side as these were sandwiched together in the collar. Being the nerds that we are, a few serious error collectors I know hope, pray, and even actively look for what is the actual matching coin to their error to complete a mated pair. This is extremely difficult to do, and who knows if its mate even made it out of the Mint and/or has since been destroyed. Since most mated pairs were discovered in the same roll or Mint bag, the chances of reuniting two mated-pair errors once they hit circulation is realistically a fool's errand. (Very rare struck with a clipped blank/planchet; $325)

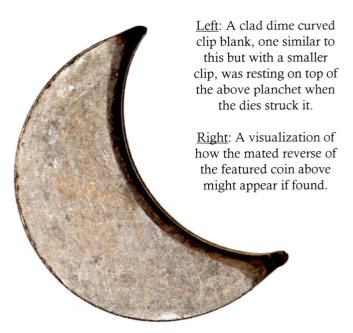

Left: A clad dime curved clip blank, one similar to this but with a smaller clip, was resting on top of the above planchet when the dies struck it.

Right: A visualization of how the mated reverse of the featured coin above might appear if found.

1959 Lincoln Cent and a 1974-D Jefferson Nickel: Full Reverse Indent/Uniface Reverse from a Split Planchet

Just as a complete planchet can sit atop another complete planchet in the chamber, it can also have a split planchet resting on a complete planchet (or another split planchet). In this case, the textured side of a split cent and nickel planchet were both rammed into the reverse of each planchet leaving the textured appearance on both reverse sides. Since the cent weighs 3.11 grams and the nickel weighs 5 grams, we can deduce these coins are not split planchets (unless they were rolled very thick) but in fact were struck with split planchets resting perfectly between the reverse die and the reverse side of these coins. Therefore, the attribution on the nickel's label is not incorrect but rather is simply incomplete. Full indents/uniface strikes from split planchets are much more rare than from complete planchets. (Rare; $50-$100 for the cent; $175 for the nickel; MS-63 by NGC)

Full Indent/Full Uniface Strike from a Split Planchet

1974 D 5C
OBVERSE HALF OF TWO
PLANCHETS STRUCK TOGETHER
MINT ERROR MS 63
2682678-007

NUMISMATIC GUARANTY CORPORATION NGC®

Partial Indents

1998–P Roosevelt Dime:
Broadstruck and Double-struck with a Partial Obverse Indent

This centered broadstrike at some point was struck with a second unstruck planchet sitting on top of and off-center to the obverse side of this coin which created a large **partial indent** to the back of FDR's head. The force and stress from the strike caused this dime to stretch so far out in that area that it led to splitting. As for FDR, he has been left with a splitting headache that will *live in infamy*. (Scarce; $90; MS-64 by ANACS; the label does not state it is also a broadstrike.)

Coin Trivia: Beginning in the mid-1960s, the U.S. Mint started using Martha Washington/Mt. Vernon "nonsense" dies to strike test pieces on different metallic compositions. This clad dime, minted circa 1965, was likely struck to test the clad composition for U.S. dimes as the Mint began to transition away from 90% silver coinage. It sold at Heritage Auctions in 2017 for $4,230. Graded MS-62 by NGC. (Photos courtesy of Heritage Auctions/HA.com)

Indents from Smaller Planchets

1971-D Eisenhower $1:
Reverse Indented by a 1 Cent Planchet

It is very rare for two planchets to get struck together for an in-collar strike, but it's even more rare when there are two different planchets for two different denominations that get struck together for an in-collar strike. Based on what we see below, a clad Eisenhower dollar planchet and a 1 cent planchet were directly on top of each other in-collar and struck simultaneously with 1971-D Eisenhower dies. The consequence of this situation left the following: (1) A 1971-D Eisenhower dollar with a reverse indent from a 1 cent planchet that failed to bond to it, and (2) a 1 cent planchet – wherever it is currently – bearing only partial reverse designs of an Eisenhower dollar along with a full uniface obverse. As to how a 1 cent planchet wound up in a coining press set for Ike dollars is anyone's guess, but regardless

it resulted in a fascinating major error. This one was photographed by me and is owned by a good friend of mine, but he wishes to remain anonymous; it's graded MS-63 by PCGS.

This error coin also serves to illustrate yet another example as to why coins make terrible investments. During my research for this coin, I noticed it sold for $1,610 at a Heritage Auctions offering in 2011 (and I assume it's where my friend acquired it). However two years earlier in 2009, a very similar 1974-D Eisenhower with the exact same error on the reverse and equally great eye appeal – yet graded *lower* at MS-62 – sold for $2,760 at Heritage Auctions. In other words, the same error type on the same denomination (and in a lower grade by the same grading service) sold for over $1,000 less two years later.

Below: An approximation of how the planchets appeared before and after striking the coin above.

Brockages (Partial)

When a planchet is struck by the dies but fails to exit the chamber, it can at times be smashed into an incoming planchet as the dies strike again. As you would expect, designs from the struck coin can become pressed into an incoming planchet. Should this occur, coins resulting from this type of mishap are known as **brockages.** (If an *unstruck* planchet is struck into a second planchet leaving no designs, it is known as an **indent**.) Brockages can be found on coins that may or may not have been broadstruck on the first strike.

For the cent on the left, a previously struck coin did not eject properly and was then sitting off-center on top of a newly-arrived planchet. The hammer die came down and struck both into each other, leaving the new planchet with both normal, raised designs from the dies and mirrored, incused designs from the previously struck coin. How sharp the mirrored and incused details are depends at what stage the brockage occurred. Obviously, the very first time a previously struck coin hits a new planchet (known as a **first-strike brockage**), the sharper the mirrored image will be. As it sticks to a die and continues hitting incoming planchets, it will become more stretched/distorted over time.

For this coin, the brockage occurred at an early stage of the striking process. They are also known as **partial brockages** because only a portion of the previously struck coin was pressed into it. On rare occasions, the entire design of one side can be struck into a planchet; these are known as **full brockages**, and can appear as a "two-headed" or "two-tailed" coin with the brockage side being mirrored. Full, first-strike brockages sell at a much higher premium, with "two-headed" first strike mirror brockages featuring full dates going for well over $1,500 even for modern cents. A mirrored brockage of the obverse design on a bicentennial Eisenhower dollar went for just shy of $14,000 at Heritage Auctions in February of 2020.

2000 Lincoln Cent:
Broadstruck with a 50% Partial Reverse Brockage
on the Obverse Face with a Mushroom Split

The impact of the die strike with the additional struck coin on top of it lead to this coin stretching beyond its limits. Observe how the splitting which occurred has transformed this once symmetrically rounded planchet into a mushroom-shaped coin. The resulting partial reverse brockage on the obverse face is from an early stage, and you can see the that the incused and reversed ONE and the "CEN" from CENT are both clear and sharp with little warping. What looks fine horizontal scratches from 11 – 1 o'clock are actually the parallel lines of the Lincoln Memorial steps. Despite the severe trauma to this coin, almost none of the reverse designs are affected and appear as normal. (Scarce; $100)

Coin Trivia: At the entrance of the U.S. Mint in Philadelphia, a stuffed bald eagle named "Peter" greets all those who come through the main doors. Apparently Peter made the Philadelphia Mint his home periodically from 1830-1836. Unfortunately Peter got caught on a coining press that badly injured his wing as it began operating. He was not able to recover and died, but he his now memorialized and immortalized for all to see.

Undated Lincoln Cent (Copper):
Full Reverse Double Brockage on the Obverse Face

It's not every day you come across a coin that has the same design on each side. In fact when it comes to genuine same-sided U.S. coins, those where the same obverse or reverse die struck both sides are among the rarest and most expensive of all U.S. error types. At first glance it may appear to some that this coin is among that exclusive class as both sides of this Lincoln Memorial cent feature only reverse designs. *Is this error genuine?* Yes, it is. *So it's worth a fortune, correct?* No, it's not. Although it is a cool, genuine Mint error, it is not a coin struck with two reverse dies.

What we have here instead is known as a **full brockage**, which is a brockage that covers the entire face of one side of a coin. (In this case, because some of the outermost designs nearest the rims are missing, it is a full but "incomplete" brockage). *O.K., but how did the error happen on this coin?* A previously-struck coin remained in the striking chamber when an incoming, unstruck planchet entered along with it. The reverse side of the struck coin – acting as the obverse die and hindering a direct obverse die strike – rammed into the planchet's obverse side, while the reverse die made a direct strike on the reverse side; as such it left (dual) backwards-facing and incused designs of the reverse on the obverse side while the reverse side is normal. But because the Lincoln Memorial looks the same whether backwards or forwards (unlike a bust or an animal), you really need to take a closer look to notice the lettering is backwards and that it's a dual brockage. This coin is an early stage (but not a first-strike) brockage as the degree of warping is not that severe. (Much scarcer than partial brockages; $125; MS-64BN by PCGS.)

1918 Mercury Dime:
Mirrored, First-strike, Full Brockage of the Obverse Design on the Reverse Face
This beauty fetched $4,887.50 at Heritage Auctions on July 10, 2009.

Photos courtesy of Heritage Auctions/HA.com

Counterbrockages

Observe the overly-enlarged and ghoulish-looking head of President Lincoln – which is cut off at the top – as well as the missing letters "LIBE" in LIBERTY and an incomplete four-digit date. This coin also features a wire rim on the obverse, yet everything on the reverse is perfectly normal.

Coin Trivia: The Lincoln cent obverse design was designed by Lithuanian Jewish immigrant (though at the time it was part of the Russian Empire), Victor David Brenner. However, the name inscribed on his tombstone at Queens' Mount Judah cemetery reads "Avigdor ben Gershon" – his name in Hebrew.

19XX (Copper) Lincoln Cent Counterbrockage of the Obverse Design on the Obverse Face

A close cousin of a brockage is an error type known as a counterbrockage. Simply put, a **counterbrockage** error happens when a coin featuring a brockage error is rammed into a planchet. Whereas the brockage coin that struck the planchet has reversed and incused designs, the planchet with a counterbrockage strike will now have designs that are correct-facing and raised. However, there will be an increase in the warping of the designs as well as their expansion on counterbrockages as the brockage error continues to strike incoming planchets. It's very common on counterbrockages to see designs that have been cut off (e.g. partial dates, busts, etc.), while those which remain appear as only faint, ghostly, and distorted images of their former selves. You can sometimes find these raw and misattributed as a "brockages" rather than counterbrockages which are a much scarcer error type than brockages. (Very scarce; $90)

Below: This undated Liberty nickel with an obverse counterbrockage on the obverse face sold for over $4,000 in 2008 at Heritage Auctions. *(Photo courtesy of Heritage Auctions / HA.com)*

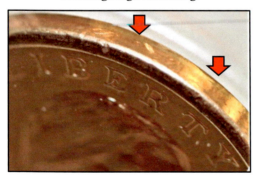

Missing Edge Lettering

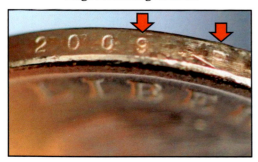

Edge Lettering Present

Missing Edge Lettering

2009 $1 Sacagawea "Three Sisters (Agriculture)" Variety: Missing Edge Lettering

Starting in 2009 with Sacagawea dollar coins, the Mint relocated the date, the mintmark, and the motto E PLURIBUS UNUM to the edge of the coin (this process started in 2007 for the Presidential Series). For some reason, the Schuler edge lettering machine was bypassed or malfunctioned and the motto, date, and mintmark on this coin are missing entirely (the same error occurred to many Presidential Series $1 coins starting in 2007). The comparison photos on the bottom left should give you a better idea of what to look for.

OK, so with no date, how do we know this is a 2009 $1 coin? Because the reverse image shown is the "Three Sisters (Agriculture)" variety for the Sacagawea dollar, and was only issued in 2009, thus an exact date can be designated. The only thing not known for certain is whether this coin was minted in Philadelphia or Denver.

Exactly how many were produced this way for each year is uncertain, but these are not hard to acquire for both the "Sac" and Presidential Series dollars. Additional edge lettering errors include "Weak Edge Lettering," "Doubled Edge Lettering," and "Doubled Edge Lettering – Inverted" along with a couple other variances, including the incredibly rare unstruck planchet *with* edge lettering. (Scarce; $50; MS-66 by PCGS)

Coin Trivia: The very first U.S. coin depicting an image of a Native American was the 1854 Gold $1 "Indian Princess." This one has particularly strong die clashes. (Photos courtesy of Heritage Auctions/HA.com)

1991–D Roosevelt Dimes: 50% Off-center Mated Pair Chain Strike

These two dimes almost look like they fit and go together. That's because they do! When two planchets are adjacent to each other (not fully or partially overlapping each other) and are then struck with the same die paring, it produces what's known as a **chain strike** (though NGC neglected to state that on either label for some reason). Of course, these are obviously struck outside the collar resulting in no reeding present on either coin. You may also have noticed the point where they would fit together is much more flat than round; this is due to them making contact with each other during the die strike.

Because these coins go together, they are also an example of a mated pair. *How is it certain that this pair was struck at the same time?* Perhaps the best answer is that they were discovered at the same time, most likely found in the same Mint bag. But beware! I often see people selling "genuine" mated pair chain strikes when they are not. It's not hard to match up different chain or off-center coins from the same denomination and have them appear to all be from the same strike. (Very rare; $375 for the pair; MS-64 for both)

Chain Strike Mated Pair

Coin #1 of 2

Coin #2 of 2

Edge Strikes

(No Date) Copper-plated Zinc Lincoln Cent: Edge Strike

Although at first glance one might think this is an unstruck planchet, it actually does have some design elements on it meaning it has progressed to being an actual coin. This error type is very rare with most of them being on cent planchets. (I have seen an edge strike on a struck nickel). What we have here is known as an **edge strike**, which transpires when a planchet enters the striking chamber and sits vertically rather than flat and horizontally. The dies then strike the edge of the coin rather than the broad and flat sides which are normally struck. Note the top right photo where you can see some designs very clearly including the lower right corner of the Lincoln Memorial and the top of the letter "T" in CENT found on the reverse of this Lincoln Memorial cent.

As to why this planchet did not bend significantly more or even fold over like a taco with a strike pressure of 65 tons, the answer is not clear. Maybe it was perfectly vertical (and not sitting at a slight angle) which caused it to act more like a brace to resist bending. Who knows, but theorizing about why it bent so little has *struck* up plenty of conversations. (Incredibly rare; $500; MS-66 by NGC)

Fold-over Strikes

1987 Copper-plated Zinc
Lincoln Cent: Fold-over Strike

Dear Lord! Beauty is definitely in the eye of the beholder concerning this poor thing, which suffered about as catastrophic an event as a coin can go through. This error type is a very close cousin of the previous coin, except instead of being struck on its edge and only bending slightly, it literally folded over and bonded to itself; these are known as **fold-over** strikes, with this one in particular exhibiting a hard shell taco-like appearance. You can also see a good deal of the zinc core very clearly as the striking process scraped away some of the thin copper plating.

How did this happen? Like the edge strike, a fold-over for some reason was sitting vertically in the chamber rather than sitting flat and the force of the die strike caused it to bend in half. Again, as to why this particular coin became a fold-over and the previous one did not is not entirely clear, though it could be due to exactly how perfectly vertical it was sitting in the chamber. *Was one leaning/slightly tilted and the other was sitting perfectly straight up on its side? Also, was one sitting more perfectly centered in the middle of the chamber while the other was off more to the side?* Possibly, but there is no way to know for sure for each coin. What we do know is that these are wildly popular, sell almost immediately, are more desirable when they are taco-shaped like this one, are astronomically rare, and even more rare with full, complete, and visible dates. As expected, Lincoln cents are the most available of any denomination, but even so there are only around a couple hundred that exist. (Very rare; $800; MS-63RB by NGC)

Coin Trivia: A "Fold-over" is an error type for both minted coins and printed paper currency. As you'd expect for currency fold-overs, a section of the paper was folded over and then the printing was added over top of the paper – including the folded area. This $20 bill featuring President Andrew Jackson was graded VF-35 by PCGS and sold for $504 at an April 28th, 2020 auction at Heritage Auctions. (Photo courtesy of Heritage Auctions.)

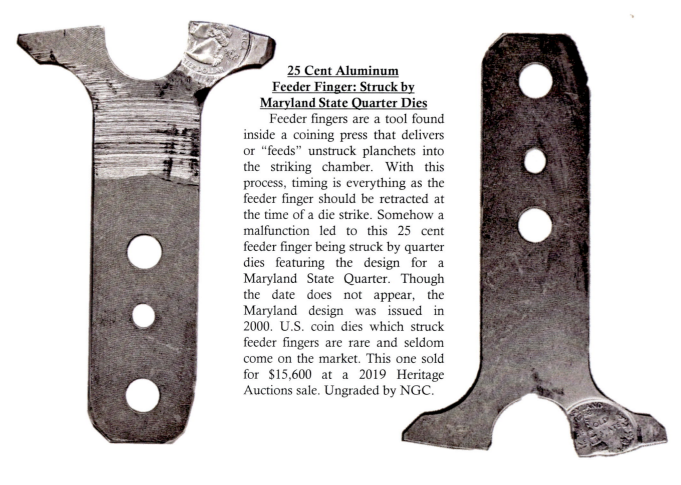

25 Cent Aluminum Feeder Finger: Struck by Maryland State Quarter Dies

Feeder fingers are a tool found inside a coining press that delivers or "feeds" unstruck planchets into the striking chamber. With this process, timing is everything as the feeder finger should be retracted at the time of a die strike. Somehow a malfunction led to this 25 cent feeder finger being struck by quarter dies featuring the design for a Maryland State Quarter. Though the date does not appear, the Maryland design was issued in 2000. U.S. coin dies which struck feeder fingers are rare and seldom come on the market. This one sold for $15,600 at a 2019 Heritage Auctions sale. Ungraded by NGC.

Magnetic (Steel) Washer: Struck by 1972-D Lincoln Cent Dies

I suppose it is conceivable that a washer – a donut-looking metal ring used both to prevent damage and to evenly distribute the force to an installed object – could wind up in a striking chamber. But then again it could have also been placed in a coin press purposely. What is truly amazing is that none of the designs on this "cent" are missing because this steel washer's diameter is pretty darn close to a cent's diameter. A few other washers struck with coin dies exist including a couple other cents, a nickel, and at least one Washington quarter. As for this coin, it sold for $4,887.50 at Heritage Auctions in 2017. Graded MS-64 by PCGS.

Photos for both featured "coins"
courtesy of Heritage Auctions / HA.com

Let's Review: What Are Some Possible Reasons Why My Coin Has Missing and/or Weak Designs?

Unstruck Blank/Planchet

Weak Strike

Rolled Thin Planchet

Split Planchet Before Strike

Grease Strike-through

Struck-through a Late Stage Die Cap

Full Indent/Full Uniface Strike

Struck on a Foreign Object

Severe Circulation Wear

Because few coin collectors truly study their coins or the minting process itself, it is understandable why so many don't know a genuine Mint error when they see one. All too often I see coins that are damaged, altered, completely fake, or are perfectly normal coins yet they're being offered for sale as genuine Mint errors or die varieties. In many cases the seller is simply uninformed and not actively trying to deceive potential buyers. Yet there are several bad apples out there who know darn well their "errors" are inauthentic and prey upon your ignorance for profit. Or perhaps it is you who finds a coin while you're coin roll hunting or looking through a collection given to you and aren't sure if one you come across is genuine. Many coins can resemble true Mint errors which are not. *O.K, but what are some tools, tests, and tips I can utilize to help give me a better idea if one is genuine or not?* Well, that is exactly why I included this section in the book. Now I don't have all the answers, and even the TPGs can be fooled sometimes. But hopefully you'll have a better grasp of what to look for and what each coin is telling you as you examine them for authenticity.

However, just because you learn your "error" coin isn't a genuine Mint-made error, that doesn't mean you should toss it. Having some fake, altered, damaged, and other categories of coins resembling genuine Mint errors are great resources to have. *Really? Why?* Because you can use these to study, compare, and educate yourselves and others on what to look for when assessing the authenticity of Mint errors. Lastly, you might want to hold on to some of your fake and altered coins because just like in the Art world, some of these "Black Cabinet" or "Dark Side" coins can actually be worth some good money!

Nope! These Aren't (or Shouldn't Be Considered) Genuine Mint Errors

Not every bizarre-looking coin is a Mint error. Below are some other categories your strange coin could be, so don't start popping champagne bottles as the odds are what you found isn't valuable. However, there's a slight chance even though it isn't a true Mint error it could still be worth some money. Some of these categories below will be explored in the pages ahead.

1. Enhanced/Assisted Error – *A genuine Mint error that was altered intentionally to make it more dramatic.* This is done to make the coin more desirable and valuable to collectors, so the intent is usually to con others. Squeezing a nickel's designs on an off-center cent to add a nickel brockage error to it is a good example.

2. Mint-assisted Error – *An error coin created intentionally at a government Mint by Mint employees, usually for personal profit.* One example which fits this description is a 2000 cent struck over a 2000 Virginia state quarter. Collectors debate whether these can be genuine "errors" since they were (a) created on purpose and (b) weren't authorized, yet they still sell for big money. However, despite the opinions of many conspiracy theorists in this hobby, the creation of Mint-assisted errors is incredibly rare.

3. Fantasy Coin – *A privately-minted coin that mimics a government-issued coin, yet it has features like a date, mintmark, and/or a design the government never issued or never officially released.* For example, Moonlight Mint owner Dan Carr produced 1963 JFK halves despite this series not starting until 1964, hence the term "fantasy" coin. He produces these by taking genuine silver halves and striking them again with dies he created (e.g. 1963 JFK half dollar dies) in a process known as **overstriking.**

4. Altered – *A genuine blank/planchet or struck coin minted by the government that was modified from its original form.* It could be from the result of accidental environmental damage, someone's boredom, or even intentional criminal mischief. Common examples include copper-plating steel cents and altering dates/mintmarks to mimic rare coins. Altered coins are considered PMD.

5. Counterfeit – *(A) A coin where both the planchet and the die strikes aren't genuine or (B) an unstruck blank or planchet that was not produced by the Mint nor its approved contractors; both were forged specifically to deceive and defraud others.* These are not produced for amusement like fantasy coins or replicas where collectors know what they're buying. Instead these pests are forgeries produced and sold to unwitting collectors who think they're buying the real thing. Some have even been slabbed by TPGs. Ugh!

6. Post-Mint Damage (PMD) – *This can take many different forms, but it normally encompasses any change or modification to a coin including its shape, surfaces (including plating, deplating, or the removal or other tampering of clad layers), the edges, lettering/numbering/designs, planchet make up, and color (except from natural toning) done after the last stage in the minting process was completed.* It can be anything from a staple scratch, to corrosion or staining due to prolonged exposure to a harsh environment, to improper cleaning, or even altering a coin. The list of what forms of damage there are and how they become damaged is endless. Lastly, it can be difficult to identify if damage (e.g. a scratch) on an error coin occurred before, during, or after ejection from the chamber.

7. Pareidolia – *A situation where your brain makes you think you see something which in reality is not there.* Examples include thinking you see a poodle in a rock formation, the Pope's face on a corn chip, or a swastika on a Roosevelt dime. (Come on! Do you really think the U.S. Mint would put a swastika on a U.S. coin?)

Both of these cents suffered post-Mint damage (PMD).

<u>Left</u>: Glue or some other adhesive has dried on this cent.

<u>Right</u>: This cent had direct contact and prolonged exposure to acid or some other form of a very corrosive substance.

8. Unauthorized Strike – *A genuine Mint-made planchet struck with government-made dies at a government Mint featuring a date and/or mintmark without government approval; these tend to feature dates that pre-date or post-date official mintage records.* For example, the five-known existing 1913 Liberty Head nickels are genuine in their composition and strike but were struck secretly by a rogue employee(s); the series officially stopped in 1912. (I've also heard they are actually altered "1912" dies where someone forged the 2 into a 3.)

9. Replica – *A coin intended to look like an original, government-minted coin; they're created for amusement purposes by a non-government entity.* Replicas often omit something found on genuine coins or the diameter was changed (top right) to help prevent their fraudulent use. They're also required to have the word "COPY" struck on them.

10. Restrike – *Coins struck with original, authentic dies but minted at a later date.* An example includes re-minting old Confederate coins using the original dies which struck them decades ago.

11. Patterns, Die Trials, and Experimental Planchets – A **pattern** *is a coin produced to evaluate a proposed new coin design.* A **die trial** *is a coin used to test a die or a pair of dies.* Lastly, **experimental planchets** *can include trying out new rim formations, surface finishes, and planchet compositions for new or existing coins (e.g. plastic, rubber, aluminum, etc.).*

12. Tokens and Medals: Both tokens (e.g. bus, gaming, and advertising tokens, etc.) and medals made to honor a person, place, or event can resemble coins with recognizable faces and patterns. However even those which do have errors (e.g. off-center) are not considered "Mint" errors because they aren't legal tender. The collection of tokens and medals is known as **exonumia.**

13. Your Coin is Normal! – I've lost count how many times someone posted an error or die variety for sale but the coin is 100% normal. One humorous situation is when sellers market "missing mintmark" coins like that 1965 dime (center right) and list them for hundreds or thousands of dollars. Just a few seconds of research would show that no coin denominations from 1965-1967 have mintmarks and that not until 1982 was the "P" added to coins (except cents). However, there is a non-proof 1982 "No P" dime die variety, and a few proof coins with a missing "S" mintmark. The Mint has also produced special commemorative re-issues of a retired series (e.g. Mercury dimes) on gold planchets (bottom right), which of course are not errors.

"Can you believe it? I'm going to retire after selling this U.S. Mint set struck on micro planchets! Yippee!"

Dear God...I really hope more people read this book than I anticipated. Ugh!

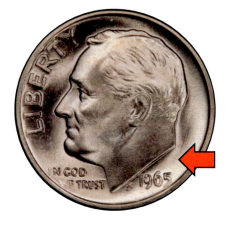

"Wow! I found a super rare 'No P' Roosevelt Dime! How Incredible!"

Sorry. It's just a normal 1965 dime.

"Amazing! I just discovered a super rare Mercury dime struck mistakenly on a gold planchet! Can you say 'Cha-CHING!!!'"

Sorry again, but this is not an error of any kind. In 2016 the U.S. Mint sponsored its Centennial Gold release of three coins struck on 24 karat gold planchets. These include the Mercury dime, Standing Liberty quarter, and the Walking Liberty half dollar. (A 2014 JFK issue was struck in .999 fine gold. *Images courtesy of PCGS® at PCGS.com/CoinFacts)*

Enhanced (a.k.a Assisted) Errors = Damaged

1967 Kennedy 40% Silver Clad
Half Dollar: 40% Split Layer Obverse

By now you should know why people purposely alter coins to appear as errors or die varieties. However, people have also been known to modify and alter genuine errors by (a) making the error more significant or (b) creating additional errors on them; these are known as **enhanced** or **assisted errors.** *Why would someone do that?* Isn't it obvious? More dramatic = higher selling price. I believe this is the case for this 1967 half dollar.

Notice the scratch marks on the JFK half indicated by the red arrows. I believe someone tried to pry off this obverse layer by using a pin or other sharp, narrow instrument. In my opinion, someone first started prying it at 2 o'clock, and then continued towards the center leaving additional scratches. However, the layer would not fully separate and then it started bending along the vertical line of separation; those raised lamination marks are evidence that it was bent backwards (blue arrow) and eventually it just broke off. Seeing that a completely detached layer as well as the remaining planchet missing the obverse layer are worth more than a simple clamshell error, I think someone thought it was worth the risk trying to completely detach it but failed. What was once a neat clamshell error thus became a split obverse layer via enhancing the original Mint error. I received a $53 refund from the seller after I pointed out it is now a damaged coin despite what is written on the label. Hopefully either the seller will inform the next buyer that it's damaged or a sharp-eyed collector will catch it.

1980-D Roosevelt Dime: Partially
Missing the Obverse Clad Layer (After Strike)

I believe this clad dime was also tampered with to try and make it a fully missing obverse clad layer, mainly because of what appears to be a ruptured puncture mark in the center of the coin in front of FDR's ear. Notice the entire edge of the curved region is raised up above the core which is highly suspicious and could have been the first point of contact to force the layer off completely. Although there are no tool marks or scratches on the coin like the JFK half dollar above, there are many objects – including toothpicks – which won't necessarily leave marks behind. In addition, observe the long, linear fold line that the top arrow is pointing to which runs from FDR's temple to the "G" in GOD. This line is sunken in and not raised, which is exactly what would happen if someone was prying off the clad layer and bending it backwards forcefully. In my opinion, ANACS totally missed this obvious sign of tampering. Like the 1967 half dollar, these are actually enhanced and therefore damaged errors.

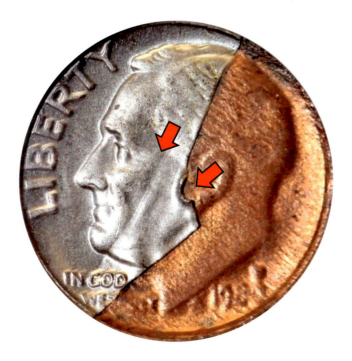

Mint-assisted Errors

2000 Lincoln Cent Struck on a 2000 Virginia State Quarter

How on Earth did this happen? Obviously a struck quarter re-entered the striking chamber and got struck a second time with cent dies. The problem is that quarter planchets are too wide to fit in a chamber set for cents. Thus the only way this got struck a second time by cent dies is that the chamber set for quarters had its dies replaced with cent dies. This scenario is too fantastic to believe, and the fact that there are cent dies which also struck other state quarters and Sacagawea dollars makes these reek of Mint-assisted shenanigans. Though these have been certified by grading companies as "Mint Errors," many collectors feel Mint-assisted errors don't meet the spirit of what it truly means to be a Mint error. Regardless, these go for big money.

The exact same error type on a New Hampshire state quarter sold for around $12,000 within the past year.

Photos courtesy of Heritage Auctions/HA.com

Fantasy Coins

1975 40% Silver Clad Washington Quarter

A 1975 quarter? Is this another unauthorized strike like the 1913 Liberty nickel? Or maybe a hubbing error with the wrong date? Not even close. Since the Mint never authorized nor produced quarters, halves, or Eisenhower dollars with a 1975 date, Moonlight Mint owner Dan Carr made them as "pretend" or "fantasy" strikes. He produced these by taking genuine coins and then striking them again with dies he made on a discontinued U.S. Mint Grabener coin press he acquired; coins like this are known as **overstrikes.** In fact you can even see evidence of the genuine first strike on Washington's face and the Drummer's arms. Though some collectors detest Carr for promoting and selling altered coins, he is upfront about what his form of art is and does not market these as genuine coins. ANACS even grades and slabs them. (Scarce; $80)

In addition to producing fantasy coins like this one, Dan Carr submitted several proposed designs for various U.S. coins including many for the State Quarter Series. Both his New York and Rhode Island reverse designs for the 1999 issues were accepted.

Altered Mintmarks

1922 "No D" Lincoln Cent? No!

Similar to how the 1937-D "3 Legs" Buffalo nickel error occurred, this 1922 "No D" cent had its mintmark removed accidentally as a result of over-polishing die imperfections caused by die clashes. Among Lincoln cent collectors, this Mint error (or die variety depending on how you define it) is one of the keys to the series and is extremely difficult and expensive to acquire in high grades. (There is a "weak reverse" and a "strong reverse" version, with the strong reverse being more desirable for Lincoln cent collectors.)

As is commonplace, someone either wanted a cheap filler coin to plug a hole in a Whitman album or tried to rip someone off by rubbing out the "D" mintmark below the date. Below you can see a depression in the mintmark area and along the rim in what is a very sloppy alteration. *(Genuine photos courtesy of Heritage Auctions/HA.com)*

**Altered 1922 "No D"
Lincoln Cent**

Highly desirable coins with rare dates and/or mintmarks should always garner much more intense scrutiny, especially when buying them raw.

Don't forget to always check a coin's rims (and the edges) carefully. Wear should be relatively even unlike this altered cent – a clear sign of tampering.

**Genuine 1922
"No D" Lincoln Cent
(Strong Reverse)**

1950-D Jefferson Nickel: Small Zero Variety? No!

The 1950-D nickel was at one time selling for a couple hundred dollars after coin investors hyped up their low production and hoped to capitalize on high demand keeping sale prices up. Large scale hoarding ensued by investors and the public, but some discovered a sloppy and rudimentary way of "finding" a 1950-D by altering 1958-D and 1959-D nickels to appear as zeros. (The featured coin here is from an altered 1959-D.) Ultimately the well-marketed hype and the reality of their availability years later saw prices come crashing down to Earth. Today Mint State 1950-D nickels can be had easily and for considerably less money – around $20 – much to the annoyance of those who shelled out almost ten times as much a few decades earlier.

Above: Observe how the "0" on the altered 1950-D (left) is the same shape as the top loop of the "9" from a 1959-D nickel (center). The "0" for a genuine 1950-D should appear as it does on the right. Like altered mintmarks, altered dates usually show depressions and/or raised areas as metal shifts.

The relative ease of me finding other altered 1950-D nickels lends me to believe this was quite a popular strategy to cash in on the hype.

Altered via Buffing/Grinding to Appear as Errors

1959-D Lincoln Cent:
Full Reverse Indent/Uniface Strike? No!

I see a lot of coins which look like this one for sale as "one-sided" or "full indent/full uniface strikes," but this one is one of the easiest calls that it's an altered coin. For one, it is not possible for a coin to only have a rim on one side if it was put through an upsetting mill. Notice even on genuine full indents/uniface strikes you can still clearly make out the raised rims (though not as defined as when they are struck). Second, there are clear abrasions all over the reverse side which were left by some sort of buffer or grinder. Third, if a significant amount of metal is removed from a coin it will greatly affect its weight. Fourth, the side (or sides) of a coin which was ground down will almost always have a much brighter appearance than the other side (if that other side was unaltered). Lastly, unlike coins that are ground down, many genuine full indent/uniface strikes have some degree of ghostly design transfer visible on the unstruck side; in some cases designs from both sides will appear.

Altered Full Indent/Full Uniface Strike

Rim is not present on the reverse.

Rim is present on the obverse.

Ghostly design transfer is not present at all.

One indicator that can often suggest evidence of a genuine full indent/full uniface strike is the presence of phantom or ghostly images of die designs (a.k.a. design transfer). Observe on the genuine full indent 1963-D cent below that you can make out both Lincoln's bust and the Lincoln Memorial clearly on the reverse side unlike the 1959-D cent above (though that's not always the case). It also has clearly-defined rims on both sides.

Genuine Full Indent/Full Uniface Strike

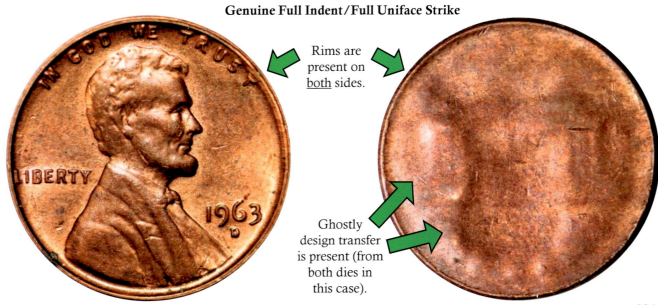

Rims are present on both sides.

Ghostly design transfer is present (from both dies in this case).

231

Altered Cents for Use as Dimes in Vending Machines

1957-D Lincoln Cent
and a 1964 Canadian Cent:
Struck on Foreign Planchets? No!

One of the most common altered errors I come across are cents which are smaller in diameter and lesser in weight. Many coin dealers/sellers attribute these erroneously as "struck on foreign planchets" while others claim these planchets were "punched out with dime-sized blanking dies." Though there are Lincoln cents struck on several different foreign planchets, this isn't one of them. What we have here is a cent shaved down to be the approximate weight and diameter of a dime; placing them in acid is another common trick (some even used both methods to get the weight and diameter as precise as possible). *Why would*

someone do that? Because sometimes these would fool juke boxes or vending machines into accepting them as dimes and rip off businesses. Seeing that a dime was worth about 85 cents in the early 1960s, perhaps some found it worth the trouble to alter them.

Canada's small cents – both copper and zinc – have been similar historically to the weight, composition, and diameter of U.S. cents; they've also been altered to use in vending machines in place of dimes. Notice both cents are close to the weight of both silver dimes (2.5 grams) and clad dimes (2.27 grams). Since cross-border trade/travel has been so open, it wasn't uncommon for either nation's altered cents to be found in their vending machines. Neither of these are Mint errors. Very sneaky, eh?

**1957-D Cent
2.6 grams**

**1964 Cent
(Canadian)
2.4 grams**

Altered for Use in Jewelry/Coin Art

1927 Lincoln Cent: Struck on a Foreign Planchet? No!

Some foreign countries do have some rather peculiar-looking planchet shapes used for coinage. I've seen square-shaped coins with rounded corners, coins with round or square holes in the center, and even those with wavy or "scalloped" edges like the Israeli 1 Agora coin below (bottom right). Therefore it's understandable someone thought this 1927 cent may have been struck on a foreign planchet; it's not.

Coins with squashed edges and rims that are uniform in shape like this one were likely once encased in some form of jewelry like a pendant, charm, or even cuff links. For example, on the bottom left is my 1902 $5 gold Liberty Head encased inside a gold rope bezel which can be worn as a charm on a necklace. I cant be 100% certain, but I think it's likely this 1927 cent was also once housed in a jewelry bezel as well. Unfortunately, though this cent looks like it could be an improper alloy error, the significant rim and edge damage from the bezel has stripped it of any numismatic value as an error coin.

An Israeli 1963 1 Agora Coin

Below: A 1902 $5 Liberty Head Gold Coin Encased Inside a Rope Coin Bezel

1946 Lincoln Cent:
Rim-restricted Design Duplication? No!

In addition to business cards and newspaper/magazine ads, one way companies and event organizers in the good ol' days used to promote their company or special event was to give away coins (usually cents) encased in specialized tokens. One common example of a token-encased cent is the "Good Luck" token seen below. This one in particular is promoting the 1901 Pan-American Exposition (World's Fair) in Buffalo, New York where event organizers encased a 1901 Indian Head cent inside it.

Anyway, it wasn't uncommon for people to remove the coins either to spend the money or to preserve them for their numismatic value. However, encasement often resulted in coins being physically damaged (e.g. rim flattening, token designs/lettering transferring to the coin, etc.). Though I don't know what type of token this 1946 Lincoln cent was in, you can see on the reverse from 8–12 o'clock that the token lettering has transferred to the coin.

Unfortunately, what some people think is a good example of rim-restricted design duplication doubling is really just a damaged coin. On the bottom right is a close-up of an actual case of rim-restricted design duplication that appears above IN GOD WE TRUST on the obverse of a 1994 Lincoln cent. *(Special thanks to Nick Reiswig for donating the 1946 cent to my collection of educational pieces.)*

<u>Right</u>:
1901 Indian Head Cent Encased in a 1901 Pan-American Exposition "Good Luck" Token

<u>Below</u>: Close-up of Genuine Rim-restricted Design Duplication (Machine Doubling) on a 1994 Lincoln Cent

Altered Coins via Staining to Appear as Mint Errors

1916 Barber Dimes (2): Struck on
U.S. or Foreign Copper Planchets? No and No!

A "copper" Barber dime would be an incredible and envious addition to any Mint error collection…if it were genuine! Stained coins often fool many people into thinking they were struck on the wrong metal, on a foreign planchet, or even improperly annealed. Though staining can be caused from prolonged exposure to a harsh environment (e.g. buried underground or underwater), it appears both of these Barber dimes were intentionally discolored (likely via wood stain) to make them appear as copper coins.

Someone also went through the trouble of attempting to file off the reeding on both coins, perhaps to make them appear as cent planchets since cents don't have reeding. However, the retaining collar for dimes is reeded. Regardless what coining metal a planchet consists of, it will have reeding if it fits inside a dime collar and is struck, so filing off the reeding actually made this "error" appear even less genuine. I think there may be several more of these out there as I found both of these in less than a week. Both actually scanned as 90% silver despite the staining. Fakes struck on counterfeit copper planchets also exist.

Right: Close-up of the weak edge reeding from the coin above. Because it is much more worn than the details on either side, I believe the attempt to remove it was intentional to try and make it appear as a cent planchet.

1964 Jefferson Nickel:
Missing Obverse & Reverse Clad Layers? No!

Too often I see brown, red, and rusty-looking nickels being marketed as "Missing Clad Layer" errors on auction sites (see bottom left photo). Unfortunately if you go through some auction histories on EBay you can see several people have been duped into buying them. The problem with these dubious listings is that normal nickels are alloy coins; this means different metals are melted together and bond to form one solid metal. U.S. nickels have never been composed of clad layers (except Mint errors like those struck on U.S. quarter stock or dime planchets), so they can't have clad layers missing in the first place. This 1964 Jefferson nickel is simply a normal coin that is stained and is not an error at all.

Special thanks to John Amirault for donating this coin for educational usage.

Below: There are thousands of incorrect descriptions of coins routinely plaguing auction sites, including this "1985-D Jefferson Nickel Missing Clad Layer." Sometimes it's tough to know for sure if a seller is being strategically dishonest or simply has innocent ignorance. Sellers who don't respond to your questions, claim to know little or nothing about the coin, and/or don't offer refunds should be avoided in my opinion. Though some auction sites will refund you if the coin wasn't described accurately, it's your responsibility to know what you are buying.

The 1976 nickel above has a wood stain stripe while the 1980-D nickel below looks to be partially covered with either brown paint or a wood stain. Neither of these are clad layer errors. *(1980 photo courtesy of Chris Rhodes.)*

1 of 3

1985-D Jefferson Nickel – Missing Clad Layer Mint Error! Unbelievable!

$10,800

Altered via Plating

**Altered
1944 Steel Cent
(Steel-plated Copper)**

Plating genuine coins is a common technique to fool others into thinking a coin is an authentic error (e.g. wrong and/or foreign planchet, off-metal, etc.). However plating a coin results in three main problems: (1) It can create an unnaturally shiny luster; (2) The wrong planchet/off-metal coin shouldn't be the same weight as the planchet it's normally struck on; and (3) Often the plating starts to wear away exposing the real planchet underneath, especially on the rims and design high spots.

Observe the genuine brown-colored planchet is showing through underneath the post-Mint plating of this 1944 cent.

**Genuine
1944 Steel Cent**

1944 Steel Cents:
Altered (Steel-plated) and Genuine Examples

Like genuine 1943 copper cents, authentic 1944 steel cents are impossibly rare and unaffordable for most collectors. For example, the genuine steel cent directly above sold for $30,550.00 in January of 2016 at Heritage Auctions. Much less challenging is finding a steel-plated/altered 1944 cent shown on the top row. Like many plated coins, over time the plating often starts to wither away from years of handling. For example, notice how the copper is showing through on

the close-ups of the altered steel-plated cent. Normally weighing these is a good first step as genuine 1944 steel cents should weigh very close to 2.7 grams vs. 3.11 grams for copper cents. However earlier I showed you counterfeits made from a steel alloy that weigh the exact weight of a genuine steel cent. Keep your guard up extra high for both 1943 copper and 1944 steel cents for sale as genuine off-metal errors, and remember some were also found in fake TPG holders. *(Steel cent photos courtesy of Heritage Auctions/HA.com)*

1943 Steel Lincoln Cent: Copper Plated

As far as Mint errors go, genuine copper 1943 Lincoln cents – as opposed to the very common 1943 zinc-plated steel cents – are incredibly rare and about as highly desired as you can get with only around twenty examples known in existence. Many collectors consider 1943 copper cents as the "King" of Mint errors, and even non-error collectors covet this most famous off-metal prize. Unfortunately, very few people on the planet have the cash on hand to purchase one regardless of the mintmark. *How much do they cost?* Well, the most recent one on the bottom row is a 1943-S which sold in 2020 for $504,000 (or 50,400,000 cents); it's graded MS-63BN by PCGS with a green CAC sticker.

With any field of collecting, rare and in-demand collectibles also draw the attention of swindlers looking to scam the ignorant, and both fake and altered 1943 copper cents have likely come into every coin dealer's shop at one point. Other common altered coins include the 1922 "No D" Lincoln Cent, the 1937-D "3 Legs" Buffalo nickel, the 1916-D Mercury dime, and many rare Morgan and Trade dollars to name a few.

How did genuine 1943 copper cents come about? Legitimate 1943 copper cents were once unstruck copper planchets that somehow got lost in machinery or stuck in coin bins during the changeover to steel planchets in 1943. Jarred loose, a few wound up among millions of steel planchets that were struck by 1943 dies and escaped into circulation.

How do they alter 1943 steel cents to look like copper? Altered examples such as this one are merely steel cents that were plated with copper. Although this cent is perhaps one of the better and more convincing altered 1943 copper cents at first glance (1st row), performing two simple checks can eliminate it as being genuine: It's weight and a magnet test. Sadly, not only does this cent stick to a magnet as do steel cents, but it weighs 2.7 grams which is what a genuine steel cent weighs; copper cents weigh 3.11 grams. So if you ever come across one of these, don't get your hopes up!

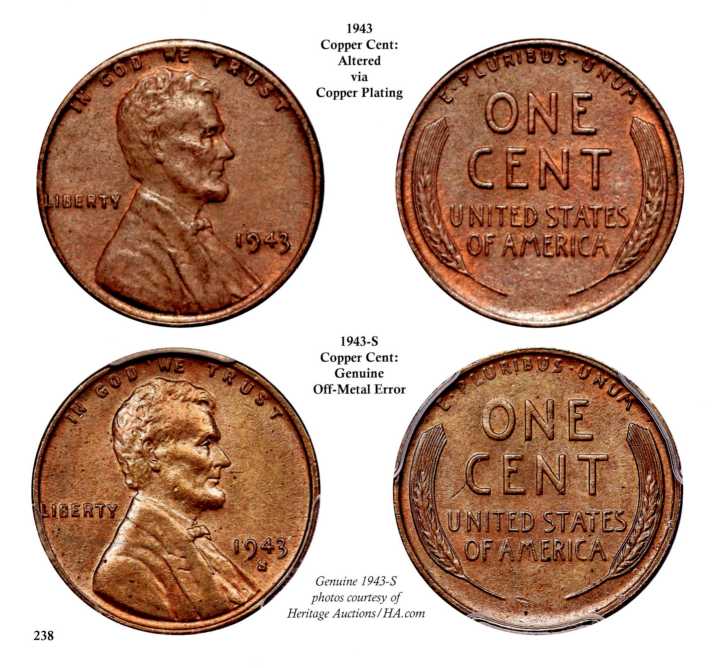

1943 Copper Cent: Altered via Copper Plating

1943-S Copper Cent: Genuine Off-Metal Error

Genuine 1943-S photos courtesy of Heritage Auctions / HA.com

1958 Lincoln Cent:
Plated to Resemble a Foreign Planchet

For several decades the United States used to mint coins for many other nations including countries like Saudi Arabia, Belgium, Australia, the Philippines, and several Latin American countries such as Panama, El Salvador, and Cuba. Just as leftover off-metal planchets caused mistakes like 1943 copper and 1944 steel cents, the same premise occurred with leftover foreign planchets in bins mixed with planchets geared for striking U.S. coins.

However, the luster on this coin is abnormally shiny and doesn't look authentic. In addition, for as little wear as there is I thought the fine details should be a bit more pronounced. After scanning this coin my suspicions were correct that it is a plated copper cent resembling a foreign planchet error. A genuine gold-colored 1959 Lincoln cent struck on a Philippine 10 Centavos Planchet is provided below, owned by yours truly. Notice designs are cut off as the 10 Centavos planchet is slightly smaller.

Altered Cent to Appear as a Foreign Planchet (Plated)

Genuine 1959 Lincoln Cent Struck on a 10 Centavos Philippine Planchet

Coin Trivia: The U.S. Mint actually had one official minting operation outside the continental United States – the Philippines – which ran under U.S. control starting in 1920 – and produced some Filipino pesos and various denominations of centavos. It stopped minting Filipino coins in 1941 after the Japanese occupied the islands during World War Two. The U.S. continued to strike some Filipino coins back in the U.S. up until 1978.

1962 Lincoln Cent: Silver-plated to Resemble a Cent Struck on a Silver Dime Planchet

Wrong-planchet errors are very popular with more affluent error collectors, and I even know a couple people whose collection is limited to that error type alone. This 1962 Lincoln cent was being offered as a cent struck on a silver dime planchet, which in MS grades can run approximately $850. At first glance I had serious doubts this was a genuine wrong-planchet error. *Why is that?* For starters, because dimes are smaller in diameter than cents, some designs/lettering are almost always missing; this one has all designs/lettering present. The coin should also be the same weight as a silver dime which is 2.5 grams; this one is 3.2 grams which is about the normal weight of a copper cent. I then had it scanned on a metallic scanner which showed its silver composition was negligible. Thus in just a couple minutes I proved that this coin is simply a silver-plated copper cent.

**Silver-plated
Copper Lincoln Cent**

Observe how the genuine cent on dime planchet below has designs cut off closest to the edge including IN GOD WE TRUST on the obverse. The above coin has no missing designs at all.

The genuine coin below weighs 2.5 grams – the weight of a silver dime. The above coin weighs 3.2 grams which is slightly more than a copper cent; this strongly suggests it was plated.

**Genuine 1962 Cent on
Silver Dime Planchet**

*Genuine photos courtesy of
Heritage Auctions / HA.com*

2005-P Oregon State Quarter: Stuck on a 90% Silver Business Strike Planchet? No!

The 50 State Quarter Series which launched in 1999 through 2008 was among the most profitable ventures undertaken by the U.S. Mint. It seemed almost everyone from kids to adults, men and women, experienced collectors to novices, and speculators to hobbyists all put forth effort into finding each mintmark for each state. In addition to circulated coinage, the Mint also issued clad and 90% silver proof sets for all states. (This has continued for the District of Columbia and U.S. Territories series in 2009 and the America the Beautiful series from 2010-2021.)

Of course the craze of this wildly popular quarter series brought with it opportunities for marketers to issue their own sets with a few twists and creative packaging. Private companies including those advertising on late-night TV infomercials and shopping channels sprang up to advertise "special collector sets" where these were plated in platinum, gold (bottom left), and silver (right column) as gimmicks to bump up prices

and profits. The plating was usually around .003 inches thick with negligible if any metallic value. Technically from a numismatist's perspective these are actually considered "damaged" and worth only face value. But so long as these weren't advertised as "silver" or "gold" coins and it was stated they are "plated" on the packaging (see below), it's the buyer's responsibility to read the fine print.

As for this Oregon state quarter in particular on the right, a friend of mine asked me if this could be a genuine silver error since the edges are silver-colored and the surfaces have convincing luster. Seeing that 90% silver state quarters were only minted (a) in San Francisco with an "S" mintmark, (b) on proof planchets, and (c) weigh 6.25 grams, it was an easy call that this 5.8 gram business-strike quarter is clad. Keep in mind the edges on unaltered clad coins can still appear as all gray depending on how the layers were rolled, but don't rule out these were once part of marketed sets or that they were simply altered by sinister, undignified malefactors looking to pull a fast one.

Above: Close-up of the plating on the reeded edges on the 2005 Oregon State Quarter.

Below: A set of privately-marketed 24 karat gold-plated State Quarters issued in 1999.

1965 Roosevelt Dime: Plated to Resemble a Silver Dime Planchet Transitional Error

When the U.S. Mint makes major changes to coins, mistakes can and do happen periodically. As we have seen so far, some blunders can be blatantly obvious while others have gone unnoticed for several years or more. For instance almost everyone would notice an unstruck dime if they were placing loose dimes in rolls, but I bet few people would notice if a 1965 dime – which is supposed to be on a clad planchet – was struck mistakenly on a silver dime planchet. *Why?* Because both clad and silver coins are similar in color. 1964 was the last date that dimes, quarters, and half dollars minted for circulation were on 90% silver planchets. Starting in 1965, dimes and quarters were produced on non-silver clad planchets, while halves were minted on 40% silver clad planchets from 1965-1970; they, too, switched to non-silver clad in 1971. Yet a few 90% silver coins minted with 1965 dates (and others) do exist. One was found in circulation after 40 years!

Coins like 1965 silver dimes and 1943 copper cents are known as **transitional** errors. With this error type the issue is not the planchet size or thickness, nor was it struck with an incorrect die pairing. However it was struck on a planchet with a different metallic makeup that was (a) intended for the previous year or (b) it was intended for a year or years to come (e.g. a 1964 clad dime). If you consider that both the Philadelphia and Denver Mints were producing 1964-dated dimes (and some other coins) through 1965 and even into 1966, you could say it practically invited opportunities for transitional errors to occur. Like wrong-planchet errors, leftover planchets stuck in bins or the coining press that became loose and mixed in with other planchets are plausible causes.

Nevertheless, the real "error" here is thinking that the 1965 dime on the top row is a genuine transitional metal error; it's not. Like many other coins people think are Mint errors, Mr. Roosevelt has been plated to merely appear as a rare and very expensive 1965 silver dime struck on a 90% silver planchet. Genuine post-1964 silver dimes should weigh what a silver dime weighs – 2.5 grams – which is slightly heavier than clad dimes at 2.27 grams. Because the color and even the weight difference is only slight between non-silver clad and 90% silver coins, it is easy to see why few people out there would notice one from the other. Perhaps it also explains why many transitional metal errors wind up with grades lower than MS because they remained unnoticed in circulation for so long. *How much is a genuine 1965 silver dime worth?* The one on the bottom left (AU-58 by NGC) sold recently for $8,400 at Heritage Auctions on September 10th, 2019 .

Plated to Look Like A Transitional Error

This coin on the top row has a highly-suspect surface finish with its unnatural color and luster, and yet has high points which are flat and dull; these are strong indications of plating. *(Special thanks to Steven Leary for the donation of this dime.)*

Genuine 1965 Transitional Error Struck on a 90% Silver Planchet. *(Genuine photo courtesy of Heritage Auctions/HA.com)*

Below: A close-up of the edges can also detect clear evidence of plating as the recessed areas of the reeding may appear "filled in."

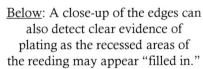

2000-P Ohio Statehood Series Quarter: Reverse Plating to Resemble a Missing Clad Layer Error

The Statehood, D.C. & U.S. Territories, and America the Beautiful Quarters Series are some of the most popular issues to collect, and many error collectors I know try to complete the series with missing clad layers. (Layers missing on the reverse are more popular as the reverse designs are what's different on them.) Since everything collectible can be faked or altered, and because MS missing reverse clad quarters can be worth several hundred dollars each (or more depending on rarity), you need to be cautious buying these uncertified.

Whether done innocently or with the intention of scamming people, many coins offered for sale as "missing clad layers" are either environmentally damaged and/or stained (e.g. metal detector finds) or were altered intentionally (e.g. use of acid, plating, etc.). For example, this 2002 quarter was listed as a "Missing Reverse Clad Layer" by a dealer friend of mine. I noticed immediately the color didn't look right as it does not look like copper. As usual my first test is to weigh a coin. A quarter missing one clad layer should be about 5.39 grams, but this one weighs 5.8; that's .13 grams more than a normal quarter! This led me to thinking the reverse side was plated, and my scrutiny of the edges confirmed it. I don't know what the plating consists of, but what really matters is that this is an altered quarter. Thankfully the dealer is honest and won't be offering this altered coin for sale as a genuine error.

Below: Genuine Missing Reverse Clad Layer
(Photo courtesy of Heritage Auctions/HA.com)

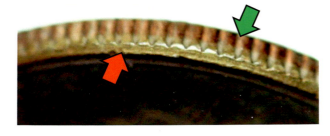

Above: Red arrow = plating;
Green arrow = actual copper center

Below: Actual weight of the suspect coin

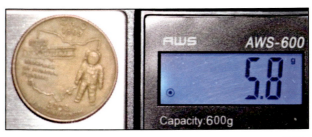

Plated and Deplated Zinc Lincoln Cents

2012 Lincoln Shield Cent:
Plated to Resemble an Unplated Cent

Because non-error cents are worth so little, there is no real financial risk in trying to alter them to appear as genuine errors. One way is to plate them with gray-colored metals in an attempt to get them to resemble unplated errors, some of which can sell for over $200. However plated coins tend to look unnaturally shiny and the plating tends to fill in areas of sharp details making them softer in appearance. Often you can also see evidence of the copper underneath as you can on this coin, including on the rims as seen on this 2012 Shield cent.

1985-D Lincoln Shield Cent:
Deplated to Resemble an Unplated Cent

Along with plating a coin, zinc cents are also altered by deplating them to look like genuine unplated errors. Harsh chemicals like acids normally leave telltale signs like a significant loss of Mint luster, a drastic reduction in the sharpness of details, and signs of pitting/corrosion on highpoints including the rims. Like plated cents, oftentimes you can see some evidence of the original copper plating which used to be there, including on the rims as seen here.

**Genuine Unplated
Zinc Lincoln Cent**

**Altered
Dual Missing
Clad Layers**

1966 Roosevelt Dime: Dual Missing Clad Layers

Coins missing clad layers are highly collectible because of how eye-catching and scarce they are. Dual missing clad layers are exponentially more difficult to find and easily reach $1,000.00 or more depending on the grade. (Only fewer than ten on dimes are known, and some are struck on pre-damaged planchets). Trapped gasses, bad mixtures, impurities, or a combination of some or all of these factors is normally what causes an outer layer to detach from the planchet either before or after striking.

What we have above was not caused by any of those circumstances; it was altered, presumably by being placed in an acid. The warped rims and fuzzy details pretty much give this away as an acid-treated coin, and it

was one of my first lessons learned about how to tell a coin was altered. (Keep in mind details will be sharper if the clad layer was missing before striking, and tend to be softer if the clad layer separates post-striking). Of the few genuine dual missing clad layers I have seen on dimes, most were struck on planchets which were damaged *before* they entered the coining press; these can still get to around $750. (This is one of those cases where the term "damaged" must be used with caution. Exactly *when* the damage occurred – before or after striking – makes a huge difference for error collectors; post-Mint damage is a death knell for many of them.) Fortunately an honorable seller refunded my money on this altered coin and even said to keep it as a memento.

**Genuine
Dual Missing
Clad Layers**

*Genuine Photos
courtesy of
Heritage Auctions / HA.com*

Altered to Appear as a Ragged Fissure/Planchet Defect

1903 Indian Head Cent:
Altered to Resemble a Ragged Fissure

Ragged fissures are particularly peculiar anomalies and are among my favorite errors. Denis McGinity sent me this 1903 Indian cent below to examine and at first glance I got excited for him. Unfortunately upon further review under a 5X magnifying loupe it took me just a few seconds to disqualify it as a genuine error. In fact, it isn't even a genuine error that later became damaged. Simply put, it is a damaged coin someone sliced with metal shears leaving it to look like a ragged fissure. *How*

do you know for sure? Because part of the raised lettering, most noticeable on the "R" in AMERICA on the obverse, slopes downward (red arrow); this would have to mean the die also slopes downward, which of course it doesn't. You can also see flattening of the rims (blue arrows) and a small additional matching cut mark at 3 o'clock, possibly from a tool that was gripping it as the coin was being cut. For comparison, a 1959 Lincoln cent with a genuine ragged fissure has neither downward sloping raised designs nor flattening of the rims.

**Close-up of the Altered
1903 Indian Head Cent**

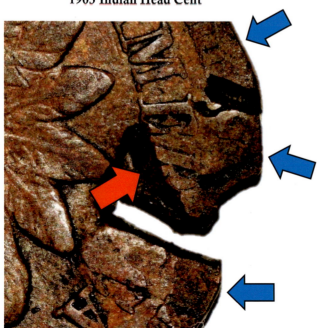

**Close-up of a 1959 Lincoln Cent
with a Genuine Ragged Fissure**

No Downward-
sloping Designs or
Flattened Rims

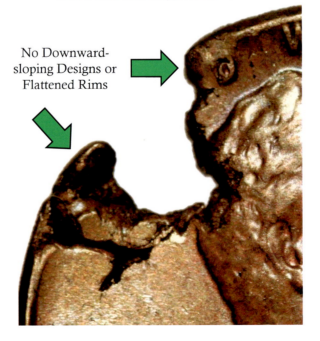

Vise Job to Appear as a Dropped Letter

1983 Lincoln Cent: Obverse Struck Through a Dropped Letter "B" on Forehead

Dropped letters/numbers are truly amazing error types and are extremely rare. In this case, it appears the letter "B" in LIBERTY was filled with grease, fell off, and was rammed into the planchet on Lincoln's forehead (See Close-up #1). However in Close-up #2, you can also see some of the other letters in the word LIBERTY, which instead indicates it was likely pressed against another coin either intentionally (e.g. a vise job) or possibly unintentionally. Either way, we can't ignore the evidence; it is not a dropped letter error. By comparison, the dropped "8" below (bottom right) is genuine and some of the filling is actually still retained on the eight's lower loop.

Close-up #1

Close-up #2 – Notice how the other letters in LIBERTY show up in a linear pattern on high points, likely from being pressed against another struck cent.

Genuine Dropped Filling Error (Dropped "8")

This is a close-up of the reverse from a 2007-D Utah Statehood Series quarter. Notice between the "T" in UTAH and above the raised "8" in 1896 you can see a phantom "8" recessed into the planchet. With dropped filling errors, sometimes the struck-in grease can remain in full in the affected area, other times it leaves a "clean" recession with no filling retained, and like this coin it can even leave only a portion of the impacted grease behind. *(From the collection of Shannon McCord; photographed by Joe Cronin.)*

Coin Trivia: Another way scammers modify coins to appear as dropped-letter errors is to use a hammer and a punch or a counterstamp kit similar to the one below. However, most sets have letters much larger and with different serifs than what would normally be seen on coins, but they are not impossible to create so they can look authentic. (Photograph of the counterstamp punch kit courtesy of Ed "Paddyman" Padilla.)

Vise Jobs to Appear as Brockages

2017-P Lincoln Shield Cent: Double-struck with an Obverse First-strike Brockage from a 2002 Lincoln Memorial Cent, and a Reverse First-strike Brockage from the Reverse of a Lincoln Shield Cent? No!

It shouldn't take you very long to find fake brockage strikes on genuine coins as you peruse some popular online sites. What's even scarier is searching the purchase histories on those sites and seeing what people have paid for them. To not get duped in buying forged brockage errors like this 2017-P cent, it is incumbent on you to actually envision in your head how an error like this could have occurred if genuine. To do that, you need a general understanding of the minting process from start to finish. You then need to ask questions like, *"At what step of the minting process would the error(s) have occurred? Is this error even possible? Even if it is possible, is it likely? What does the physical damage (whether it's Mint-caused or not) tell you about the coin? Could I have forged this myself? If so, how? How does it look in comparison to other genuine examples? Do other known, certified examples even exist to compare it to?"*

There are so many troubling features on this coin that it shouldn't take you more than a minute to know the brockages are fake. For example, the likelihood that this coin has two first-strike brockages – one on each side – is beyond ludicrous despite being theoretically possible. Also, the 2017-P die strikes had to come first. So did it not eject from the striking chamber, and then these two previously-struck cents not only (a) entered the chamber with it, but (b) they sandwiched this coin *and* (c) all three fit perfectly inside the retaining collar for another strike? If they were all squarely inside the collar, why is part of the rim damaged? And exactly how did the 2002 cent get in there in the first place? Was it floating around inside that striking chamber for 15 years? Perhaps it was stuck inside the coining press, came loose, and landed in the striking chamber at the *exact same time* these two other coins were in there? Was there no unstruck planchet fed into the chamber while all this happened? Hopefully it is blatantly obvious that all of these brockage strikes were forged post-Mint.

Unfortunately altering genuine coins to produce fake brockage errors is simple, and you likely have the tools to forge them right in your own home. I used the vise below to forge the above coin. How I did it is explained in the diagram to your right.

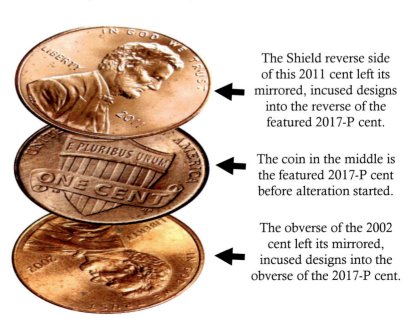

The Shield reverse side of this 2011 cent left its mirrored, incused designs into the reverse of the featured 2017-P cent.

The coin in the middle is the featured 2017-P cent before alteration started.

The obverse of the 2002 cent left its mirrored, incused designs into the obverse of the 2017-P cent.

Altered to Appear as an Indent From a Dime Planchet

2000-P Washington Quarter; State Quarter Series, New Hampshire: Indented In-collar by a Dime Planchet? No!

I don't know exactly what the person who made these alterations was trying to do or why, but it was for sale at $125 as a "dime planchet indent" when I came across it at a Buffalo-area coin show. After I had a very cordial conversation with the dealer, he was convinced there's no evidence this New Hampshire Statehood quarter had a dime or other denomination's unstruck planchet rammed into it, at least not at the Mint. However there is evidence another quarter was hammered into it, but not on the reverse where the indents are.

To me it looks like someone placed another quarter under this one and then used a hammer to smash in an obverse brockage; it also explains the indents on the reverse where the hammer would have made contact. (Evidence of the brockage can be seen on Washington's neck with incused, warped lettering.) If a smaller-sized dime planchet were struck in-collar into a planchet in the coining press, it would look similar to the reverse side of the 1935 Quarter below. Notice the rims are not corrupted with an in-collar strike and there are no clear, sharp, or even worn details where the indent is. Why would there be since it didn't come into direct contact with a die to leave them there? As for how an unstruck dime planchet got in the striking chamber with that 1935 quarter, it could have been left in a bin that later had quarter planchets poured into it, or was stuck in machinery, jarred loose, and landed in the press with it. (I was allowed to keep the altered coin so long as I promised to include it in my book, though I vowed to keep the dealer's name private.)

2000-P Quarter: Altered to Try and Resemble an Indent from a Smaller Planchet

1935 Quarter: Genuine Indent from a Dime Planchet

Observe the differences in what the opposite sides of the indent look like. Genuine examples generally maintain their normal shape as both the collar and dies help prevent coins from expanding and warping.

1935 genuine photos courtesy of Heritage Auctions/HA.com

Same-sided Coins

1954/1964 Two-headed Jefferson Nickel? Yes, But Altered

On occasion I have people asking me if their two-headed or two-tailed coin is real, and I have seen just about every U.S. denomination in existence with two heads/tails. Though an error like this two-headed 1954/1964 nickel could occur theoretically, the likelihood of a two-headed coin with two different dates is unlikely to the point of being ludicrous. However, PCGS actually certified a real two-headed 2000-P nickel (bottom row), but there's only one known to date plus three known two-tailed U.S. coins.

This 1954/1964 two-headed nickel was made from real nickels that were ground down and bonded together with some form of epoxy or glue. The dead giveaway here is the edge where you can see a clear dividing line separating the two, plus having dates a decade apart is also highly suspicious. If no line is present, it could be from having one coin hollowed out while the other was slightly ground down and dropped inside the other. Two-headed and two-tailed coins are often created as **magician coins** for amusement only and not to deceive error collectors.

Altered Two-headed Nickel

Obvious uneven wear from one side to the other is a good sign your same-sided coins aren't genuine.

Left: Coins made from casts or cut in half and glued together often have clear seams which genuine coins shouldn't have.

Genuine Two-headed Nickel

This 2000-P Jefferson nickel, which sold for $20,520 at Heritage Auctions in 2018, is the only known genuine two-headed U.S. coin. (PCGS MS65)

2000-P two-headed nickel photos courtesy of Heritage Auctions/HA.com

Altered to Appear as a "Mule" Error

(2000)-D Sacagawea $1 Reverse Muled with a Statehood Series Washington Quarter Obverse? No!

Though genuine mule errors aren't the most expensive error coins ever sold, they're about as rare as they come. The few dollar/quarter mules known to exist have sold for over $45,000. One reached $192,000 in March of 2018! *What is a mule?* Well, silly, a mule is a crossbreed of both a horse and a donkey!

OK, seriously, a **mule** error exists when a coin is struck with mismatched dies. Some possibilities include a coin with two obverse dies, two reverse dies, or with one side featuring one denomination (a dollar) and the other side featuring a different denomination (a quarter). For example, both coins featured on this page are examples of mules, albeit one is altered (top row) and the other is genuine (bottom row). *How did the genuine mule error occur?* An inattentive Mint worker(s) simply paired the wrong obverse die denomination – a Washington State Quarter Series obverse die – with the correct Sacagawea reverse die and then struck some manganese dollar planchets meant for Sacagawea dollars (exactly how many is unknown, but so far only eighteen have been discovered and certified by grading companies as of this writing).

Mules can be a relatively easy error to fake with the right tools. *How was this altered one on the top row created?* Someone hollowed out the obverse side of a Sacagawea dollar, then filed off the reverse side of a Washington quarter, plated the quarter to match the color of the dollar, and used some form of epoxy to bond it to the dollar. *But since the coin weighs only .1 gram off (8.2 instead of 8.3) and the color is kind of close, how can you tell it was altered?* (1) The quarter side has a raised rim as it sits inside the planchet, but that area should be recessed into the coin; (2) The outside rim of the planchet is flat and not rounded like all known genuine examples; and (3) there are no known Denver Mint examples of this error type. Diagnosis: Altered. *(Genuine mule photos are courtesy of Heritage Auctions/HA.com)*

Altered (2000)-D Sacagawea Dollar Struck with a Washington Quarter Obverse Die Mule

Genuine (2000)-P Sacagawea Dollar Struck with a Washington Quarter Obverse Die Mule

251

1995 Roosevelt Dime Struck with a
Lincoln Cent Obverse Die: Mule Error

Below is a cent – I mean a dime...wait...What is it? Struck with the obverse die of a Lincoln cent yet paired with a Roosevelt dime reverse die, this fascinating (and genuine) coin is one of the other few known mule errors among American coins. To be precise, this coin is technically a dime, and to be even more precise it is a cent on dime mule. *Well isn't it also by default a dime on cent mule?* The answer is simple: No. *Why?* Because the planchet is a clad dime planchet – not a zinc cent planchet, and that makes a difference because it's the obverse die that is wrong. (There are two known dime on cent mules struck on zinc cent planchets: 1993-D and a 1999). This mule graded MS-64 by NGC was sold in January of 2010 at Heritage Auctions for $57,500.

*Photos courtesy of
Heritage Auctions/HA.com*

2014-D $1 with a Sacagawea Obverse
and a Presidential Series Reverse: Mule Error

This is the only known mule of a Sacagawea dollar combined with a Presidential Series dollar. The reverse should be the "Native Hospitality" design. However since the Mint produced both series in 2014, if this were meant to be a Presidential Series coin the obverse should feature either Warren G. Harding, Franklin D. Roosevelt, (John) Calvin Coolidge, or Herbert C. Hoover. This amazing discovery piece was certified and graded AU-58 by NGC in January 2021. Being the only one known to date, despite an AU grade it could likely fetch over $100,000+ at an auction. And of all the known U.S. mule errors, this is the only one where the planchet is the same regardless of what series it was for as well as each side being the same denomination as the other. It's a Sac-adential dollar!

*Photos courtesy of
NGC® at NGCcoin.com*

Genuine Mint-struck Coins Altered with Fake Die Strikes

1943 Lincoln Cent Struck on a 1943 Mercury Dime: Double Denomination (Altered via Fake Cent Dies)

Like rare non-errors, rare and unique errors which make headlines and sell for big money will eventually be copycatted by opportunistic forgers. At some point these pests always will make their rounds on dealers' tables and auction sites with sellers either knowingly or unknowingly pushing these as genuine. (Always be even more cautious if uncertified). Some are so good that even experienced collectors and dealers get fooled. TPGs have even slabbed a small number of fake and altered coins! Yikes!

1943 Lincoln cent errors and die varieties are among the most popular and expensive coins with many being financially out of reach for most collectors. For example, in the second row is a genuine 1943 Mercury dime that was then struck by 1943 Lincoln cent dies; this double denomination sold for $33,600 at an August 2018 auction on Stacks & Bowers' website. However, there are several forged specimens of that coin floating around, including the one in the top row. Though it is a genuine 1943 Mercury dime, it was overstruck by counterfeit 1943 Lincoln cent dies. If not for the partially misshapen rim and some flattened designs, this one is a pretty decent alteration that would likely fool a lot of people, but it was an easy call for authenticators at NGC who rejected the submission.

Altered Cent on Dime
Double Denomination

Genuine Cent on Dime
Double Denomination

Genuine photos courtesy
of Stacks & Bowers®
at StacksBowers.com

The Good, the Bad, & the Very Ugly:
Other Genuine Coins Struck Again with Fake Dies

1963 Washington Quarter Struck Over a 1963 Roosevelt Dime: Double Denomination

This is a very "good" attempt to make one of these rare errors, but both the weakness of the quarter's details and some of the lettering just don't match up to a genuine strike; it's simply an altered dime. *(From the Fred Weinberg collection; Photographs by Joe Cronin.)*

1977 Lincoln Cent: Triple Struck, Rotated In-collar on a Dime Planchet

Since rims don't get flattened on in-collar strikes, and because this coin weighs slightly more than a cent (3.3 grams), this "bad" boy was not only clearly struck with two fake die strikes, but to go even further it was plated with an unknown metal; it's just an altered cent.

1964 Jefferson Nickel: Double-struck, 2nd Strike Off-center, Flipover Strike

Can you see Jefferson's face (left) on the reverse side and an upside-down Jefferson Memorial (right) on the obverse? Notice its disfigured shape and extreme flattening on both sides; it was struck at least once with fake dies. I have seen multiple similar examples of these "ugly" 1964 nickel errors hit with fake dies, possibly all made by the same person.

1960-D Lincoln Cents (3) Double-struck/Multi-struck & Rotated In-collar Coins: A Very Common Altered Date via Fake Dies

The worst part of this hobby for me is telling people – including even experienced dealers – that their errors are simply altered coins. Just because you see multiple strikes with raised designs, it doesn't mean what you have is genuine.

1960-D (and 1964) cents are among the more common altered cents from the 1960s I come across, specifically those which are rotated-in-collar double or multi-struck errors like these three coins here.

It is possible the same person used a set of fake 1960-D Lincoln cent dies to forge extra strikes on all three coins, and it is highly likely several more exist. (It took me less than a year to find these three). Look for warped rims and soft details on the additional strikes as these are possible signs a rotated in-collar strike isn't genuine.

1957-D Lincoln Cent Struck Again (Post-Mint) with Crystal Club and Montesano Smoke Shop Token Dies

Genuine U.S. coins struck over previously-struck, privately-issued tokens are astronomically rare. In fact they are so rare that all known examples could easily fit in one hand. (All known examples are also very likely Mint-assisted errors.) However there is a big problem with this 1957-D Lincoln cent that proves it isn't genuine. *What's the problem?* Answer: The token's die strikes – on both sides – are *on top of* the cent's designs. *OK, but what does that prove?* This proves the cent was struck first and the smoke shop strikes came after. Since the U.S. Mint never made "Smoke Shop" tokens nor had the dies to make them, the overstrike error couldn't have happened at the Mint; it is a post-strike alteration.

The best explanation is that since token dies are cheap and readily available, someone used one token die to strike the obverse side of this cent and a second die for a different token to strike the reverse.

Token experts told me the markings overstruck on the obverse side of the 1957-D cent (top left) match those for a "Crystal Club" Casino token (top right), likely for the casino's smoke shop. (I was told it was located in Nevada, possibly the Reno area). However the markings on the other side of the Crystal Club token (bottom right) don't match those found on the reverse side of the cent (bottom left). Instead, those markings match designs for one of the many smoke shop tokens in the Montesano, Washington area. I guess this cent won't be *lighting up* an auction.

Special thanks to Steven Leary for donating this coin for educational use.

Did the U.S. Mint ever strike a U.S. coin on a token planchet? **Yes! See an example on the next page.**

Token photos courtesy of Richard Greever at TokenCatalog.com

1970-S JFK Half: Struck Over a Shell Oil Company "States of the Union: Missouri" Aluminum Token

As a promotion for their gas station customers in 1969-1970, Shell Oil Company had the Franklin Mint produce various aluminum tokens to collect. One such gimmick was the "States of the Union" Coin Game, where if certain groupings of U.S. state tokens were all acquired, a customer could redeem them for cash prizes ranging from $1 to $5,000. Somehow a very small handful of these Shell tokens wound up being struck at the San Francisco Mint, including some JFK halves like this 1970-S and an Eisenhower dollar. Seeing proof coin production is so much more controlled, it's highly likely these were intentionally struck and should probably be considered Mint-assisted errors.

This coin in particular was struck on the "Missouri" issue Shell Gas aluminum token. In fact, above the word DOLLAR on the reverse you can make out most of the word MISSOURI. You can also just barely see the "M" in GAME on JFK's cheek and some of the circular rings on his face and in the fields on the coin's obverse. Graded PR-62 by PCGS. (This coin went unsold at a January 2021 Heritage Auctions sale, though I estimate its value at around $3,500.)

JFK photos courtesy of PCGS ® Used by permission at PCGS.com/CoinFacts

Actual Shell Oil Company "States of the Union: Missouri" Coin Game Aluminum Token

(No Date) Indian Head Cent: Struck 60% Off-center

One of the many dirty tricks forgers use to try and make their fake and altered coins more convincing is to use genuine unstruck blanks and planchets rather than to produce their own fake ones. Acquiring unstruck type 1 blanks (no raised rims) and planchets (rims added) that were intended to be minted as 95% copper cents, copper-plated zinc cents, nickels, and non-silver clad dimes and quarters are neither difficult nor expensive with some being only a few dollars each. Silver blanks and planchets, or those on denominations no longer minted that aren't silver (e.g. large cents, half cents, steel cents, etc.) can be a bit more tricky to find and prices shoot up as denominations rise. For example, unstruck silver dime planchets go for around $30, silver quarters for around $100, and silver dollars can be around $1,000. But since major errors (e.g. off-centers) on Trade, Morgan, and Peace dollars can reach hammer prices well over $15,000, many forgers will assume the financial risk if it can lead to monstrous profits.

In addition to simply having the coin metal look like it is the proper metal (for example, many older silver coins have toning, but there are even ways to induce and fake that as well), producing forged coins on genuine unstruck blanks and planchets will show proper compositions if they are analyzed on industrial metallic scanners. Thankfully grading companies do more than just "scan" a coin before they authenticate them, but I have been at several shows where a dealer will simply scan a coin that "doesn't look right," yet not question anything else if the metal content is kosher.

Checking the edges of coins is equally important to help authenticate them. After being punched out by the blanking dies, unstruck blanks do not have rims until they are added later via squeezing them in an upsetting mill. Thus type 1 blanks should have a rough and "squared" edge as if they were torn out of the planchet strips (which they are). During the upsetting process, that rough texture is smoothed out and the edges are more "rounded." This is another reason why some forgers only want genuine blanks and planchets because it is difficult to not only make your own planchet metal, but also to have the tools and know-how to punch out blanks and add realistic rims to them. A majority of counterfeit coins on fake planchets have the appearance of a rim, yet the edges are rough like a type 1 blank – a dead giveaway they likely aren't real.

The greatest difficulty in forging a coin is producing quality fake dies. Creating them with extra fine details along with known die markers is just too challenging and time-consuming for most people. For example, this undated Indian Head cent appears to look good at first glance. Though it is on a genuine planchet and appears Mint State, the denticles, feathers, hair, and wreath are much too soft and undefined. The lettering on the obverse also has problems as some letters are tripled or even quadrupled while others are not. Despite using a genuine copper cent planchet to try and fool others, it simply does not pass muster after examining the die strikes closely. *(From the collection of Fred Weinberg; photos by Joe Cronin.)*

Fake Die Strikes on Genuine Unstruck Planchets

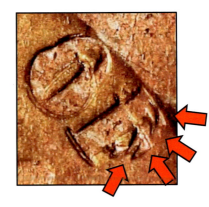

Somehow only the word "OF" has four sets of letters while no other letter on the obverse has more than two. This is very strange and highly suspect indeed.

(1964) 90% Silver JFK Half Dollar: 60% Off-center with an Obverse Brockage on the Reverse Face

Coming across off-center silver half dollars doesn't happen too often, and when/if it does it's unlikely you've seen many this far off-center with a dramatic brockage of the obverse side on the reverse face. Despite the date missing, only 1964 JFK halves were struck on 90% silver business strike planchets, so a specific date can be identified (though there are a few transitional errors with other dates struck with 90% silver by mistake). The trouble is that although the planchet is genuine and is 90% silver, it was struck with fake JFK dies. We can therefore assume the brockage is not genuine either (meaning these striking errors did not occur at the Mint).

PCGS error authenticator and nationally-respected Mint error specialist, Fred Weinberg, informed me that several 1960s error coins – including silver Washington quarters and JFK halves – "started surfacing in Southern California in the late 1960s." It is not known exactly who made them, but these are above average fakes and would likely fool most collectors and dealers. Genuine and extreme half dollar errors like these, especially on silver coins, sell easily for $900 and up; proof errors regularly reach multiple thousands of dollars.

Obverse

Reverse

Below is a JFK Half dollar struck on a nickel planchet. Strangely, it not only features a brockage of the obverse on its reverse side, but was also struck a second time off-center by the reverse die of a Jefferson nickel; it also lacks an obverse die strike on the opposite side. This coin is also likely part of that 1960s fake and altered coin error dump that first hit the Southern California market in the late 1960s. *(From the personal collection of Fred Weinberg; photos by Joe Cronin.)*

Counterfeits

I know that for years many numismatic experts have expressed the opinion that a counterfeit die strike on an genuine, unstruck planchet (e.g. the JFK half and Indian cent on the last two pages) constitutes a "counterfeit" coin. However, as I stated before, in my opinion a coin in its totality really shouldn't be considered a "counterfeit" if its base – the planchet – is itself genuine; I feel the term "altered" should be used. At the very least, in a case like that it should be noted that only the die strikes are counterfeit, not the coin itself as a whole (just as I did for the previous two coins). To me, a true **counterfeit coin** is one where both the planchet *and* all the die strikes are inauthentic. For example, all of these coins in the right column are not only made of lead but weren't struck by any dies at any U.S. Mint. Absolutely nothing about these coins is genuine and thus they're 100% counterfeit.

Now what's the difference between the terms "counterfeit" and "forgery?" I guess that really depends on who you ask. In my opinion, **forgery** means to intentionally produce a copy or imitation of a genuine product and then market that product as an authentic item to consumers. In this respect, altering a genuine coin by adding or removing a mintmark to make it more valuable is just as much an act of forgery as it is to make one of these 100% fake lead coins. Others distinguish the specific intent of the forger. For example, some feel the word "counterfeit" is more appropriate if the coin is made to be used in commerce, while "forgery" should be used if someone is producing it in order to scam a collector for far more than just its monetary value. Again, it really depends on your point of view on what term is best so long as other people understand what you mean.

1963-D Jefferson Nickel, 1952 Roosevelt Dime, 1974 Washington Quarter, and a 1976-D Bicentennial Eisenhower Dollar: Struck on Lead (Counterfeit) Planchets

Off-metal errors? Not a chance. What we have here are counterfeit coins made out of lead, but it isn't hard to find coins like this for sale as genuine Mint errors. Many lead fakes are made via casting as it is an incredibly soft and inexpensive metal, and sometimes you can even see a raised line along the edges where the casting plates separated. Because they're cast and not struck with fake dies, details are incredibly soft and undefined. Lead-based coins can also tend to have a very distinctive "white metal" look to them. Since none of these are rare dates or were created to mimic other errors, it is likely these were produced to be used as cash in business transactions to rip off retailers.

Coins Struck on Lead Planchets

1963-D Jefferson Nickel

1952 Roosevelt Dime

1974 Washington Quarter

1976-D Bicentennial Eisenhower Dollar

1866 Indian Head Cent: 40% Off-Center – 100% Fake

Though the lettering and numbering style – including the serifs – and many of the designs are not terrible, this coin has several red flags. Like many forged coins, notice by comparison how the fake (lower left column) has very weak details on the headdress feathers, the lines on the top of the shield, the wreath's leaves, and even the denticles unlike the genuine coin (lower right column). Both would be considered Mint State, yet the fake has way too many soft and weak devices which should not be on an MS coin. The rims on the fake are also inconsistent and even lacking on some of the unstruck area, yet it doesn't meet the diagnostics for a type 1 blank either. Raised bumps on the obverse are equally troubling.

Close-ups of the Counterfeit Off-center 1866 Cent

Close-ups of a Genuine 1866 Cent (Non-Error)

Genuine coins with denticles normally show a consistent pattern throughout (thickness, spacing, height, etc.). Forging uniform denticles on a die is one of the hardest features to replicate and is a good place to examine closely. Though errors like off-centers can distort some details (e.g. stretching) including denticles, it doesn't explain the differences in their width and spacing.

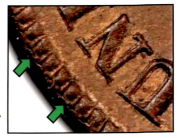

261

1955 Lincoln Cent: Doubled Die Obverse and Struck 15% Off Center – 100% Fake

Incredible! Not only is this the most popular and coveted die variety of the 20th century, it is also 15% off-center! *Did I manage to find a discovery coin? Can it actually be real?* The answer to both questions is a resounding "No!" First, let me say that when a major die variety like a 1955 doubled die cent also happens to be a major Mint error like this one, the chances of it being authentic are incredibly slim. Second, it fails some pretty basic diagnostic tests for being genuine: (a) The rim pattern on both sides is uneven; (b) The edges of the coin should be smooth if this were a true planchet with raised rims, not looking punched and torn as blanks do with a rough surface (see close-up photo below); (c) It has very uneven wear as the letters and date are very strongly defined, yet Abe's face is mushy and lacks detail; and (d) The color doesn't look right. Copper coins do tone some very interesting colors, but this one stands out as very unnatural. So even though the diameter is good and the weight is close at 3.09 grams, visually this coin screams fake and should be an easy call for most experienced dealers and collectors.

However even if this coin were real, there are still a couple issues that would make it difficult to sell. One is that those who collect expensive rare dates and die varieties like a 1955 doubled die cent generally do not want flawed or "problem" coins (e.g. stains, scratches, or those containing Mint errors which by definition are considered flawed); most collectors want their rare date coins "clean" (i.e. free from flaws). Another issue is that most error collectors care more about the type of error and how dramatic the error looks. The fact an error is on a low-mintage or key date coin is irrelevant to most and they won't pay extra for that. Thus sometimes major errors on desirable and expensive rare coins can be a much tougher sell to both error and non-error collectors alike. Now would I love a genuine off-center 1955 doubled die? Absolutely!

It's very likely the same (Chinese) counterfeiting operation which produced the off-center 1955 Doubled Die also produced this off-center 1909-S VDB below.

Though this planchet appears to have a raised rim, notice the edges are rough and have a torn-looking appearance; they should be smooth. This is usually a good sign a planchet/coin is counterfeit, which this 1955 DDO cent is.

1955   **1C**
ICG - NOT GENUINE

Dbl.Die Obv.,Off Center

1974 Aluminum Lincoln Cent – 100% Fake

As the price of copper rose during the Vietnam War era, Mint officials had two major concerns that soon (1) it would cost more to make a 95% copper cent than they were worth and (2) people would hoard copper cents and sell them as scrap. The Mint thus started looking into alternative metals, one of which was aluminum. So in 1973, the Mint produced about 1.5+ million 1974-dated experimental aluminum cents (some had a "D" mintmark; there were also about 66 with a 1975 date). To gain support, a few Mint officials and select members of Congress were given some. The idea was soon rejected partly because of concerns that they wouldn't work in vending machines nor show up on x-rays if swallowed. The Mint demanded all examples be returned and were later destroyed, but about a dozen are still unaccounted for. In fact, these aluminum cents are one of the few U.S. coins that are illegal to own and subject to seizure because they were never "officially" released and no one at the Mint had authorization to take, keep, or give them away.

Though the coin on the top row is aluminum and weighs only .03 grams less than a genuine 1974 aluminum cent (.937 grams), the mushy details on Lincoln's face and missing designer initials on the obverse make this an easy call that it is a fake. (I acquired the fake cent from China.)

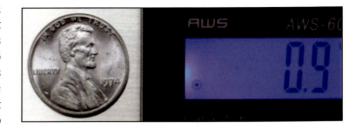

Coin Trivia: In 2016, Randall Lawrence from San Diego was told to surrender his 1974-D aluminum cent to the U.S. Treasury which he acquired from his father (a former Mint official). The story is featured on an episode of Fox Business Network's Strange Inheritance titled "Pretty Penny."

Counterfeit 1974 Aluminum Lincoln Cent

Genuine 1974 Lincoln Cent Struck on an Experimental Aluminum Planchet

Used by permission PCGS ®
www.PCGS.com / CoinFacts

1888 Liberty Nickel with Clashed Dies
Dies: Struck on a Foreign Planchet? Nope!

Even to an experienced collector, this Liberty nickel doesn't really stand out as a fake unless you take the time to examine it much more closely. For example, weakness at the end of LIBERTY on her crown, soft details on the wreath and some of the reverse lettering, and inconsistent denticles on both sides along the rim should draw one's suspicion; it also only weighs 4.1 grams instead of 5 grams and is not within tolerance. At first I thought it could be struck on a foreign planchet (there are several known examples) because details and designs can have weak spots on such coins, but other diagnostics simply didn't add up to known, genuine examples. However, one interesting feature about this fake is that it has significant die clashing on the obverse which you don't see too often on counterfeit coins. It is my opinion that the clashing was accidental and wasn't created to market this as an error; both the planchet and die strikes are 100% fake. *But would why would someone fake this particular year?* In terms of mintages 1888 didn't have the lowest production level for this series, but Mint State coins can fetch well over $300 – certainly high enough to drive someone to fake them. *(Die clash overlay created by me.)*

Clash marks can be seen surrounding Lady Liberty's head.

Coin Trivia: Within the entire Liberty nickel series from 1883 – 1912, only its last year of 1912 had production at Mint facilities outside of Philadelphia; they were also produced in Denver and San Francisco. Even the controversial 1913 date (of which there are only five known) was only produced in Philadelphia.

1895 Liberty Nickel: Double-struck 50% Off-center? Yes, But it's 100% Fake

Error collector or not, just about everyone loves dramatic-looking double strikes – including the Chinese counterfeiters who are always making them! In case you haven't already picked up on it by now, there is a reason why China seems to get the brunt of the blame for most of the fakes plaguing the U.S. and world coin markets: Because they deserve it! In fact, China is notorious for counterfeiting almost everything from fake bottles of Dom Perignon champagne to New Era caps to U.S. coins, and every world government and major corporation knows it. As a former U.S. Customs inspector in the Port of Buffalo, NY, I can attest I have seen both declared and smuggled counterfeit merchandise originating from China on several occasions for several name brand products; our government only finds a fraction of what actually gets through. With the U.S. being the number one consumer culture in the world, and Chinese counterfeiters making millions of better and better fakes each year, it's no wonder why so many of their counterfeit coins wind up here.

As far as coins go, Chinese counterfeiters are permitted to continue making fake coins so long as they are all dated before 1949 (the year when communist China was founded under Mao Zedong.) In addition, counterfeits made in China are not required to be marked with the word "COPY" unlike those produced in the U.S. This is why taking the time to study U.S. coin minting processes is critical including understanding things like metal flow, die markers, and other key diagnostic indicators.

This double-strike could easily fool beginning collectors and even many long-time dealers, but like the 1888 Liberty nickel on the previous page, both the planchet and the dies which struck it aren't genuine. Details on some of the lettering, Liberty's hair (obverse), and the wreath (reverse) appear much weaker than they should. In addition, the off-center strike has what appears to be a mirrored proof-like finish while the first strike does not and the denticles are not uniform in size or shape. Lastly, the shape and serifs on the date appear to be off compared to genuine 1895 nickels (see comparison below).

Coin Trivia: This series is also known as the "V" series for the Roman numeral "V," which of course is the number 5.

Red arrows = different widths; Purple arrows = different shape loops; Blue arrows = different serifs and lower positioning; Green arrows = protruding bottom loop of 5 instead of rounded.

Close-up of the date on a genuine 1895 nickel. *(Photo courtesy of Heritage Auctions / HA.com)*

Close-up of the date on this counterfeit 1895 Liberty nickel

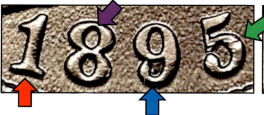

265

Nail Struck with 1907 Barber Dime Dies

Below is yet another example of someone copycatting a widely-publicized crazy error. Below is a 1907 Barber dime struck on a nail. I actually own two, and a friend of mine owns another. Now the fact that there are several of these known to exist should be all you need to know these are fakes. In addition to that, one has to ask whether or not this exact style of nail would have been used in the early 1900s. (It turns out rounded, flat-head nails similar to this one were being produced beginning in the 1890s, but the specific cut of the nail, its metal content, and if it is plated – and if so, with what – would have to be researched and compared to known examples from that era.) Also, the fact that this nail has very little rust for being over 110+ years old makes it highly suspect (although this fact wouldn't immediately disqualify it just for that reason. After all, there are ancient Roman coins a couple thousand years old in existence that are considered to be almost uncirculated and even Mint state).

There are a handful of genuine coins struck on screws and nails, including Lincoln cents, Roosevelt dimes, and Washington quarters. *OK, but were these produced as Mint-assisted coins by Mint employees as the cents struck on quarters are, or are they genuine errors produced and released accidentally?* Though you're always going to have skeptics, nationally-known Mint error experts insist there was no funny business in their production. *How would a screw or nail wind up in a striking chamber?* I have read reports that screws could likely have been loosened over time during the striking process and fallen into the chamber, and also that nails had been used to pry off stuck planchets blocking and jamming the coining press. So, theoretically it is at least plausible as to why and how screws and nails would have landed in the striking chamber by accident. On the bottom right is a nail struck with 2000 New Hampshire Statehood Quarter Series dies that was sold by Mint error dealer Jon Sullivan for an undisclosed amount. (Some experts suspect this is a Mint-assisted error.)

Nail Struck by Genuine 2000
New Hampshire Quarter Dies
(Photos courtesy of Sullivan Numismatics)

(No Date) Trade Dollar:
Struck on a Dime Planchet? No!

What are Trade dollars? A Trade dollar is a special unit of American currency produced from 1873-1878 (with proofs being produced through 1883; a handful of 1884 and 1885 proofs were also discovered) mainly for overseas trade in China and the Far East. *Why didn't American merchants just use Morgan silver dollars?* Because Chinese merchants preferred the Mexican silver peso which had more silver than U.S. Morgan dollars. This meant merchants had to exchange Morgans for pesos and pay expensive brokerage exchange fees. In response, the U.S. government started minting Trade dollars which now contained slightly more silver than the Mexican peso. The concept was a huge success as it became the preferred silver coin in Asia and was approved as legal tender in the U.S. However, increased silver mining flooded the silver market, devalued the Trade dollar, and so it was later discontinued.

As for the chances of this "error" being genuine, I'd say they're about as good as finding a set of hen's teeth. To suggest that significantly thicker dollar planchet metal was fed into a press set up with dime blanking dies and then struck – perfectly centered – by U.S. Trade dollar dies is incredibly far-fetched. Unfortunately these are readily available from Chinese merchants and sold on popular online shopping sites, so don't be fooled into thinking they're real. Some are even silver plated to further convince you they're authentic. Morgan examples also exist.

The 1873-CC Trade Dollar shown here helps put the featured coin in perspective. Though it tested as 90% silver, this complete 1873-CC Trade Dollar is also 100% counterfeit.

Obverse

Reverse

Edge View

267

1884-O Morgan $1: 10% Off-center – 100% Fake

Despite being what many collectors feel is one of the most unattractive designs of any circulated U.S. coin in history, Morgan dollars are exceedingly popular in the numismatic community. (It also explains why there are so many fakes.) Not many people can complete a genuine set as there are several key dates and mintmarks which are quite expensive. However even fewer can afford major errors on silver dollars, including those two coins below, which would be several thousands or even tens of thousands of dollars if they were genuine. This coin may be the same weight, diameter, and thickness of a genuine Morgan, but it has no luster at all and is not silver. In addition to other flaws on it, it has full edge reeding; this would not be possible as it would have been struck outside the retaining collar (see explanation on the next page).

1893-S Morgan $1: Double-struck 65% Off-center – 100% Fake

A genuine 1893-S is so rare that even a lower grade of Very Fine can be around $5,000, but this double-strike is a forgery. Everything from the denticles to the toning is fake. It's tough to estimate a value if it were genuine because many error collectors won't pay more just because the date is rare, and many non-error collectors don't want errors on rare coins.

Coin Trivia: Morgan dollars were once nicknamed the "Buzzard" dollar as people felt the eagle on the reverse looked more like a buzzard than an eagle.

Clues that Edge Reeding Can Tell You About Genuine Off-center Coins

Coins featuring reeded edges have the reeding pattern adding during the striking process. The pattern is located on the inside of the retaining collar (below). As the planchet is struck, it expands very slightly and presses the edges into that reeded pattern. Thus the retaining collar for coins with reeded edges serves two main purposes: (1) Preventing expansion/maintaining symmetry and (2) applying the reeding pattern.

A U.S. Dime Reeded Retaining Collar

Close-up of the Reeded Inner Ring

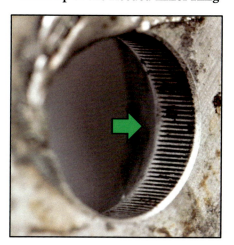

Genuine off-center coins struck completely outside the collar should have no edge reeding at all like the dime on the lower right. Though it is possible for planchets struck partially inside the collar to have some edge reeding, it should be weak in some areas with other areas missing completely. Seeing that the off-center 1884-O Morgan dollar (top right) has complete reeding throughout – which is impossible – it cannot possibly be a genuine strike; the planchet also is not silver.

**Fake Off-center
1884-O Morgan $1 (Edge Reeding)**

**Genuine Off-center 1990-D
Roosevelt Dime (No Edge Reeding)**

Straight Clip

Ragged Clip

90% Silver Dime Type 1 Blanks (No Rim); Various Clips – 100% Fake

Many error collectors love the incomplete and freakish look of clips. But there's something to be said about silver and gold Mint errors which have that added attraction simply because they're made from precious metals. *But are these silver dime blank clips in fact made with silver?* Yes, they are, and they're actually 92% silver (plus 3.5% copper and 2.5% tin; the remaining combination was a list of over 15 different metal types all less than .5%, which is common when scanning metals). For those that can have their diameter measured, they're the same diameter for a silver blank. *So then I guess it's a no-brainer that these have to be genuine, right?*

Wrong! Thanks to the great memories of a few long-time error collectors and professional authenticators, a few of them contacted me directly after I posted the ragged clip online (center left) and delivered me some bad news. Apparently during the late 1960s in Southern California, counterfeit silver dime planchet strips were being made by someone or possibly a group of people. From those fake silver dime strips came many various unstruck types of clips including ragged, curved, and even those with both types on them. PCGS Mint error authenticator Fred Weinberg told me on the phone that "all of a sudden" these "fake silver type 1 clips flooded the market" and drew quite a bit of attention. But with hype and attention comes deep study and skepticism. Word got out that these were nothing but clever fakes and people started to catch on. *But how did the counterfeiter(s) create such convincing fakes?*

Some people have told me these are something a very capable and experienced jeweler could make, including producing silver sheets and using punches to cut out rounded blanks. As for the ragged clip look, supposedly by rolling out non-annealed silver ingots, eventually the ends of the strip will start to crack and split apart resembling ragged clips, and from that you punch out your blanks to create what you see here. (Thankfully, I paid very little for it.) Clearly the seller didn't know these were fake and had even less of an idea what a genuine error like this would sell for. But it was a good learning experience and I even bought three more just to showcase the many kinds of clips that were faked: Ragged clips; strait clips; curved clips; and combinations of multiple clips all on one blank. Unfortunately, a few counterfeit clips made from the fake silver planchet strips wound up getting slabbed by some TPGs as genuine pieces.

Ragged Clip & 2 Curved Clips

Ragged Clip & 2 Curved Clips

Special Feature: "Some Fakes are More Equal Than Others"

There is no doubt that fake and altered coins made to duplicate rare collectible coins – including errors and die varieties – are victimizing numerous collectors and investors every single day. Dealers I know tell me they see fakes coming into their shop several times a week. Recent published media reports indicate counterfeiting rings inside China alone are producing fake U.S. coins and bullion (both in bar and coin form) to the tune of hundreds of thousands per month. In addition, they are also counterfeiting certificates of authenticity, U.S. Mint packaging (boxes, inserts, wrapping, etc.), CAC stickers, and even slabs, labels, and holograms from professional grading companies. To complicate things further, many of these coins have the same weight, diameter, thickness, metallic make up, and Mint luster as genuine coins.

However, there is something you can do to help yourself avoid being tricked by this dark side of numismatics (and what some people refer to as **black cabinet** coins). Despite that some may find my recommendation unpopular, I strongly urge all collectors to acquire some fake and altered coins to study, especially from a series you collect. (I'm willing to bet most of you reading this already have a few, but hopefully not for nefarious purposes.) *Wait, isn't this promoting the problem and incentivizing people to fake and alter coins?* Absolutely not. There is a huge difference between acquiring some to educate yourself and acquiring them to sell as genuine coins to scam people. They aren't hard to find, and you might have a few friends or trusted dealers who might give or loan you some to evaluate.

Once you have some, compare them to your genuine coins or from high-definition photos you can view on the PCGS and NGC websites. Scrutinize numbering, lettering and mintmarks (e.g. shapes, spacing and placement, serifs, etc.), and the sharpness of fine details like hairstyles and feathers on birds. Look for known **die markers** on coins – flaws and imperfections on dies that transferred to coins; these can include attributes like die chips, cracks, abrasions/polish lines, clashes, gouges, etc. (I highly recommend John Wexler's website "Wexler's Die Varieties" at *DoubledDie.com*. Among other great features, it has photos of several die markers for numerous coins). Interestingly, there are many mass-produced counterfeits which can also be identified by specific die markers. Above all, what's most important is that you share what you have learned with others. Knowledge is useless if it isn't shared, which in this case can help protect others and improve the hobby overall.

With all this being said, though 99.9% of fakes are equally worthless in terms of their numismatic value, there's a very small number of them which can be worth money; in some cases even hundreds of dollars. Thus if I may borrow and modify a line from George Orwell's *Animal Farm*, you can say that "some fakes are more equal than others." Just like in the Art world, occasionally a fascinating story behind a known fake can draw the appeal of collectors and drive up prices, especially if there is a known forger. Presented next are five "black cabinet" coins that made national headlines and – for better or worse – became an infamous part of American numismatic history. Details surrounding a few of their stories include humorous marketing strategies, design blunders, a brilliant attention to detail vs. great detective work, and if you can believe it, even murder!

1944 "No P"
Jefferson Nickel

Which of these three fake FIDOs is worth some money?

1937-D
"3 Legs" Buffalo Nickel

1942/41
Mercury Dime

The Mysterious Case of the "Hofmann Mule" Cent: 1959-D Wheat Reverse Lincoln Cent

Arguably one of the most controversial coins in American numismatic history in terms of its authenticity is a disputed Mint error known as the "Hoffman mule" cent. Though the coin on the top row is a replica of it, the one on the bottom row is the "real" thing, and by "real" I mean the "actual" Hofmann mule cent. *O.K., what's the error here?* In 1959, the Lincoln cent premiered its new reverse design – the Lincoln Memorial – in honor of both the 150th year since Lincoln's birth and also the 50th anniversary of the Lincoln cent's commencement; it replaced the "Wheat" design which was minted from 1909-1958. However, this is the only coin known since 1959 to still have the Wheat reverse pattern. Thus it is considered a "mule" coin because it was struck with a pair of mismatched dies. *A handful of genuine mule coins do exist, but is this one genuine?* The alleged forger, Mark Hofmann, says it isn't and grading companies refused to certify it as being authentic. Yet forensic examiners at the U.S. Treasury stated it is genuine on two separate occasions. *So, is it genuine or not?* Before we get into that debate, it is important to first learn exactly who Mark Hofmann is and what he did that thrust his name into this intriguing story of deception, forgery, and even a double homicide. Truth really is stranger than fiction here in a fascinating case that totally shocked and absolutely horrified America.

During the early-mid 1980s, a rare-documents treasure hunter and dealer in Salt Lake City, Utah named Mark Hofmann gained notoriety by "discovering" historically significant early Mormon Church documents (including Mormon paper currency), some of which served to potentially change the course of Mormonism's recorded history. In addition, he seemed to somehow come up with very rare documents featuring signatures of America's Founders and signers of the *Declaration of Independence*, classical writers/poets, and other historical notables.

**Counterfeit 1959-D Lincoln Cent
with Wheat Reverse
("Hofmann Mule" Copy)**

**Actual 1959-D Lincoln Cent
"Hofmann Mule"
(Authenticity in Question)**

*Photo used with
permission from
Ira & Larry Goldberg
Coins & Collectibles*

Hofmann found buyers easily and sold his treasures for multiple thousands of dollars to private collectors and Mormon Church officials. (However, Hofmann spent much more than he was earning and was hundreds of thousands of dollars in debt). His documents were initially deemed genuine by professional museum curators, university professors and researchers, forensic document examiners, and even the FBI; this only furthered his reputation and the prices of his artifacts continued to sell quickly to eager buyers. (It's also reported that as a teenager he supposedly added a "D" mintmark via electroplating to a 1916 Mercury dime – a highly prized and rare coin from the Denver Mint – that was certified as "genuine" by the U.S. Treasury before grading companies existed.)

However, one set of documents in particular appeared to lend Hofmann some trouble. He claimed to have a series of papers written by William E. McLellin, an original leader of the Latter Day Saint Movement, who became a harsh critic of Mormon founder Joseph Smith and later parted ways with him. Steve Christensen, a document collector and Mormon bishop who was interested in purchasing Hofmann's "McLellin Collection," repeatedly pressed Hofmann to present the controversial documents for review. But around the time Hofmann was supposed to meet with Christensen and other Mormon officials to present it, a series of unthinkable tragedies took place. Incredulously, Christensen was killed at his office while opening a package containing a motion-sensitive pipe bomb. That day another pipe bomb killed Kathleen Sheets, the wife of one of Christensen's business associates, J. Gary Sheets. Police were then alerted to a third pipe bomb explosion. This time it was Hofmann himself who was severely injured, and claimed a package exploded as it fell to the floor in his car. *Exactly who wanted to kill these people, and why would they want these people dead?*

After police questioned Hofmann about what happened to him, they immediately suspected he was the bomber at all three locations (despite the fact he actually passed a polygraph exam) because his account did not match forensic evidence found in his vehicle. Also, the nature of his injuries (e.g. losing many of his fingertips) could only be explained by him holding the bomb and that it didn't fall on the floor of his car as he claimed. Police believed Hofmann was not an innocent bombing victim but merely became injured while attempting to deliver his third bomb; it simply went off prematurely due to his carless handling of it. His ties to the other two victims also reeked of suspicion. *But why would Hofmann want potential customers of his documents dead, especially when he was deep in debt?*

The answer: Prosecutors theorized Hofmann planned these attacks because he feared he was finally going to be exposed as a fraud by Steve Christensen and that all his documents – including all his previous sales and offers to other clients – were forgeries. Police believe the bombs were intended to buy him some time and get his nagging, suspicious clients and the police

(who were looking into possible forgery/fraud) off his back. In fact, police obtained a warrant to search his home and found several forging instruments and other incriminating evidence leaving no doubt this brilliant man was deviously devoting his talents to a very complex criminal operation. New document examiners discovered there were similar writing styles on vastly different documents written by different people from different time periods, that the ink didn't match what was used during some of the time periods, and even problems with how the ink had bled and dried into the paper. Rather than be discovered, he needed a distraction which turned out to be lethal. Hofmann later pleaded guilty to theft by deception, forgery, and two counts of second degree murder rather than face a trial leading to a conviction and maybe a death sentence. He is currently serving a life sentence at the Central Utah Correctional Facility.

Anyway, when reports of this 1959-D "mule" cent hit the news in 2002, Hofmann immediately took credit for it. He claimed it was secretly confiscated from his home during the police search after the bombings and it wasn't turned in for evidence. Hofmann did have a better-than-average knowledge about counterfeiting coins and fooled numismatic experts before. If anyone had skills to forge this mule cent, it was Mark Hofmann. But then perhaps he didn't create it and just wanted more attention, and after all he is an accomplished liar.

Forensic experts at the U.S. Treasury stated on two occasions that the Hoffman mule cent is a genuine Mint product. Expert numismatists at professional grading companies vehemently dispute those findings. Regardless, the very controversial coin has sold a few times including just recently for $50,000 in June of 2019. *So is the Hofmann 1959-D Lincoln cent mule genuine?* I doubt it. *Did Hofmann forge it as he claims?* Who knows. In any event, it remains an enigma and a captivating conversation piece, but the story doesn't end there.

It turns out the Mormon Church didn't need Hofmann's McLellin Collection after all (which he would've had to forge). *Why?* Because the Church forgot they already acquired McLellin's papers in 1908. The one item still missing was McLellin's personal notebook, which was later acquired by a collector named Brent Ashworth. Interestingly, Ashworth was not only one of the interested parties of Hofmann's supposed McLellin Collection, but people close to the story believe he was the intended target of Hofmann's third pipe bomb.

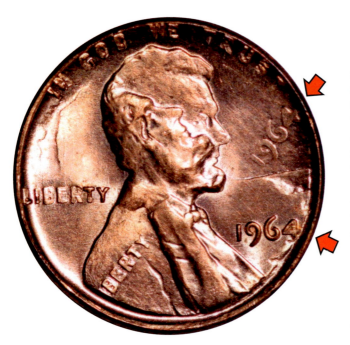

Notice the two mottos of LIBERTY and IN GOD WE TRUST, as well as two Lincoln profiles and two dates (red arrows). The lack of similar raised doubling on the reverse strongly suggests the coin was tampered with.

1964 "Piacentile/Sheiner" Lincoln Cent: Double-struck Rotated In-collar (Obverse Only)

Because the coin business can bring in some big money, naturally it also draws the attention of a criminal element looking to cash in by knowingly selling fake and altered coins. Sadly, very rarely are these individuals caught. However nearly a half-century ago two N.Y. City men were caught and sent to prison for their involvement in selling altered coins knowingly with the intent of defrauding error collectors.

In the mid-1960s in N.Y. City, Victor Piacentile (a.k.a. Victor Pease) and coin dealer William Sheiner were marketing 1964 Lincoln cents that were double struck, rotated in-collar errors which they claimed were discovered in U.S. Mint bags. Not only did they advertise these for sale (including in *The New York Times)*, but they even staged a presentation to collectors at a N.Y. hotel where they opened up a "sealed" bag and "discovered" some inside. The idea that both men were able to "predict" there would be this very Mint error inside an unopened Mint bag made their story too fantastic to believe.

Upon investigation by the U.S. Secret Service after receiving some complaints, charges were filed against the pair which included mail fraud, fraudulent possession and sale of altered coins, and conspiracy; roughly 100 were sold with a couple hundred more discovered after searches were conducted. At trial, Mint experts testified there is no way the defendants' coins were produced at the Mint, especially because the diameter was much wider than normal and wouldn't expand if struck in the collar. It was suspected with a great deal of certainty that a fake obverse die struck the coins after leaving the Mint. (There are a few genuine proof cents with only one side being double-struck and rotated, but proofs are produced a bit differently.) The court agreed the two conspired to commit fraud, and because they used the U.S. Mail as an avenue to conduct their illegal activity, both men were found guilty of mail fraud and conspiracy (plus additional charges separately) and sentenced to three months in prison with two years probation.

In terms of what these are worth, there aren't any formal records of sales that I can find, and very few people actually know what this particular coin is or the story behind it. I have seen people trying to sell these as genuine errors for several hundred dollars, and thankfully many of them pulled their listings after I informed them these are altered cents. If I had to put a value on these, I know of a couple unpublished sales where these sold as altered coins for $10-$40 depending on condition. (MS-64RB by ICG)

1883 Liberty Nickel, Type 1 No CENTS: Struck on Gold Stock? Nope! It's a "Racketeer" Nickel

Theoretically this Liberty Head nickel could have been struck on gold stock making it a wrong stock/off-metal error. After all, there are genuine Indian Head cents and a Buffalo nickel struck on gold planchets, so it is at least plausible there could be a gold Liberty nickel on one as well. But as you can see, it was plated long ago to appear as gold. It even had edge reeding applied after it was minted as genuine gold/silver coins have, however the pattern is inconsistent. *But why plate this Liberty nickel in particular?*

On February 1st, 1883, the Mint released this new "Liberty" nickel series to the public. However, no one at the Mint at first realized or was too concerned that the new 5 cent nickel lacked the word CENTS on it; the reverse simply had a Roman numeral "V" meaning "five." Its nonexistence opened the door for criminals who sought to capitalize on an opportunity to plate them in gold, add edge reeding, and then pass them off as $5 gold pieces. However, the U.S. Secret Service was soon receiving complaints from business owners and bankers that racketeers – people who purposely engage in fraudulent business dealings – were passing off these gold-plated "racketeer" nickels as $5 gold coins. Newspapers from California to Washington, D.C. to North Carolina reported the scam to inform the public.

After weeks of complaints and bad media publicity, the government finally caved and began production of new reverse dies on March 11th, 1883. The word CENTS was added to the bottom (lower left) which also saw the motto E PLURIBUS UNUM being moved to the top to accommodate the change (and are known as "Type 2"). Today, "Racketeer" nickels are one of the more popular altered coins. Dare I say "genuine" ones should (a) be in a very high grade but dull in color and (b) have very slightly worn and dull edge reeding (center left). Like 1944 steel cents, these are often faked/altered and plating or replating leaves an unnatural shine. Rumors that these were plated initially by a deaf-mute man named "Josh Tatum" are still unsubstantiated. (Scarce; Around $80 for reeded examples.)

Edge Reeding Added (post-Mint)

Type 2 Reverse: With "CENTS"

Type 1 Reverse: No "CENTS"

The 1944 Jefferson "No P" Henning War Nickel

One of the most widely-known and interesting American counterfeit coins are Jefferson nickels produced by Francis Leroy Henning. His fakes are among one of the few "Dark Siders" where their numismatic value is higher than their genuine counterparts. In fact, some of the dates he produced have sold for over $500. But unlike other forgers, although he wanted to make a profit with his operation Henning was not looking to swindle collectors out of their hard-earned money.

In the mid-1950s, Francis Leroy Henning from Erial, New Jersey began minting his own Jefferson nickels with dates including 1939, 1944, 1946, 1947, and 1953. Many experts speculate he made about 500,000 with roughly 100,000 entering circulation. (The 1944 date is the easiest and cheapest to acquire.) It is believed he created several dates in order to avoid suspicion, and that he may have created dies to make his coins appear worn and circulated for the same reason. (I imagine in the mid-1950s or later people would take notice that he always had new and shiny nickels from 1939 or the mid-1940s; circulated-looking coins draw much less attention.) However it was his 1944 date with a careless blunder on the reverse that did him in.

Starting in 1942* through 1945, the Mint added silver (and manganese) to nickels, removed the nickel from them, and also enlarged mintmarks significantly which were moved to the top of Monticello's dome on the reverse (center photo). This larger mintmark in a new location would help banks and the government know which ones to pull from circulation after the war to recoup these 35% silver "war" nickels. However, in his haste Henning failed to add the mintmark to his 1944 fake (top photo). After collectors noticed and reported the anomaly, it didn't take the U.S. Secret Service long to discover Henning's operation. Since coins without mintmarks traditionally indicate minting at the Philadelphia Mint, his 1944 blunder became known as the "No P" Henning nickel. Over time collectors have been able to point out certain identifying die markers on some of his fakes. Although there are a couple specific flaws to look for, the most pronounced one is something called the "Looped 'R'" in the word PLURIBUS on the reverse (bottom right); it developed a flaw in the bottom left leg of the "R," but not all his have this defect.

Learning the Secret Service was on to him and before he skipped town for Cleveland, Ohio, Henning tried to hide the evidence by dumping most of the remaining 4000,000 nickels in two different rivers: New Jersey's Cooper River (with some being recovered) and Pennsylvania's Schuylkill River (where none have been reported recovered). Upon his arrest in Cleveland in 1955, a federal judge sentenced him to three years in prison and a $5,000 fine. But after learning Henning was also faking paper currency, the judge added three more years. Interestingly, because his metallic composition was so similar to genuine nickels, several of his confiscated fakes were melted down to make real nickels.

Both non-silver and 35% silver nickels were produced in 1942, and are referred to as "Type 1" and "Type 2," respectively.

1944 Henning "No P" War Nickel (Reverse)

Genuine 1944–P War Nickel (Reverse)

Close-up of the Looped "R" in PLURIBUS

276

Because Henning did not use silver for any of his fake nickels, silver won't be detected when you scan them for metal content. However his other dates without the Lopped "R" are harder to identify because the metal composition is close to genuine nickels. Some people claim weighing them is effective (many of his fakes weigh slightly more or less than 5.0 grams), but I disagree. A lot of genuine coins weigh slightly more or less than their target weight and fall within thcir weight tolerance. *How is that?* Because sometimes the planchet metal gets rolled thick or thin resulting in overweight and underweight coins respectively.

Only one of the four major grading services encapsulates fakes and grades them: ICG. You can even say they certify your counterfeit Henning nickels as…*genuine?* If you can believe it, people actually alter genuine nickels to mimic his counterfeits by removing mintmarks from genuine 1944 nickels (see top right photo). I've also seen tool markings trying to emulate the "Looped R" on his other known dates which sell for significantly more money because they are much more scarce.

Perhaps if Henning studied U.S. coinage more carefully and/or simply avoided dates from war nickels, the world may have never known about his clandestine mint. He claimed he made no profit off this scheme, but many people who sold his counterfeits may have. (Scarce; $60; graded F-12 by ICG, which is one of three grades you usually find them in besides G and VG.)

Henning Nickel Reverse Die Markers
Some Henning nickels have all or some of the following diagnostics on the reverse side.

Looped "R"

Vertical Die Crack

Rough Texture "Altocumulus Clouds" Pattern Above Left Side of Monticello

Minor Die Flaw Above and In Between the "EN" of CENTS

A Poorly-altered 1944-P Nickel Intended to Appear as a Henning Nickel

Genuine "Missing Mintmark" Die Varieties
The 1971 "No S" proof Jefferson nickel and 1982 "No P" Roosevelt dime below are just a couple examples of coins missing their mintmarks. *(Photos courtesy of Heritage Auctions/HA.com.)*

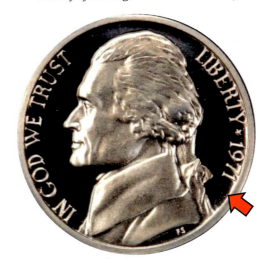

**Henning Nickels: Three of
His Five Known Dates**
(All with the "Looped R")

1939
($325)

1944
"No P"
($60)

1947
($500)

*Prices determined
by 2019 auction sales.*

278

The Alarming Caper
of the "Charles Silverstone" Errors

No other situation in modern American numismatic history has created a greater sense of panic among collectors, dealers, and professional grading companies than when a large group of altered error coins hit the market in the mid-2010s. Literally hundreds of coins were being offered for sale on sites like EBay and directly to dealers and collectors featuring absolutely fantastic and unbelievable errors, many which have never been seen before. Errors like Eisenhower dollars struck on 1 cent planchets with massive curved clips, Susan B. Anthony dollars struck on proof nickel planchets, and Washington "50 State Quarters Series" on 1 cent planchets wowed and amazed coin nerds everywhere. Sale prices reached multiple thousands. Major grading companies boosted the confidence of wary buyers by certifying a small handful of them causing sale prices to climb even higher. The craze was peaking for coins being offered by a man who called himself "Charles Silverstone" (a.k.a. "Mike McCoy"), who was selling these errors both in-person at shows and on EBay under the seller name of "National1966." Then suddenly the frenzy crashed when it was discovered several weeks later that these were masterfully-made coins forged to resemble genuine errors. *What tipped off the experts?*

Mint error dealer and numismatist, Jon Sullivan (Sullivan Numismatics), informed me he discovered what was going on "by having a group of the coins in one place to compare them." He noticed very quickly a few weren't genuine, which only aroused suspicion that the others weren't either. Through Jon's research and close examination in conjunction with a group of other dealers, he began to notice that "some of the same dies were being used on different errors of wildly different dates." Many of them also featured mintages from different Mints. Basically, this means that the same fake dies must have been passed around constantly from Philadelphia, to Denver, to San Francisco over a long period of different years. Sullivan suggests the probability of this happening is "totally impossible in any remotely reasonable scenario."

What made them much more difficult to detect was that the error coins consisted of "authentic Mint planchets, genuine error coins, or normal coins, and then [he] created errors over top of them" with fake dies. Because the quality of these fakes is so convincing, Sullivan suspects Silverstone or someone else likely created them "at some minting institution which would have had excellent equipment." Many experts suspect their production was in Eastern Europe, possibly Bulgaria where Silverstone once listed his location on EBay. (I suspect this was part of a larger criminal racket and he didn't work alone.)

Grading companies like PCGS, NGC, and ANACS took immediate and appropriate action to inform the public and remedy the situation. Everyone who submitted these coins for certification was refunded what they paid for them if they returned them and provided appropriate paperwork. EBay and PayPal also refunded people who bought from Silverstone. Even Silverstone himself refunded some people electronically, but many never got their money back.

Who Silverstone really is, what he's doing currently, and where he is now is unknown (he listed both a St. Petersburg and Clearwater, Florida address while he was actively selling). As of yet he hasn't been held accountable. A few of his errors – both slabbed and raw – still pop up occasionally for sale online, but many people like myself actively try to get these removed. Hopefully after reading this you will have your guard up as well. *Is it possible some day these "Silverstone Errors" will be just as collectible as Henning nickels?* Possibly, but I think as of right now it's still too fresh in people's memories – especially those he scammed – to view these as potential collector's items.

2000-P Virginia State Quarter
Struck on a 1 Cent Planchet
I acquired this Silverstone creation
for educational purposes.

Below is one of the few remaining "Silverstone" errors still encapsulated in a major TPG holder. It is not known exactly how many still sit inside a certified slab, but since EBay, PayPal, and the grading services themselves were willing to give full refunds, I can't imagine very many still remain in plastic. That being said there is still a collector market for fake coins that managed to get certified, and they certainly make great educational pieces.

**2002 Louisiana State Quarter
Struck On a 1 Cent Planchet;
Straight-graded at MS66-BN by NGC**

The owner paid $2,500 for this "Silverstone" coin but was refunded by EBay. *(Photos by Joe Cronin. The owner wishes to remain anonymous.)*

Coin Pareidolia: What You See Isn't What You See

1943-D "Ghost 4" Steel Lincoln Cent: Misplaced "D" Mintmark

Perhaps you may have noticed earlier when I showcased this 1943 "Ghost 4" cent that it has what appears to be a severely off-centered, misplaced, and crooked "D" (Denver) mintmark. *Is this a one-of-a-kind error?* Unfortunately, no, and in fact it isn't a mintmark at all. What you "see" here is an example of a phenomenon known as pareidolia – in this case, **coin pareidolia** – where your brain interprets and formulates a recognizable image on a coin that simply is not there. Seeing Jesus' face in cumulus clouds, the devil in the flames of a forest fire, or a mintmark on a coin that isn't there are all examples of pareidolia. The raised area you see could simply be gunk struck into the coin, a chip from the die, a gas bubble, a planchet flaw, or a contact mark from another object. Upon closer inspection you can see very plainly it is not a mintmark at all, but many people will see what they want to.

1964-D Washington Quarter: Misplaced "D" Mintmark

Here is yet another "misplaced mintmark," which tends to be one of the most common "discoveries" (and forms of pareidolia) people think they have found. Here, instead of the "D" being below the center of the branches and above the last "R" in QUARTER on the reverse (bottom right), it appears to have been struck on the arrowheads. It does in fact have a strong resemblance to both the shape and size of the "D" mintmark, but sadly it just took a hit from something causing metal to shift around. *(Photos courtesy of Gary Meziere.)*

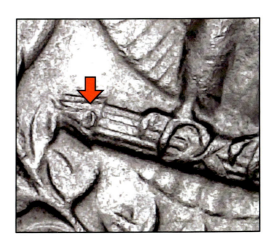

Upon closer inspection, clearly the area in question is not a mintmark at all. This is where a 10x loupe comes in very handy.

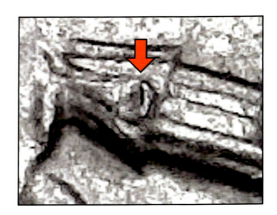

Below is where the mintmark appears on normal silver Washington quarters (1932-1964).

Environmentally Damaged Coins Appearing as Mint Errors

Prolonged exposure to our planet's harsh environment causes some of the most common and catastrophic forms of damage to coins. Naturally-occurring acids and man-made pollutants found in soil and standing water (as well as contact with salt water and air) can slowly corrode almost anything, including coining metals. Though environmental damage is usually easily discernable for most collectors, several misdiagnose these as errors. For example, it is not uncommon to find environmentally damaged coins being offered for sale as "improperly annealed" coins, "off metal/wrong stock" or "struck on copper" errors, coins "missing clad layers," or even coins "struck on foreign planchets." The truth is that these coins below and others like them are damaged. They also have no numismatic appeal or value on top of their monetary value – that is, if you can even tell what denomination they are. Lastly, just because it is round and flat doesn't mean a badly corroded round metal disk is/was a coin; keep in mind it could also be a slug or a non-monetary metal part or fragment. Coins like these are found quite frequently by people who go metal detecting. *(Thanks to Ed "Paddyman" Padilla for these donated coins.)*

Zinc Cent
If it weren't for the partial motto of IN GOD WE TRUST at the top, you might not even know this is a coin.

Nickel
Corrosion left this nickel appearing without a date and missing most of its details.

Clad Dime
It's not an alloy coin like Jefferson nickels, but this 1970 Roosevelt dime still winds up with almost identical surface colors.

Clad Quarter
All that's left is the copper core of this 1996-P Washington Quarter; each side's clad layer has withered away.

Manganese Dollar
Little of its original golden manganese layer exists on this John Tyler $1 Presidential Series coin.

Your "Mint" Error is Actually a "Token" Error

1863 Broas Brothers Pie Bakers Civil War Store Card Token: Reverse Die Clashes on the Obverse Face and a Reverse Shattered Die Strike

For a coin to be considered a "coin" it needs to be produced by a *government* mint for the purposes of being used as legal tender in transactions. Even proof coins – which are intended to be collector issues – can still be used as real money if taken out of the special packaging. "Tokens" on the other hand are struck at *private* minting facilities for a variety of purposes, including payment of some *government* services. For example, some were (and still are) used for bus fare, road and bridge tolls, border and ferry crossings, and subways in American and foreign cities. Many businesses which made tokens also accepted them as forms of payment including gaming tokens at video arcades and casino slot machines, or to redeem a free drink or appetizer. Of course the main goal for private sector token production is/was to advertise a business and/or a product and get your name out there, especially when there was neither radio nor TV to help you years ago.

One clever marketing trick for token production that many businesses employed was to create tokens resembling genuine government-issued coins. For example, many tokens produced in the late 1700s up through the mid-1900s feature popular U.S. political figures like Benjamin Franklin, George Washington, and Abraham Lincoln. Others have iconic images like bald eagles, Lady Liberty, and Native American Indian chiefs. (See this token's similarity to the 1863 Indian Head cent on your right.) It makes you take a second look especially when an establishment rejects it as a form of payment. (Some businesses actually accepted these copper tokens as 1 cent coins.) You'll also be more likely to remember it and talk about it with others. This is exactly what advertisers want: Exposure. (It also often explains why some companies do bizarre, rude, and even illegal things to try and grab the public's attention.)

On the top right is an 1863 Civil War store card token advertising "Broas Pie Baker," which at least in 1863 was located at 131 41st Street in NY City (Queens). While it displays patriotic messages during the chaos of the Civil War (e.g. UNITED WE STAND and ONE COUNTRY), the primary purpose was to advertise the business. Notice how the token's obverse side has very strong die clashes of it's reverse designs. In fact it's so strong you can see details of the Indian Chief's eye, headband, and feathers in addition to some of the reverse lettering on top of his head. On the token's reverse side, you can make out several raised cracks as a result of being struck with a shattered die. Several examples of this token error and other Civil War tokens exist. (Scarce; $80)

Notice the similarity of the designs and lettering between the reverse of the 1863 Broas Pie Baker token above and the obverse of the 1863 Indian Head cent below. *(IHC photo below courtesy of Heritage Auctions/HA.com)*

Coin Trivia: During the Civil War, many people and businesses accepted copper tokens as coinage as a shortage developed due to the hoarding of copper as copper prices rose. In response, part of the 1864 Coinage Act *outlawed the production of privately-minted coinage.*

Chapter 12: Mint Canceled Coins – Are They "Errors?"

Sadly for error collectors like myself, the U.S. Mint introduced a new process in 2003 to immediately "condemn" or "cancel" their imperfect coins and blanks/planchets directly at Mint facilities. This process, in addition to no longer selling batches of loose coins in those cloth Mint bags, has greatly reduced the chances of finding modern errors. Now FIDOs which get caught are gathered up and fed into a contraption called a Dutch Waffling machine where they are crushed and left resembling an actual waffle. Once they become "cancelled" via waffling, they're immediately stripped of their legal tender status and become formally known as "**Mint Canceled**" coins. (Though technically they aren't "coins" since they can't be used in transactions.)

What is done with them after they are "waffled?" Since they no longer have monetary value, one option is that companies who have contracts to make coin metals for the government can acquire them as "scrap" to be recycled into new planchet strips. However, some people acquire them to market and sell these waffled coins as collectible "coins," which is entirely legal. I have even seen coins which were purposely altered to resemble actual Mint canceled coins as a way to scam collectors if you can believe it.

Should errors that get discovered and wind up waffled/canceled still be considered "Mint errors?" Some claim that because these defective planchets and coins are canceled right at U.S. Mint facilities, they should still be considered Mint errors. But seeing that they were canceled *after* the last stage of the minting process, I don't see how they can be viewed as anything other than "Mint-destroyed defects," which is merely an unsympathetic euphemism for "post-Mint damage." (I also heard the first batch of blanks from every new planchet strip is automatically sent to be waffled as well regardless of whether or not they find any defects.)

Many other error collectors I know also consider Mint canceled coins as PMD and want nothing to do with what they categorize as a marketing gimmick. *Are they neat to look at?* I guess. *Are some incredibly rare?* Sure, especially Martha Washington test pieces. PCGS and NGC will even certify and slab waffled coins, but neither company denotes them as "Mint Errors"; they simply identify them as "Mint Canceled" or "Waffle Cancelled." They also don't assign them grades, though they do classify some that qualify as "Brilliant Uncirculated" for some reason.

What are Mint canceled coins worth? To many collectors these don't have any real value even if you can tell it is a 60% off-center Sacagawea dollar struck on a Roosevelt dime with a readable date. Like everything in life it is worth what someone is willing to pay for it, though some people have paid hundreds of dollars or more for some. As for a dollar amount, who knows?

2003 Washington Quarter (IL)   **2015-D Roosevelt Dime**   **2017-D Jefferson Nickel**

2012-D "Grover Cleveland" Presidential Series Dollar

Chapter 13: The End of an Error?

While I was giving a presentation on error coins a while back, someone from the audience asked me, "Do you think the top managers at the Mint purposely and secretly create errors to generate interest in the hobby?" I answered quickly with a definitive "No." Why would they want to do that? Sure, the Mint sells coins directly and always hopes to increase sales, but they do not sell errors nor would they want to. Mistakes released into circulation and then popularized in the coin community make them look foolish and incompetent during their tenure as bosses. In fact, big money is actually spent at all locations producing U.S. coins, currency, stamps, etc., to ensure errors are not happening. *Have rogue employees purposely created errors for fun and/or to sell?* Absolutely, but not often and not through any kind of formal directive from the Mint's top brass.

Many production and quality control changes have been put in place just in the last few years, let alone since the first U.S. Mint (Philadelphia) started minting coins in 1793. Regrettably, desirable Mint errors produced from recent years are quickly becoming incredibly rare and are much more costly to acquire. The Mint not only has highly-trained people looking for mistakes and error coins, but also has machines and computers at various stages of the minting process helping to weed out those freaks and oddities. They even have several U.S. Mint Police officers watching over the employees (and other officers) to ensure there is no funny business like smuggling out errors to be put on auction sites, and both visitors and employees are searched going in and out of Mint facilities. Error coins that get discovered during the various stages wind up being corralled, forcibly separated, and are then exterminated by waffling machines in an act of error coin genocide. The remains of these deformed, innocent errors are then unceremoniously discarded as "scrap."

Fortunately the good news is there are more genuine errors minted in years past out there and ready to be given a good home than you can possibly count, buy, and store. However, don't give up looking through your change for newly created errors just yet as Mint officials can't possibly catch or stop everything; a small number still sneak out. But if you get tired of searching your stashes of loose or rolled coins you've kept in old coffee cans over the years, don't forget there are local coin shops to visit, coin shows to attend, estate sales to browse through, flea markets to peruse, online auctions to place bids on, and reputable dealer websites waiting for your mouse clicks. Hopefully now that you're armed with some of the knowledge I have shown and shared, combined with a readiness to learn more and build up your skills to judge things for yourself more accurately, you will soon have and be able to show off your very own collection of *Mint Errors to Die For.*

Chapter 14: Joe Cronin's "Twenty-one Numismatic Truths"

Before I conclude, I thought it would be a good idea to provide you with a recap of some helpful suggestions and words of wisdom I mentioned throughout the book. Some of these are obvious while others I learned from experience (and some the hard way). These don't cover everything, but I hope my "Twenty-one Numismatic Truths" will help save you money, time, and aggravation as you continue to learn more about the wonderful pastime of Mint error collecting.

1. Learn the minting process for how coins are made and how methods changed over time. This can be among your best defenses to avoid buying fake, altered, and/or damaged coins resembling genuine errors.

2. A digital scale, a 5-10x magnifier, a magnet, and a digital caliper are great and inexpensive tools to help you better detect fake, altered, and damaged coins.

3. Coins make bad investments as the market is volatile. You'll be lucky to get back what you paid for them. Treat this as a hobby and you'll sleep better at night.

4. Just because a coin is old, had a low mintage, or is a Mint error, it doesn't always mean it's valuable.

5. Recent auction prices are the best way to keep up with approximate values. (Heritage Auctions, Stacks & Bowers, Great Collections, EBay, etc.)

6. The overall eye-appeal of a coin (e.g. its luster, toning, color, dramatic look, error placement, etc.) is often much more important than its grade.

7. Avoid buying cleaned/damaged coins as they will eventually bother you and can be very tough to sell.

8. Do not attempt to clean or restore coins yourself. Please leave this skill to the professionals.

9. Research how to store your coins properly. This includes not only the products your coins will be placed in but also the environment/climate in which you live.

10. Study an error type first before you start collecting them. Look at known, certified examples for different series and denominations to become familiar with what you can expect to see (and not see) on them.

11. Learn how to grade coins yourself, and be sure to research each denomination, series and type you're interested in. Keep in mind that for errors, grading can be much more subjective as a portion or all of a coin's details could be warped and/or missing.

12. The number of collectors and dealers who focus on errors is a small percentage of the hobby; this can make it much harder to find dealers and buyers. Be patient!

13. Error coins with no visible date are less desirable and valuable than those with a date. Errors which have more than one full date are more desirable and valuable than errors that have only one.

14. With errors, the value generally goes up as the denomination increases. For example, a 1971 dollar with a 10% curved clip is more valuable than a 1971 cent with a 10% curved clip (assuming a similar grade and eye appeal exists).

15. Errors with more than one major error (e.g. an off-metal that's double-struck) tend to be more valuable than those with only one error type.

16. Normally errors on "type" coins (e.g. war nickels, steel cents, bicentennials, etc.) are more valuable than those struck on standard designs.

17. In general, major errors on silver/gold coins are worth more than those on modern, non-precious metal coinage (all things being equal).

18. Be extra cautious when buying raw (i.e. uncertified) errors. There are literally thousands out there for sale which are garbage (e.g. damaged, altered, fake). Study what different types of damage look like (e.g. harshly cleaned, vise jobs, etc.). There may be a very good reason why it isn't certified!

19. Avoid sellers who can't answer questions about the errors they're selling and/or who fail to respond to you, don't or won't guarantee authenticity and/or won't accept returns, use gimmicky language (e.g. "it's one of a kind!"), have poor feedback, etc. Trust your gut: If you think something is shady about the coin and/or the seller, don't buy the coin.

20. Wise collectors spend much more time studying coins and reading about them than they do looking for coins to buy.

21. BUY THE COIN, NOT THE HOLDER and treat every coin – raw or certified – as if it's raw. Experts can make mistakes, labels can be wrong and/or have missing information, and there are fake slabs out there. It is really up to YOU to stay informed and know what you're buying!

Select U.S. Coin Weights (gm), Diameters (mm), and Compositions*

Half Cents: 1793-1795 → 6.74gm; 23.50mm; 100% Cu
1795-1857 → 5.44gm; 23.50mm; 100% Cu

Large Cents: 1793-1795 → 13.48gm; 23.50mm; 100% Cu
1795-1857 → 10.9gm; 28.50mm; 100% Cu

Small Cents: 1856-1864 → 4.67gm; 19.0mm; 88% Cu, 12% Ni
1864-1942 – 3.11gm; 19.0mm; 95% Cu, 5% Sn/Zn
1943 → 2.7gm; 19.0mm; Zinc-coated Steel
1944-1946 → 3.11gm; 19.0mm; 95% Cu, 5% Zn
1947-1961 → 3.11gm; 19.0mm; 95% Cu, 5% Sn/Zn
1962-1982 → 3.11gm; 19.0mm; 95% Cu, 5% Zn
1982- ___ → 2.5gm; 19.0mm; Copper-plated Zinc

Two Cents: 1864-1873 → 6.22gm; 23.0mm; 100% Cu

Three Cents Cu/Ni: 1865-1889 → 1.94gm; 17.9mm; 75% Cu, 25% Ni

Three Cents Ag "Trime:" 1851-1853 → .80gm; 14.0mm; 75% Ag, 25% Cu
1854-1873 → .75gm; 14.0mm; 90% Ag, 10% Cu

Half Dimes: 1853-1873 → 1.24gm; 19.2mm; 90% Ag, 10% Cu

Nickels: 1866-1883 → 5.0gm; 20.5mm; 75% Cu, 25% Ni
1883-1942 → 5.0gm; 21.2mm; 75% Cu, 25% Ni
1942-1945 ("War" nickels) → 5.0gm; 21.2mm; 56% Cu, 35% Ag, 9% Mn
1946- ___ → 5.0gm; 21.2mm; 75% Cu, 25% Ni

Dimes: 1853-1873 → 2.48gm; 17.9mm; 90% Ag, 10% Cu
1873-1964 → 2.5gm; 17.9mm; 90% Ag, 10% Cu
1965- ___ → 2.27gm; 17.9mm; 75% Cu, 25% Ni on pure Cu

Twenty Cents 1875-1878 → 5.0; 22.5mm; 90% Ag, 25% Cu

Quarters: 1853-1873 → 6.22gm; 24.26mm; 90% Ag, 10% Cu
1873-1964 → 6.25gm; 24.26mm; 90% Ag, 10% Cu
1965- ___ → 5.67gm; 24.26mm; 75% Cu, 25% Ni on pure Cu
1976 → 5.75gm; 24.26mm; 40% silver clad

Half Dollars: 1853-1873 → 12.44gm; 30.61mm; 90% Ag, 10% Cu
1873-1964 → 12.5gm; 30.61mm; 90% Ag, 10% Cu
1965-1970 → 11.5gm; 30.61mm; 40% silver clad
1971- ___ → 11.34gm; 30.61mm; 75% Cu and 25% Ni on pure Cu
1976 → 11.5gm; 30.61mm; 40% Silver Clad
1982 → 12.5gm; 30.56mm; 90% Ag, 10% Cu

Trade Dollars: 1873-1888 → 27.21gm; 38.1mm; 90% Ag, 10% Cu

Dollars: 1840-1935 → 26.73gm; 38.10mm; 90% Ag, 10% Cu
1971-1978 → 22.68gm; 38.10mm; 75% Cu, 25% Ni on a Cu core
1971-1976 → 24.6gm; 38.10mm; 40% silver clad
1979-1981 and 1999 → 8.1gm; 26.5mm; 75% Cu, 25% Ni on pure Cu
1983-2018 (Commem.) → 26.7gm; 38.10mm; 90% Ag, 10% Cu
2000- ___ → 8.1gm; 26.5mm; 77% Cu, 12% Zn, 7% Mn, 4% Ni on pure Cu

American Silver Eagles: 1986 - ___ → 31.10gm; 40.60mm; .999 Ag

Weights of Clad Coins Missing One Complete Clad Layer (Approx.)

Dimes: 1.9gm
Quarters: 4.7gm
40% Silver Clad Quarter: 4.8gm (Est.)
Half Dollars: 9.25gm
40% Silver Clad Half Dollars: 9.5gm
Ike Dollars: 18.9gm
40% Silver Clad Ike Dollars: 20.2gm (Est.)
Susan B. Anthony Dollars: 6.0gm
Sacagawea/Presidential Dollars: 6.0gm

Does not include all years for all denominations, or gold coins, or all special-issue or proof coins; some dates were also minted on planchets with different weights/diameters/compositions.

Mint Error / Die Variety Collection Log

Date/Mintmark	Denom.	Error Type(s) or Die Variety
1.		
2.		
3.		
4.		
5.		
6.		
7.		
8.		
9.		
10.		
11.		
12.		
13.		
14.		
15.		
16.		
17.		
18.		
19.		
20.		
21.		
22.		
23.		
24.		
25.		
26.		
27.		
28.		
29.		

Date/Mintmark	Denom.	Error Type(s) or Die Variety
30.		
31.		
32.		
33.		
34.		
35.		
36.		
37.		
38.		
39.		
40.		
41.		
42.		
43.		
44.		
45.		
46.		
47.		
48.		
49.		
50.		
51.		
52.		
53.		
54.		
55.		
56.		
57.		
58.		
59.		

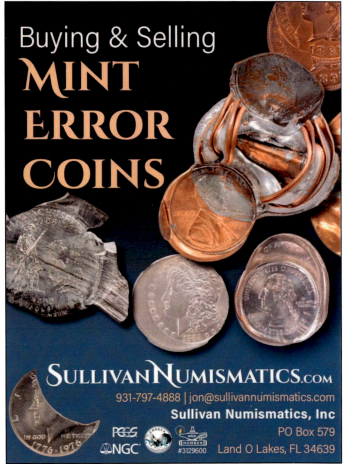

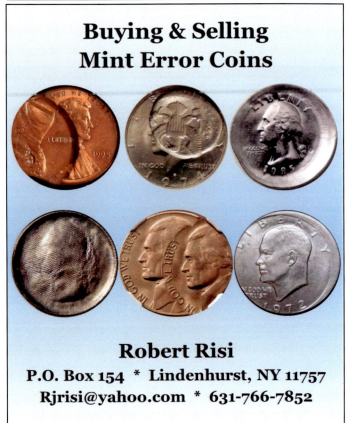